Families and States in Western Europe

This collection of essays traces the relationship between families and states in the major countries of Western Europe since 1945, examining the power of states to shape family life and the capacity of families to influence states. Written by an exceptionally distinguished team of scholars, *Families and States* follows many narratives, allowing comparisons to be drawn between different countries. The essays point to numerous convergences, illustrating how states have coped with common problems arising at the level of family life, and exploring issues such as secularism, the pressure of multiculturalist demands and the growing rejection of welfare state principles. *Families and States* will be of interest to anyone analysing relations between civil society and the modern democratic state, and the place of the family within this relationship. This collection makes a significant contribution to current political theory and to our understanding of European family life in its many different forms.

QUENTIN SKINNER is the Barber Beaumont Professor of the Humanities at the School of History, Queen Mary, University of London.

Families and States in Western Europe

Edited by

Quentin Skinner

CAMBRIDGE
UNIVERSITY PRESS

CAMBRIDGE
UNIVERSITY PRESS

University Printing House, Cambridge CB2 8BS, United Kingdom

One Liberty Plaza, 20th Floor, New York, NY 10006, USA

477 Williamstown Road, Port Melbourne, VIC 3207, Australia

314-321, 3rd Floor, Plot 3, Splendor Forum, Jasola District Centre, New Delhi - 110025, India

79 Anson Road, #06-04/06, Singapore 079906

Cambridge University Press is part of the University of Cambridge.

It furthers the University's mission by disseminating knowledge in the pursuit of education, learning and research at the highest international levels of excellence.

www.cambridge.org
Information on this title: www.cambridge.org/9780521128018

First published 2011

A catalogue record for this publication is available from the British Library

Library of Congress Cataloging in Publication data
Families and states in Western Europe / edited by Quentin Skinner.
p. cm.
Includes bibliographical references and index.
ISBN 978-0-521-76257-1 (hardback) – ISBN 978-0-521-12801-8 (paperback)
1. Families–Europe, Western. 2. Family policy–Europe, Western.
I. Skinner, Quentin.
HQ611.F349 2011
306.85094′09045–dc22
2011006725

ISBN 978-0-521-76257-1 Hardback
ISBN 978-0-521-12801-8 Paperback

Contents

Contributors

MARIA ÅGREN Professor of History, Uppsala University
LAURA DEN DULK Assistant Professor, Department of Public Administration, Erasmus University Rotterdam
TONY FAHEY Professor of Social Policy, University College Dublin
PAUL GINSBORG Professor of Contemporary European History, Università degli Studi di Firenze
SARAH HOWARD Fellow of Christ's College, Cambridge
NATALIA MORA-SITJA Lecturer in Economic History, University of Cambridge
DAVID RUNCIMAN Reader in Political Theory, University of Cambridge
DEBORAH THOM Fellow of Robinson College, Cambridge
ADAM TOOZE Professor of History, Yale University
ANNEKE VAN DOORNE-HUISKES Emeritus Professor of Sociology, Utrecht University and Erasmus University Rotterdam

Acknowledgements

This book originated in a one-day conference held at Downing College, Cambridge, on 8 May 2008. The meeting took place under the auspices of the Cambridge Historical Society, of which I was then the President, and David Pratt the Academic Secretary. David and I worked together on the programme, which centred around Paul Ginsborg's work on the relations between family, civil society and the state in contemporary Italy. Paul opened the proceedings with a lecture on this topic, and we invited three colleagues from the Faculty of History at Cambridge to offer comments, and at the same time to contrast the Italian experience with that of some other European countries. Natalia Mora-Sitja spoke about Spain, Deborah Thom about Britain and Adam Tooze about Germany, while David Runciman supplied a theoretical framework for our day of discussion and debate.

The task of organising this occasion mainly fell upon David Pratt, and I should like to offer very warm thanks on behalf of everyone who took part for his efficiency and thoughtfulness. The cost of holding the meeting was met by the G. M. Trevelyan Fund of the Cambridge Faculty of History, to whose managers we are likewise greatly indebted. Downing College provided splendid facilities, and we owe special thanks to Jacqui Cressey, the College's Conference Services Manager. A word of appreciation is also due to the members of our audience, who raised many searching questions throughout a highly enjoyable and instructive day.

The conference proved so successful that I decided to approach Richard Fisher, Executive Director of Cambridge University Press, about the possibility of turning our proceedings into a book. Richard solicited several reports on my proposal, which were not only highly encouraging but full of good counsel about the best scholars to approach with a view to extending our coverage and producing a more systematic analysis of our theme. I was delighted when all the scholars I had been advised to contact agreed to contribute, and when all the original commentators on Paul's lecture agreed to expand their talks and bring them up to a comparable level and length. During the preparation of the resulting book everyone met their deadlines without the least fuss and agreed to my suggested revisions with great goodwill, for all of which I am deeply grateful.

As always, I have received exemplary help throughout from Cambridge University Press. Lucy Rhymer supervised production with the greatest care. Linda Randall acted as subeditor, bringing to bear much tact and patience as well as a wonderful eye for detail. Richard Fisher guided the project at every stage with his invariable combination of expert advice, exhilarating enthusiasm and unwavering efficiency and dispatch. My warmest thanks to everyone.

QUENTIN SKINNER

1 A theoretical overview

David Runciman

I

What stands between families and states? The conventional answer of modern political theory is civil society: the sphere of voluntary associations and relationships that provides individuals with a means of escape from both the confines of family life and the rigours of state politics. This can be either a descriptive or a normative claim. One of the distinguishing features of modern societies is the sheer scale and variety of civil associations for which they allow, whether in economic life, cultural life, communications, religion, sport or education. That is an observable fact, but it is also often held to be one of the major benefits of modern existence, and hence something to be celebrated and cultivated. We need civil society in order to avoid being trapped in the binary, pre-modern world of household and polis, in which the opportunities for human expression and experimentation are more limited.

Modern civil society is valuable because it helps to take us away from purely private concerns. It offers a route out from family life through to the wider perspectives of social and political justice. In Susan Moller Okin's terms, quoted by Paul Ginsborg in his chapter in this book, we need 'a continuum of just associations' in order to 'enlarge [our] sympathies'. But civil society is also valuable because it can provide some respite from the relentless pressures of public life, organised by and for the state. It offers some protection for families from the intrusions of the state by providing a buffer against coercion.

For these reasons, the tendency is to see civil society as intermediating between families and states, whether in an expansive or in a protective capacity. The expansive view can be traced back to Hegel, as Ginsborg shows:[1] on this account, we move up from the particularity of the family through civil society (and *only* through civil society) to the majestic vistas of the state. The protective view can be traced back to Tocqueville, for whom local and civil associations provided the best possible defence against the oppressive powers

[1] As well as the brief discussion in his chapter in this book, I am also drawing here on Ginsborg 1995.

of a democratic state motivated by the totalising principle of equality. The loss of this intermediary layer, as local civic life becomes increasingly dissipated and atomised, is one of the things that modern day Tocquevillians, like Robert Putnam, most lament.[2] But either way, whether celebratory or admonitory, ascending or descending, extensive or restrictive, these accounts of the family–civil society–state triad are linear. We move one way or the other, but we move *through* civil society.

Linear accounts of this kind are capable of considerable complexity, and indeed they may be dialectical, as in Hegel's case, or in the well-known account of the evolution of the 'public sphere' given by Jürgen Habermas, in which the emergence of civil society out of bourgeois family life comes eventually to sideline and diminish the civic capacity of families.[3] The historical relation between state and civil society is also potentially dialectical, and not simply in Hegel's terms: the development of the modern state form was in part a response to the pluralisation of civic and religious life that followed from the Reformation; at the same time, the pluralisation of civic life was greatly enhanced by the legal and bureaucratic structures developed by the form of the modern state.[4] Thus even when viewed in broadly linear terms, the institutions of family, civil society and state may be seen as interacting in intricate ways.

Nonetheless, these linear accounts, for all their potential complexity, still rest on a common assumption: that modern politics separates out states and families by interposing civil society between them. There is, however, another way of understanding the family–civil society–state triad. This is as a circular (or, as Tony Fahey suggests in his chapter on Ireland, 'triangular') rather than as a linear relationship. Ginsborg touches on this alternative picture in his chapter on Italy. I want to try to offer a fuller development of it here, since I believe that it is better able to make sense of the multifarious and multifaceted relations between families and states in the recent history of Western Europe that are described in the different parts of this book.

Figure 1 shows a picture of family–civil society–state relations with no single entry point and no fixed line of development, either up or down. Seen in this way, a circular account suggests that the relationship between state and family does not have to pass through civil society. Equally, it implies that the relation between state and civil society may pass through the family, depending on where in the circle you enter. But there is a further possible variation, which follows if the direction of the circle is reversed, as in Figure 2.

Now, it is possible for the relation between family and civil society to pass through the state. A circular picture makes it clear that any one member of the

[2] See Putnam 2000. [3] See Habermas 1989. [4] See for example Figgis 1913.

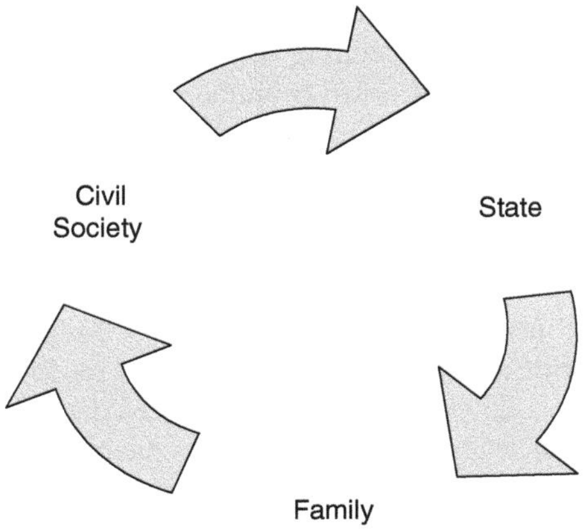

Figure 1

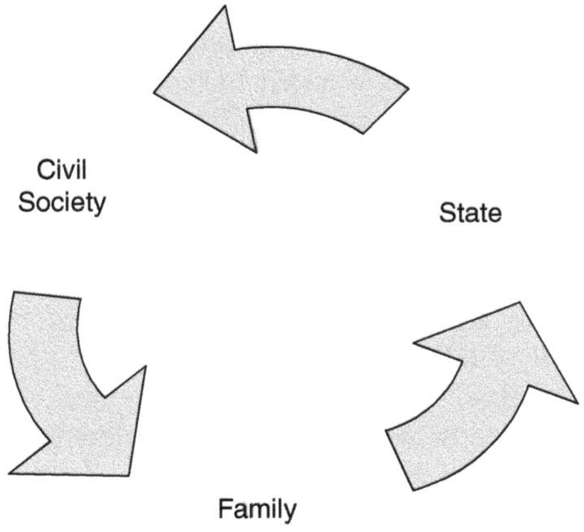

Figure 2

triad may be the mediator or the barrier, interposing between the other two. It also makes it possible to bypass one of the three altogether, since all can be related to each other directly without the need of an intermediary. As we shall see, these possibilities are reflected in the recent history of Western Europe. States regulate family life in order to sideline civil society; families look to states to rescue them from the pressures of the market; economic pressures on states produce direct impacts on families; family pressures on states lead to the regulation of civil society. These recognisable features of recent history are hard to describe according to a linear model.

A circular model also makes it easier to resist the idea that political force in modern societies is always either ascending or descending: that is, either moving up towards the state or coming down from the state. Politics does not necessarily work like that. More often, power moves through the system in an interconnected chain, as different actors react to or anticipate the behaviour of others. This makes it much harder to identify where power starts and where it ends. It would be better to say that power *circulates* through modern societies.

In this chapter I want to illustrate these ideas in two ways. First, I shall discuss the thought of another of the foundational theorists of modern politics, though, unlike Hegel and Tocqueville, one who is not often discussed in this context: Thomas Hobbes. Hobbes has some claims to be the most linear of all modern political theorists – certainly it ought to be clear on his model how power moves up to the state and how it is meant to come down again. Yet I want to argue that even Hobbes's model is not plausibly linear when it comes to the relations between state, civil society and family, and seeing why helps us to understand how hard it is to avoid some circularity. Secondly, I shall explore the implications of the recent emergence of what is sometimes known as the 'neo-liberal' or 'market' state in Western Europe. The liberalisation of the state – the limiting of its welfare functions, the preference for light-touch governance over direct intervention, the legal recognition of a plurality of different lifestyles – has not happened at the same time nor in the same way across the different countries and regions covered by this book. But it is something that has affected them all, and this is reflected in the chapters that follow. I want to suggest that by exploring these changes in broad theoretical terms – by looking at what they tell us about the changing character of the state as a source of status, of welfare, of loyalty – we can see something of the variety and circularity of relations between states, civil society and families. I shall attempt to illustrate this claim with examples drawn from elsewhere in the book.

II

For Hobbes, the power of a state derives straight from its individual subjects. It does not pass through families or other civil associations – it is an unmediated relationship between rulers and the individuals over whom they rule. However, the purpose of this arrangement is to achieve peace, and peace for Hobbes meant a flourishing civil society, with associations dedicated to learning, religion, trade, culture and leisure. His famous description of the state of nature, in which the life of man is 'nasty, brutish and short', also describes it as a place without 'Industry ... Navigation ... commodious Building ... Arts ... Letters ... Society'; sovereign power was required in order to make these things sustainable.[5] But sovereigns also needed to control the bodies that constituted civil society, which included local organisations, trading companies, universities, and so on. In chapter XXII of *Leviathan*, Hobbes makes it clear that this is to be achieved by limiting their power, and by making sure that they operate only according to the rules established by the state. All 'systems' (Hobbes's term for 'any number of men joined together in one Interest or one Business') must be subordinate to the state. In the same chapter he identifies families as a distinct category of 'system', because they are formed naturally and without specific political sanction. But they too must be subject to political control, so that the power of heads of families extends 'as far as the law permitteth, though not further'.[6]

This is evidently a descending theory of state power, and it looks highly linear: power passes down from the state to lesser political and non-political bodies until it reaches the family (that is the order in which Hobbes discusses them in chapter XXII; the only groups that come after the family are 'illegal systems', meaning crime organisations). But it is not straightforwardly descending. For example, it is not the case that the family stands beneath other civil associations; rather, it exists alongside them, in a separate category ('lawful, private bodies'). Moreover, Hobbes is clear that other non-state bodies do not have the power to interfere with families; only the state can do that. Above all, though, what comes through from Hobbes's account are his reasons for wanting such tight political control: all 'systems' must be subject to the state because they are all potentially in competition with the state, even families. Hobbes was so insistent on a linear account because he understood very well the ways that power might otherwise circulate.

As Hobbes saw it, families, civil associations and states all work according to the same basic model: as members of the group, individuals must be spoken for by others. So just as states have sovereigns, colonies have governors, cities have councils, businesses have boards of directors, universities have governing bodies and families have parents. In every case, the group is controlled or directed by representatives claiming to act on behalf of its members. Some groups, Hobbes accepted, are best run as democracies, like trading corporations, where all the shareholders will expect to have a say. Others are suited to monarchy, such as families, which Hobbes describes as 'little monarchies' and whose rulers – parents – he calls 'sovereigns in their own families' (which included not just children but servants too).[7] What this means is that even in a Hobbesian commonwealth individuals will have plenty of different people able to speak on their behalf. There will be overlapping claims, there will be conflicts of interest, there will be rivalries, even between states and families

[5] Hobbes 1996, p. 89. [6] Hobbes 1996, p. 163. [7] Hobbes 1996, p. 163.

(or, one might say, especially between states and families). The state needed to keep a tight hold of this panoply of representative associations precisely because of its inherent tendency to spin out of control.

The peoples of contemporary Europe do not live in Hobbesian commonwealths: their governments do not have that kind of power. Our rulers are subject to extensive popular oversight and they can eventually be replaced if we have had enough of them, something that would have been anathema to Hobbes. Modern families do not fit the Hobbesian model either: children, including quite young children, are no longer happy with the idea of 'absolute domestic government', and there are few if any servants around to be spoken for by their masters. States now provide all individuals who are subject to the authority of others – children, students, employees, shareholders, passengers, even spectators – with extensive rights to guard them against abuse. But it does not follow from any of this that the core Hobbesian insight into the potential for overlap between family, civil associations and state is obsolete. If anything, the reverse is true. As states have become less able to direct their power straightforwardly downwards, so we see more and more opportunities for rivalry and competition between the state and other bodies. And as Hobbes knew, where there is rivalry, there will always be shifting alliances. Families look to states for protection against the pernicious influence of civil society; civil society looks to families to guard against the failings of the state; the state looks to civil society to break the hold of family; and so on. Hobbes was wrong if he thought this sort of fluidity would lead to political breakdown and ultimately civil war. But he was right if he thought it destroyed the possibility of a purely linear account of politics.

Hobbes's particular preoccupation with the family as a rival to the state reflected the early modern (and in some senses pre-modern) setting of his thought. He was especially concerned about the standing of what he called 'great families', whose pretensions to power and consequent vulnerability to accusations of treachery he understood well after a lifetime of service to the Cavendish family (the Earls of Devonshire). Hobbes was, at various points, secretary, tutor, confidant, man of business, intellectual ornament and political embarrassment to one of the most powerful families in the land. He never married and lived as part of an extensive household that more closely resembled a mini-state than a modern nuclear family. Yet he also recognised that these great families were inherently fragile and could not be called 'properly a Commonwealth', because they might not hold together under pressure: 'every [member] may use his own reason in time of danger, to save his own life, either by flight or by submission to the enemy'.[8] Hobbes himself fled England for

[8] Hobbes 1996, p. 142.

Paris in 1640, fearing for his life in the run-up to the Civil War, and though he maintained contact with the Cavendishes, he did not resume working for them again until his return in 1652. Families, in Hobbes's terms, could mimic states, but in the end it was up to individuals to judge where their best chances of protection might lie.

The age of the great aristocratic families of Europe is long past, and dukes no longer threaten the security of states with bodies of retainers so large that they resemble private armies. Modern societies, in this sense, have successfully separated out the public from the private domain in order to minimise the possibility of conflict. It is much harder now for a family to mimic a state. But it is not impossible: the Italian case, described in this book, demonstrates that ostensibly modern societies can still retain strong pre-modern echoes of family favouritism and patronage, both lawful and unlawful. Moreover, in the case of a politician like Silvio Berlusconi, the separation of public and private domains shows signs of breaking down altogether. And it is not just in Italy that family life and high politics overlap. In different parts of the Western world, family ties continue to run through many political elites. Under the recent Labour government, the British cabinet contained both a husband and wife (Balls/Cooper) and a pair of brothers (the Milibands), with a brother and sister (the Alexanders) linking the Labour establishments in England and Scotland. In the United States, but for the intervention of Barack Obama, the presidency would have remained in the hands of two families (the Bushes and the Clintons) for an entire generation. We should not imagine that modern democratic politics is immune from the tendency of families to colonise the political sphere, bypassing civil society along the way.

This overlap between blood ties and political power might look archaic in the context of twenty-first-century politics. Contemporary democracies are meant to favour the impersonal claims of individual citizens over the personal hold of family connections. But by extending Hobbes's line of argument, we can see that the blurring of public/private boundaries is a function of the individualism of modern political life, rather than simply an affront to it. Underlying Hobbes's whole body of thought is the idea that individuals and their personal choices are the basis of all social groupings, even families – we choose where and how we want to be spoken for by others. This means that all forms of human association – whether natural or non-natural, state or non-state – are potentially political, because any association can offer a means of escape from the hold of any other. We can use family ties to negotiate political relationships just as we can use political relationships to negotiate family ties. Of course, this opportunity was always there, and it hardly serves to distinguish modern from pre-modern societies. But Hobbes's point is that individualistic societies offer more, not fewer, chances for people to utilise the social relationships that suit their particular interests – that is why he was so insistent on the state remaining in control of it all. As individuals weigh up whether their prospects are better served by private or public associations, the line between them is bound to become a little blurred. Sometimes, the results will be distinctly old-fashioned, as when politicians continue to give preferment to family members. But this is consistent with the general trend of modern societies towards greater individualism, since the greater the individualism, the harder a linear distinction between family, civil society and state will be to maintain.

Hobbes also saw that the competition between families, civil associations and states for the loyalty of individuals was unavoidably ideological. If these groups are seeking to mimic each other in their ability to represent their members, then they have to compete with each other in the domain of public reason as well. Families, just as much as states, need to explain what they can do for people to justify making claims on them. Moreover, they will adopt whatever tools are at hand. For Hobbes, these arguments were almost certain to get mixed up with wider questions of religion and morality, and from there lead to conflict. In this sense, family life could prove a battleground in civil war just as easily as the high politics of church and state (and famously, the English Civil War did split some families down the middle, pitting fathers against sons). Nowadays, violent conflict arising out of the rival claims of families and states seems less likely (though as Sarah Howard shows in her chapter on France, in the deprived and alienated suburbs these can sometimes still be burning issues, literally). But the ideological component of family–state rivalry is still there. The different chapters in this book show that questions of religion, morality, public welfare and social justice remain bound up with family life, even in an apparently post-ideological age. Indeed, this is what we ought to expect: as the lines between public and private become less rigid, so political argument will migrate across them. Hence political claims about justice can end up being couched in the language of family, just as family ties can end up trumping the claims of political justice. A more individualistic, post-ideological society is also a more fluid one, and with fluidity comes increased opportunities for political arguments to move round the state–civil society–family circle.

Finally, there is a dialectical aspect to the Hobbesian account, although not a linear one. Hobbes believed that a successful, peace-promoting state would lead to a flourishing civil society. However, a flourishing civil society will produce many more potential rivals to the state. An optimistic reading of Hobbes suggests that he hoped people would learn how to deal with this tension, and with peace would come a greater understanding of the importance of political stability, so that an expanded civil society would not threaten the ultimate dominance of the state. But any optimistic reading of Hobbes always runs up against his strong sense of the lingering potential for conflict in all human relations, even when stability seems to be assured. People will always find new things to argue about. So this is not a view of politics that can guarantee steady progress towards greater cooperation and understanding on the part of states, civil associations and families. Such cooperation is always possible, but so is its breakdown. As states introduce the rules that free up civil associations and families to enjoy the benefits of political stability, so they will also look for new forms of control, to make sure that civil associations and families do not try to dispense with state altogether. Political stability does not necessarily make states feel secure; it can also make them feel irrelevant. Cooperation creates the conditions for new forms of competition, which is why the political rivalry between states, civil society and families in Western Europe continues to evolve.

The open-endedness of a Hobbesian account, with its emphasis on fluidity, competition and the cross-cutting claims that groups make on individuals, fits reasonably well with the recent history of families and states in Western Europe. So too does its uncertain mixture of optimism and pessimism.[9] Of course, as I have said, we do not actually live in Hobbesian states. Western Europe is now made up of liberal democracies, offering citizens extensive forms of redress against the abuse of political power. Moreover, these states are something less than sovereign in Hobbes's terms, having partially pooled their sovereignty in the European Union. But they are still *states*, with all the capacity for power-grabs and paranoia that this implies. And as states, they have evolved in recent years in ways that chime with some of Hobbes's concerns. Hobbes wanted states that protected citizens while granting them the scope to pursue their own ends: in that sense, he was a liberal. Modern European states have retained much of their security apparatus (they have not, for instance, either pooled or privatised their armies) while handing over other functions to the EU or to the market. They have become less prescriptive in how they regulate family life, without giving up their capacity to intervene when they think necessary. They have sought to encourage the growth of civil associations, while reinforcing some of their own central powers. This 'liberalisation' of the state has not produced neat, linear outcomes. Instead, it has created new sources of tension and competition with families and civil society, as well as new kinds of alliances. That is what I will try to illustrate in the remainder of this chapter.

III

The idea of the 'market state' (the phrase is borrowed from Philip Bobbitt) is primarily an Anglo-American invention.[10] It refers to the market-oriented,

9 There is a mixture of optimism and pessimism in Tocqueville's *Democracy in America* too, but it is more linear: plenty of optimism in volume I (1835), greater pessimism in volume II (1840). See Tocqueville 2000.

10 See Bobbitt 2002.

individualistic, security-conscious forms of politics which emerged out of the Thatcher/Reagan years (hence its alternative title: the 'Anglo-Saxon model'). Many Europeans – including many European politicians, and even a few British ones – would like to see Europe continue to offer an alternative to this, in the form of a more traditional, social democratic, corporatist model of politics, with a greater emphasis on welfare provision and less focus on market reforms. Yet this resistance is in itself a reflection of the increasing pervasiveness of the market model, and the anxiety it has provoked. Its presence is something that is reflected throughout this book and across the continent, from Scandinavia to Spain, and from Ireland to Italy. Nowhere has been immune to the forces of liberalisation and globalisation of which the market state is both a symptom and a cause.

The essential feature of the market state, as described by Bobbitt, is that it seeks to help individuals make use of the market and prosper through it, rather than trying to control the market and protect them from it. This hands-off approach means that market states are broadly tolerant of different ways of life and willing to accommodate a certain amount of personal experimentation in the domain of family and civil associations. It is what Bobbitt calls an 'umbrella' association, offering the basic protection needed for people to do their own thing. Liberalisation also goes along with an increased interconnectedness between states, as they reallocate some functions (communications, transport, trade regulation) to international bodies. But market states jealously guard their basic security functions, and they retain the capacity to take decisive action in an emergency. Finally, market states purport to be less ideological than their predecessors, and more pragmatic, sticking to 'what works'. One of the watchwords of this form of politics is governance, not government, implying that impersonal rules are to be preferred to structures of command and control.

Nowhere does the market state exist in a pure form: it is simply an ideal type. Yet aspects of it can be seen almost everywhere, including in Europe. Over the last twenty years, all Western states have had to adapt to the increased pressure for a more liberal – in the sense of a less *dirigiste* – politics. But this has not been a linear process, either in its causes or its consequences, especially as these changes have related to the family. In some countries, social changes at the level of the family have driven liberalisation, with the state frequently struggling to catch up (as in Spain and Italy); other states have sought to embrace market reforms while retaining control of the forces of social liberalisation (as in Britain during the Thatcher years or France under Nicolas Sarkozy). Sometimes, states have attempted to influence family life through the institutions of civil society (as in France and Germany); alternatively, they have tried to bypass civil society altogether by dealing with the family direct (as in Spain). Some of the most heated confrontations have been between state and civil institutions (as in Ireland, if the Catholic church is included in that category as it is by Tony Fahey here); but equally, civil institutions have tried to forge new alliances with the state (again, as illustrated in the Irish case) to retain their influence over the family in an increasingly individualistic society. Meanwhile, in Scandinavia, we encounter the long history of families looking to the state to protect them from the arbitrariness of the 'individualistic' market, even if that means allowing more state regulation than before.

Equally, we can see that the idea that the market state moves politics away from and above the domain of family life – that the state becomes an 'umbrella' rather than an interventionist association – is mere fantasy. All the states described in this book have carried on intervening in the family as and when they see fit. Moreover, states have not separated themselves out from families by becoming depersonalised governance bodies, in implied contrast to the purely personal domain of family life. State politics remains highly personalised and, as I have suggested above, shot through with family relations. This has tended to squeeze out civil society, as states and families ally against it. Nor have market states simply devolved their welfare responsibilities down through civil society and on to the family: we do not see a linear descent, with civil society taking over where states leave off, and families taking over where civil society leaves off. Often, the impact is directly on families, to which individuals turn as a first line of defence. Families are also proactive associations, as Adam Tooze shows in his chapter on Germany, ready to change their own shape (i.e. the number of children they have) in order to fend off the pressures coming from above. They do not need to wait for civil society to act as mediator or intercessor.

Liberalisation is a messy, convoluted process, and states, civil society and families are all capable of playing multiple roles within it, active or passive, as initiators as well as followers. It is perfectly possible to move both ways round the circle, and, as Paul Ginsborg says in his chapter on Italy, 'analytically, it is possible to enter the circle at any point'. The possibility of moving in different directions is illustrated if we enter with the state, and look at the changing role of the state in the performance of three of its traditional functions (ones that Hobbes would have recognised as foundational): as an allocator of offices, as a provider of welfare and as a site of loyalty.

A primary function of the state is to allocate offices (we could also call these jobs, but 'office' serves to highlight their public nature), ranging from top government positions through to posts in the bureaucracy. Offices give office-holders power, though how much power partly depends on the office, and partly on the office-holder. Personal attributes, such as charisma and ambition, can make a big difference. Hence not all presidents and prime ministers exercise the same amount of power: it depends a good deal upon their personal style of government.[11] However, the ideal form of the market state, founded on the principles of impersonal governance, may seek to break the link between office-holding and the exercise of personal charismatic authority by reducing all offices, including government ones, to the level of the bureaucracy. If the state is just an umbrella organisation, providing the rule-based framework for civil and family life, then there ought to be less room for personal intervention by politicians. Market states should provide fewer opportunities for office-holders to accumulate power to themselves.

That is the theory. The practice of recent years suggests something quite different. Nation-states (as opposed to intergovernmental organisations like the EU) continue to provide full scope for personality politicians to dominate, powered by charisma rather than bureaucratic competence. If anything, the period of market liberalisation has been accompanied by a hyper-personalisation of domestic politics, and a greater centralisation of power. This has been the age of Blair and Berlusconi, of Schroeder and Sarkozy, not of faceless administrators. Personality politics has also provided an opportunity for the personal connections of the best-known politicians to achieve greater prominence, including their families. It has been the age of Cherie Blair and Carla Bruni-Sarkozy as well.

These are some of the ironies of liberalisation in its impact on family/state relations: as states have become more distant from families in the way they exercise control, so they have come more to resemble families in the way personal connections dominate power relations within them. Indeed, one of the striking features of politics in the twenty-first century is the way it is simultaneously becoming more personal and more impersonal.[12] Enhanced individualism and pluralism requires a hands-off approach from government; yet a hands-off government can also be harder for outsiders to control, and easier for insiders to dominate. One consequence is a greater hostility between state and civil society, even in an age when states are seeking to exercise less of a direct hold on the way individual citizens choose to associate among themselves. What is presented as liberalisation often looks more like a pulling up of the drawbridge by the political elite, as the state and its office-holders retreat into their own private world of clientelism and corruption. We see this most clearly in Italy, but there is evidence of it elsewhere, including in Britain and in France, where liberalisation has gone along with a shutting out of civil society from the inner workings of government, and where non-state organisations are frequently used as nothing more than window-dressing for the decisions of the powerful few.

[11] An excellent illustration of this is given in Hennessy 2000.

[12] I discuss this in more detail in Runciman 2006, chapter 1.

This is a function of liberalisation; it is also a function of the age of celebrity. It is not only in political life that the attention of the public is focused on the minute doings of a small number of individuals. As Sarah Howard notes, the politics of family in France now embraces the personal arrangements of Brad Pitt and Angelina Jolie, absurd as that seems. Private citizens may have the opportunity to experience an increasingly wide variety of different lifestyles among themselves, but the public sphere is thin and repetitive when it comes to contemplating the lives of others. This, in a sense, was Tocqueville's insight: the enhanced individualism of democratic states, in levelling the playing field of public life by undercutting traditional forms of authority, makes it easier for the select individuals who do capture the public's attention to dominate it. But it also prompts a Hobbesian conclusion. Individualistic societies make it all the more important for states to stake their claims over the individual in personalised terms. They cannot do this through the mediating sphere of civil society. Instead, they do it directly, by projecting a form of intimacy back on to their citizens. Family life is very useful for this. As a result, individualism can serve to bring states and families closer together.

Market states do not want to take direct responsibility for the welfare of their citizens. Instead, they aim to act as facilitators, creating the conditions in which other organisations can provide some of the services traditionally associated with the welfare state. Often, the ultimate goal is to devolve as much responsibility as possible back on to the citizens themselves. There is potentially a linear model for this process, by which states hand over welfare responsibilities to religious and other voluntary associations, who then emphasise to the individuals on the receiving end their personal and family responsibilities. But that idea is primarily an American one (it is sometimes identified with the neoliberal phrase 'compassionate conservatism'). It does not have much purchase in Europe, either ideologically or practically.

Instead, what we see in Europe is that changes in the way states provide welfare can produce a range of different interactions between state, civil society and family. Where traditional family structures remain relatively strong, as in Italy and Spain, states wishing to liberalise their welfare functions may choose to delegate responsibility direct to families. However, given that market forces also threaten traditional family structures, by promoting the rapid mobility of both people and property, the same states often need to intervene in the family to support it. In Spain and Italy, liberalisation has coincided with new forms of alliance between states and families, often at the expense of civil society. But this is not simply a southern European phenomenon, nor just a recent one. There are echoes here of the earlier Scandinavian story, described in this book, of how attempts by the state to free up areas of civil society (in this case, the laws governing testation) weakens families in ways that may result in state and family being drawn closer together (since families, threatened by market forces, end up looking to the state for protection). States which devolve powers to other bodies do not necessarily end up with fewer responsibilities themselves.

Likewise, civil society organisations do not just pick up the slack where the state leaves off. Some established bodies (like trade unions) will try to forge new alliances with the state in order to control and if possible reverse the trend towards liberalisation; others (like the Catholic church) will assume responsibilities from the state in some areas (such as welfare provision) only as a means to retain some control over the state in others (such as family policy). The actors in this process are not simply the passive recipients of whatever powers and responsibilities the state chooses to dole out. They are part of the same circle as families and states, and they will adapt to changing conditions as they see fit. These changes may mean that civil associations look to the state in order to retain some hold on the family; alternatively, they may end up looking to the family in order to retain some hold on the state. It is because civil associations are active agents in this process that the state may feel the need to bypass them altogether, and interact with the family direct. Hence market states, whatever their liberalising aspirations, do not necessarily produce flourishing civil societies, as many of the case studies in this book demonstrate.

There is also the possibility that any neat distinctions between state, civil society and family, and more broadly between the public and the private sphere, will collapse altogether. As Adam Tooze makes clear in his chapter on Germany, we need to consider the biopolitical implications of recent changes, whereby questions of welfare provision merge into wider issues of demography, fertility, gender relations, environmental sustainability and raw state power. So, for instance, when the German state cuts back on nursery care, this does not produce neat linear outcomes (i.e. intermediary bodies stepping in, or more mothers staying at home to look after their children). Instead, families exercise direct control over their own fertility, which generates fresh anxieties at the state level regarding demographic pressures and unsustainable welfare obligations towards an ageing population.

There is nothing linear about the idea of biopolitics. If anything, it represents the closing of the circle, so that there are no entry points and no exit points – state, civil society and family become inextricably bound up together. But another way to see it is as the ultimate domain of Hobbesian competition (it is no coincidence that a theorist like Giorgio Agamben, who engages directly with the concept of biopolitics, also draws heavily on Hobbes).[13] State power, civil society, the family unit all represent claims on the individual, and the claims of any one of these are therefore implicated in and overlap with the

[13] See for example Agamben 1998.

claims of the others. This is as true for market states as it is for any other kinds of state – there is in that sense no such thing as a 'hands-off' approach to the regulation of civic and family life. Some conceptions of biopolitics can be apocalyptic – either pointing towards the anarchy of a Hobbesian state of nature or towards 'totalising' conceptions of ultra-authoritarian political regimes. The recent history of Western Europe contained in this book suggests we are still a long way off from either of those visions. But there is unquestionably a biopolitical (and hence a Hobbesian) aspect to what is described here: the relentless and unstable competition between states, civil society and families for control over individuals and their bodies.

All states worry about competition for the loyalties of their citizens. Sometimes this comes from other states, but more often for modern democratic states it comes from non-state bodies, either domestically or internationally. The range of these bodies has proliferated in recent years to include multinational corporations, non-governmental organisations, social networking sites, as well as more traditional organisations like religious bodies, labour associations and sports communities. The fear that states have is not that these other organisations will pose a direct political challenge, leading to violence and war, but that they will chip away at the hold states have over their citizens, making them much harder to govern. Market states are particularly vulnerable to these anxieties. By encouraging market forces, freedom of movement and enhanced communication, these states make it easier for individuals to associate with each other in multiple different ways. The symbol of this new freedom is the information technology revolution, which over the past two decades has both driven and been driven by the trend towards market liberalisation. Market state politicians have encouraged these changes, but they have also been deeply unnerved by them. They have made it harder for politics to stake its claim over individuals, in a world where so many other things are competing for their attention and their time. States cannot be sure whether anyone is listening to them any more.

One means to address this is to focus back on the family. Families, even in such a rapidly changing world, are relatively stable as sites of loyalty, and also reasonably geographically contained. Though many families are more dispersed than they used to be, they remain quite easy for states to access, both in material and in ideological terms. Market state politicians, from Thatcher to Berlusconi, have continued to fixate on the family as a means of holding the state together. In this respect, families are the natural allies of states worried about the disruptive effects of market liberalisation. This helps to explain the schizophrenic character of much contemporary state policy towards the family, of which the case of France described by Sarah Howard provides a clear illustration. The state's impulse to step back from family life goes along with a deep reluctance to let go, for fear of losing control of one of the few institutions that still retains a manageable shape. States and families, as she says, remain trapped in a 'folie à deux' of interlocking loyalties in the face of an uncertain world.

However, as she also points out, it is not just states that are having to deal with the changes wrought by rapid social and technological change. Families are too. As always these changes can work in different directions. Just as the television, once believed to mark the end of meaningful family life, also served to bring many families together by providing them with a focal point and common source of interest ('the box in the corner', discussed by Deborah Thom in her chapter on Britain), so new information technology can unite families even as it provides them with the means to live further apart. Email, heartless and impersonal as it often seems, nonetheless brings distant families together. Even computer games, which for many observers appear to spell the death of childhood, social interaction and family intimacy, can be surprisingly useful devices for allowing families to communicate in relatively harmless and mutually involving ways. Technology does not by itself destroy traditional loyalties. Only people do that, and only if they choose to.

The new technology has also had a profound impact on civil society. It has made it much easier for individuals to link up with like-minded individuals in order to share common interests and concerns.[14] New civil associations spring up online every moment. But these groups, easy to form, are also hard to hold together and rarely generate a long-lasting identity for their members. Their political impact is often limited. The internet has allowed micro-activism to proliferate but has made sustained, durable activism much harder to come by. There is no evidence that civil society has been able to exercise any greater influence on state politics during the period that politicians have been so worried about the divided attention of their individual citizens. The truth is that this same divided attention has served to weaken the hold of civil society associations and can often help to strengthen the hold of the state. One possible reason for this is that states, like families, do not depend on being the centre of attention in order to exist; they can survive extended periods when their members' minds are focused on other things. New forms of civil association are much weaker in this respect: when individuals get distracted, the association begins to disappear.

So it may be that civil society also needs to find links to families in order to compete successfully with the state for the loyalty of individuals. We see some evidence of this competition across the different parts of Europe described in this book, in the activities of churches, sporting associations, unions, advocacy bodies – it is all part of the circle that ties states, civil society and family

[14] An eye-opening if somewhat breathless account of the sheer diversity of online communities, drawn from the United States but with implications for Europe as well, is given in Penn 2007.

together. It is a mistake to think that this competition for loyalty between them is a zero-sum game, and that one group's gain is another's loss. In fact, loyalty to family may provide states with more opportunities for control, just as new civil society associations might require some links either to state or family loyalties in order to sustain them. This is not a story of linear relationships, but of constantly shifting alliances. The arrival of the market state, such as it is, has only served to accentuate that process.

IV

Over the past half century, and particularly over the past two decades, Western Europe has shared in the global trend towards individualism and liberalisation, driven in part by the information technology revolution. Many traditional forms of authority have gone into decline or at least into retreat over this period, as new means of communication and social interaction have sprung up. One might expect this period to coincide with a separating out of state and family, with a vibrant civil society interposing between them. But that is not what has happened. States and families have established new kinds of connections, frequently squeezing out civil society in the process. States, including market states, have not backed away from the family. If anything, the reverse is true, as states have looked to the family to maintain control of a rapidly changing and ever more diverse social sphere. As Sarah Howard writes in her chapter on France: 'Within an increasingly fluid society, which is less and less governed by traditional codes, legislation has become ever more vital as a way of managing social relationships.' States have continued to exploit the family when it suits their purposes. But families are not the passive victims of this process – they have also continued to exploit the state as and when it suits them.

In framing this recent history in Hobbesian rather than Hegelian terms I am not suggesting that there are no broad dialectical rhythms to be uncovered. Nonetheless, I believe one central theme of the Western European experience is the constantly changing nature of the interactions between states, civil society and families, driven by the overlapping claims being made by each on their individual members. This is a competitive as much as it is a dialectical process, and it is oriented around power relations. The circle that links states, civil society and families means that changes that happen in one place almost always have knock-on effects elsewhere, creating new threats and new opportunities for all involved. There is nothing to suggest that this process is anywhere near at an end.

2 Britain

Deborah Thom

I

Margaret Thatcher, speaking to the general assembly of the Church of Scotland on 21 May 1988, praised 'the basic ties of the family which are at the heart of our society and are the very nursery of civic virtue. And it is on the family that we in government build our own policies for welfare, education and care.'[1] Family was the basic building block, as she saw it, of modern society. This argument has returned again and again to political discourse, since it was used by Aristotle, and has most recently appeared in the same narrative of fragile social bonds under pressure in speeches by the then leader of the opposition, David Cameron, talking about the failure of the family as the central problem of broken Britain. His solution was to operate through taxation reform to privilege propertied families by reducing the tax on those who had children while legally married. But Thatcher's speech also demonstrates another intellectual problem in a narrative of the family as building block. The state is to build on it but, in order to do so, needs to intervene in it. State policy has historically attempted to preserve an ideal of an integrally private domain in which social and psychological health can be left to flourish. The family raises difficult questions for politicians and officials about the inequality of power and resources between ages and sexes in the family and hence can be seen not as an entity or unit but as a site in which different people share a location but have different tasks within it.[2]

Family remains a contentious political theme in that there is also a central and historical narrative of a vanished golden age when family relationships were strong and secure, just before the present day. One of the reasons that this story has been so powerful has been the way in which it was newly addressed by advertisement and commercial culture as well as the social sciences in post-war Britain.

Part of the difficulty in assessing changing family patterns historically is that the family has multiple identities and histories. It means variously

[1] Thatcher 2010. [2] Donzelot 1979.

households, kin groups, lineage. It includes dead kin when seen as a historical process and may include fictive kin as well. It also relates to two central social relationships – marriage or other arrangements for reproduction and the social arrangements for a large part of rearing children and making them full members of society. The questions that narratives of family failure raise include whether it remained unaltered, as many have argued, until divorce rates rose, marriage rates fell and 'the family' began to go into decline. Part of the problem of a politicised history may well lie in the glacially slow change by which reproductive cultures may alter despite the express legislative intentions of government. I shall not attempt to discuss all the meanings of family that have been important historically – family as inheritance or lineage; family as wider kin. I shall focus mainly on the nuclear family, usually of two generations, occasionally three, which overlaps with the household in public policy and public discourse – although not nearly as much as in Italy.

There are three turning points for the relationship between the British family, civil society and the state in the second half of the twentieth century. The first shows the highest level of state regulation of all aspects of life during the war emergency, under emergency powers, as well as full employment and labour market participation for all those previously limited or excluded in the work they could do. The sick, the wounded, the old and the very young were all hauled in to contribute to the war effort. However, much of the war effort was also the result of activities within civil society. There were large numbers of volunteer workers – the Women's Voluntary Services (the WVS), the British Legion, running canteens and sandwich bars, the fire watchers, who spent long nights scanning the skies for planes and then dowsing the flames in the Blitz. This mixed economy of civil society and state was blurred to contemporary observers who often saw volunteers as just another form of bureaucracy. In fact, though many activities were effectively voluntary, they were thought to be state inspired. The most dramatic demonstration of this was the evacuation of schoolchildren. This never came to be compulsory, as the government of the day was not prepared to risk being seen to be behaving like its Fascist opponents in Europe, nor could it spare the personnel to enforce compulsion. There was also precedent for moving large numbers of children around in wider European society – the *kinder transport* bringing unaccompanied minors out of Fascist Europe to seek refuge and the large numbers of Basque children brought over from Spain after the Civil War. The idea of the citizen child so evident in British war propaganda was here given full demonstration by the mixture of Quaker and social democrat organisations that sponsored or housed these children living without their own families. Evacuation tried to save all children from the anticipated risk of aerial bombardment once war had broken out. The plan was that the nation's children were to be removed from danger and cared for in homes up and down the land for the duration of war.[3] Homes were opened up to city children in the country and the suburbs and the experience has often been seen as a time of communal responsibility and social solidarity as well as the occasion for challenging the deprivation and dirt of city slums. The short film made by Ruby Grierson in 1940, *They Also Serve*, just before her tragically early death, dedicated to the housewives of Britain,[4] used the evacuee child as a synonym of the treasure of the national future. Instead of depriving all children of family life all families became responsible for all children. The reality of evacuation was often different from the fiction of the post-war years such as in *Goodnight Mister Tom*, where evacuation saves, or *The Machine Gunners*, where evacuation is rough and ready support for otherwise endangered children who roam the streets unsupervised by adults. But what both fictions demonstrated was the imaginative understanding of the popular history which informs television and film portrayals of Britishness and British civilisation down to the twenty-first century. But these fictions also demonstrate a complex mixture of family as place of safety and society as a place of mutual aid which provides an implicit contrast to the present.

War administration also changed the household as a place of labour. There was communal life in bomb shelters during London's bombing especially; there was socialised childcare[5] as women were first lured, then encouraged, then compelled into war factories;[6] regular hot meals came in factory canteens and civic restaurants. During the war much of this provision was very popular but once war was over in 1945 speedily lost all attractions. Writers and filmmakers satirised war bureaucracy and, although 1943–51 was a period of substantial legislative innovation and social change, many appeared to see the situation negatively, seeing an uncontrolled depressed economy and poor-quality public housing. The Labour party's short film on housing problems in 1945 opened up working-class homes to public view and found them wanting. Five housewives from Wales, London and the Midlands showed damp patches, poor cupboards, dangerous wiring and homes designed by men who never did washing nor managed prams. The household was made visible and the drama of squalor chimed with the other 'giants' of Beveridge's report *National Insurance and Allied Services* – 'Want, Disease, Ignorance, and Idleness', making the home visible in a new way. Here the idea of separate public and private spheres as outlined by Jürgen Habermas in his account of modernity needs a challenge.[7] The idea of the home as workplace and the presentation of that workplace for inspection was not new, but the extent and power of these images was, as was the development of social policy to overcome them.

[3] Macnicol 1986. [4] BFI 1940. [5] Riley 1983a. [6] Summerfield 1998.
[7] Habermas 1989; Fraser 1990.

John Maynard Keynes summed it up elegantly in arguing for change in the income tax policy to support the family, by which he meant the married couple and their dependent children: 'The strengthening of the economic position of the family unit should be a main purpose of social policy now and after the war.'[8] This proposal was to take deferred pay to pay for the war and to tax married couples as one unit but to add an allowance for a non-working wife. In many ways the state's taxation regime is the primary way in which the concept of the family and the household is made most visible and can most easily be measured. Other ways showed the same concern for the family in the war period and echoed the explicit intent of eugenists and others with demographic concerns summed up in the Royal Commission on Population, which reported in 1949 after taking six years to assess the causes of the declining birth rate, which had been at its lowest in the 1930s, and concluding that public welfare could encourage earlier marriage and more frequent child bearing.[9] A state pro-natalist policy was made explicit in the years after the war when fears of an ageing population and a birth strike were much discussed; this discussion did not last much beyond the construction of a welfare state designed to encourage more children in all households. The birth rate had already begun to rise, partly because the war was over and deferred births increased, but also because the new Labour government was busily addressing precisely those concerns which the Royal Commission had raised – building affordable public housing, providing free secondary education for all 'allocated according to age, ability and aptitude' and healthcare.

War and reconstruction saw ideals of citizenship and communal institutions which reflected the ideal, as the editorial of the *Times Educational Supplement* said in 1943, that 'every child is a ward of the state'.[10] The years 1945 to 1948 saw the reconstitution of both civil society and family after the end of the war. New ministries of health and education, a children's department at the Home Office, a family allowance paid for the second child (to encourage people to have more than one), national insurance based on the family wage and an expanded housing programme – all show a commitment to decency and basic standards despite austerity and controls. The Royal Commission on Population report had shown the influence of hereditarian thinking in the assumptions about descent and the nature of the family as the transmission of the future and the need to encourage a rising birth rate. Soldiers and war workers demobilised and enthusiastically followed the new commitment to the birth rate by both marrying and reproducing in rising numbers. Post-war prefabs, laundries and continuing childcare allied to raised school-leaving age, free secondary

[8] J. M. Keynes, 'Notes on the budget', 3 Nov. 1941, cited in Daunton 2002, p. 161.
[9] Report of the Royal Commission on Population, PP 259 Cmd 7695, June 1949.
[10] *Times Educational Supplement*, 28 June 1943, p. 303.

education for all and a surge in the rate of marriage and later divorce, which peaked in 1947. This rise in marriage as well as divorce demonstrated that for many people the ideal of family life seemed a fitting way to enjoy the freedom of an end to world war.

Family reconstruction was seen as essential and government still found money and time to think about the fate of children without homes or families. The Curtis report of 1946[11] argued that the state should do everything it could to keep children in their own families, following the theory being developed by John Bowlby.[12] The theory and politics of the family was partly reactive to popular sentiment in supporting an idea of a return to pre-war stability, calm and happiness and partly constructive and egalitarian about building a new Jerusalem. For example, the Royal Commission on Marriage and Divorce in 1951, which reported in 1955, was set up to avoid discussing the private member's bill proposal of irretrievable breakdown as sole cause of divorce. The intention was to encourage marriage by ending unhappiness and hypocrisy but contemporary society was not yet ready to end the double standard between the guilty and innocent alike. This was a popular politics designed to remedy injustice and prevent social division but it did not operate through stigma of the dispossessed or deprived but more through an idea of citizen entitlement.

The construction of the citizen during the war and in the 1950s focused around the image of the radio. Radio ownership was virtually universal after the war and the nation had acquired the habit of listening during the war. One can see the most significant component of a truly national culture in radio programmes such as *Forces Favourites*, playing songs to connect conscript soldiers to their families and friends at home. The war-time programme was followed by *Family Favourites* in the late 50s, while *Workers Playtime*, introduced to keep factory morale high and rising, also continued after the war.[13] Here the economy was sponsored by the state for war purposes but civil society kept the activities of war in time of peace from a sense of citizenship and communal culture. The idea of the population as all entitled citizens was developed in various places by both state and civil society. For example, the new children's department of the Home Office set up in 1948 produced a pamphlet called *Making Citizens* in that year to illustrate the work of approved schools in reforming the delinquent child.[14]

Narratives of the social sciences flowering just after the war encouraged the family as the best place for developing a new civilian society. John Bowlby had analysed the life histories of forty juvenile thieves and had found that thirty-eight of them had endured substantial periods of life away from their families and the other two had had shorter periods of isolation. He began to publish the

[11] Report of the Committee of Enquiry into the Care of Children (Curtis committee) 1946.
[12] Bowlby 1951. [13] Kynaston 2009. [14] *Making Citizens*, HMSO 1948.

works deriving from this insight and to argue for the increase of care by parental figures in institutions after the war when he became head of the Tavistock clinic, especially in hospitals, where children were routinely separated from their parents. His most effective summary of his belief that children should always remain with a primary loving care-giver, especially in infancy, was the Penguin book he produced from his UNESCO study of twenty-four-hour nurseries for the children of war workers, evocatively titled *Child Care and the Growth of Love*. This text summed up its findings pithily: 'Better a bad home than a good institution.'[15] The children's department of the Home Office was headed by one of the first psychiatric social workers who had worked in child guidance before the war, Sybil Clement Brown, and she too was motivated by the same assumptions about the need to support families rather than provide alternative institutional places for children in difficulties. Feminist scholars have pointed out that these arguments and their development into social institutions assumed that primary care-giving was what women did. Others have pointed out that many women who had worked in arduous, uncongenial factory jobs during wartime found this priority given to families a most attractive part of the post-war reconstruction of civil society. The state was ambivalent about these ideas. Acute labour shortage meant that some departments argued for more childcare to increase the workforce while others argued for the home as the best place for all young children. Certainly, one of the effects of the social science and the government alike was to increase thinking about a gender division in society where women made homes and cared for children and men worked and trained to work better. In politics, women participated less than they had in the 1930s in local government and to some extent in central government. The 1950s saw the smallest proportion of working mothers in the labour market and the highest proportion of working fathers at any time in the twentieth century.[16]

This was a period of pro-natalism in public discourse and in private practice, especially among those educated middle-class people who had been most prominent among those parents whose revolt from parenthood had reduced the birth rate very far in the 1930s. (This may partly explain why the notion of a baby boom was so important at the time, although demographers point out that much of the increase of births was deferred births after the war, just like the similar, smaller boom in the 1920s, not a change in reproductive expectations.) Families got larger, then smaller, as ages of marriage fell for both sexes and the proportion of the population who were married reached a high. Divorce also peaked in the post-war period in 1947. But, if the total population growth of the post-war period did little more than replace deferred births from the war

[15] Bowlby 1951, p. 78. [16] Spencer 2005.

period, it did briefly place pressure and rising expectations on the growing welfare state as well as provide a population prepared to defer consumption for a while to provide it. Here the relationship between state, civil society and family was constructed by a profoundly paternalist, even patriarchal, set of assumptions about collective interest and the mutual benefit of deferred consumption and high rates of government spending. This view of the state as essentially benign did not last for very long once the world war was over. The view of the family and household as the central unit of social administration lasted much longer. One of the reasons it could do so was that popular representations of family life were informed by a sense of recent history of the 1930s and depression in which the inaction of the state had been seen as a failure to protect family life. Housing and the labour market remained as important in constructing expectations of family social life as cultural histories. But the cultural history of the mutual aid and solidarity of wartime was not undermined by losing a war, as elsewhere in Europe, nor by social insecurity, as the new welfare state was extremely effective in complementing private cultural desires. Many of the social policy analysts of the 1950s pointed out that children and young married women gained more from its provisions than the old.

II

The second major shift in British family was in the late 1960s where civil society led and government implemented. Paul Ginsborg sees 1968–73 as a turning point and I would see it as one too but in a different direction and starting earlier. One might see this as being the breakdown of normative assumptions and practices around the family in favour of not one, but several, discursive communities. For students, some young women and fewer homosexual men, the period was described as one of liberation in which sex could be divorced from marriage and work combined with parenthood in new ways. For many young workers, housing shortage and rising prices meant that family life had to wait for the council house list to reach their names before they could set up on their own. Class tended to divide people on the question of freedom to experiment and meant that for a majority there was not as much change as rhetoric suggested. In 1967, the Abortion Act, allowing abortion with the agreement of two doctors if pregnancy endangered the physical or psychological health of the mother, and the decriminalisation of homosexuality after the Steel Act, removed two legal restrictions on private practice which had barely existed for the rich in any case; 1970 saw the introduction of equal pay and equal opportunities which protected women in the labour market and helped increase labour market participation. Public childcare increased slightly and commercial provision increased also. The 1971 Finer committee investigated the situation of lone mothers in the report on one parent families, arguing for support rather than stigma.[17] In 1969 divorce legislation saw easier access to divorce and more egalitarian distribution of family property and child custody. The arrival and distribution of the contraceptive pill helped married couples limit births still further and young women enjoy a variety of sorts of sexual experience just as their brothers had done before. The birth rate fell to 1.89 children per couple. State policy no longer sought to encourage a rising birth rate. Although eugenics remained influential in discussing questions of reproduction in Britain, it was rarely discussed in relation to either society or economy as in Germany or Franco's Spain in terms of encouraging a rising birth rate after the late 1960s. Reproduction became more a matter of personal choice, epitomised in the slogan of the National Abortion Campaign formed by feminist campaigners to protect and extend the 1967 Act: 'A woman's right to choose'. This new language of reproduction as an individual choice rather than a social contribution demonstrated that biopolitics had become central to discussion about the concept of what was a civil society. Most European societies liberalised their laws on abortion in this period but in Britain discussion about the question remained rooted in questions about medicine and women's rights rather than a more economic or cultural debate about the future of the labour market or the population.

These changes reflected a powerful shift in the position and opportunities of women and reflected both rising educational qualifications and increased presence in the labour market. In 1979 the Trades Union Congress agreed to sponsor a demonstration against the Corrie bill on abortion which was probably the largest such event on an issue around reproduction, with over 100,000 marchers.[18] But this too was based around the idea of a woman's choice, not social needs. In a report prepared for the House of Commons at the end of the twentieth century members of parliament were told that the general fertility rate in the UK had fallen to 91 live births per 1,000 women aged 15–44 and by 1997 to 59.[19] But when population did begin to be discussed again at the millennium it was about its being too large, not in need of growth.

Cultural consumption continued to follow a national culture in that television replaced radio as the dominant single national experience – itself feeding into associational culture in, for example, reflecting on housing in *Cathy Come Home* which described the distressing history of a young mother who fell through the provision of housing and became homeless. Comprehensive education was becoming general in the early 1960s as numerous local authorities found the problems of selection more and more difficult and more and more

[17] Report of the Committee on One-Parent Families (Finer committee) 1974.
[18] Lovenduski 2005, p. 82.
[19] Century of Change: Trends in UK Statistics since 1900, www.parliament.uk/commons/lib/research/rp99/rp99-111.pdf, accessed 26 April 2010.

indefensible. Comprehensive schooling was made compulsory for secondary schools (as it had been for a long time in primary schools) in 1965, though selection remained in Kent and elsewhere. Schooling thus became more equitable for the two sexes, especially after the leaving age was raised to sixteen in 1968, and young women became more ambitious and more discontented as a result. New universities were opened in the 1960s. Dependence in young lengthened among the educated middle class but the advantage of inherited social capital diminished as schooling became more effective in narrowing equality. The marker for this change was the publication of *The Home and the School* by J. W. B. Douglas in 1968.[20] Here the assumption that the state could undermine class distinction was challenged by the observation that destinations in life were far more affected by the social and cultural capital of family life in childhood than by schooling itself. Sociologists wrote about 'restricted codes' in working-class families and that the absence of 'elaborated code' or substantial parental attention limited working-class children's capacity to rise in a mobile society.[21]

Mass communications helped to expose the virtual reality of family life. In Britain, the development of a popular and populist sociology allied to legacies of an egalitarian anthropology from Mass Observation in the 1930s, published by Penguin Books, had an impact through professional formation on social workers, teachers and the numerous graduates of the universities in the social sciences appearing from the early 60s. This was a reflexive society in which the state of the family was frequently discussed. For example, *New Society* and the *New Statesman* published the results of sociological and psychological research to a growing audience. Politics was, to some extent, informed by such investigation. Community studies had a particularly effective way of describing social class in everyday domestic life, in which Phyllis Willmott and Michael Young showed how the life of the home still reflected a female-dominated sociability rooted in family through young mothers' continuing close relationship with their own mothers, despite slum clearance and mobility to new housing estates.[22] Britain was different from Italy in that families were far less likely to live in three generation households and women were more likely to be wage-earners, although many of them worked part time as encouraged by regulations for National Insurance, which limited employer contributions for less than sixteen hours' work a week. Britain was not in the same way still a decaying patriarchy although it remained fairly patriarchal. Rehousing and the council estate did not jeopardise family relationships which remained, as in Italy, matrifocal. Community studies described the old working class in the East End of London and the way in which its habits remained familial in the suburban estates of outer London. Cheap family cars and public transport as

[20] Douglas 1972. [21] Bernstein 1971. [22] Willmott and Young 1957.

well as the telephone ensured that families stayed in regular personal contact despite substantial movement. Holidays kept people in touch, and the practice of regular family reunions at Christmas became general. Internal migration was less intrusive than in Italy as the telephone spread and rehousing tended to take families about twenty miles away from their original place of residence, rather than across the whole country. The workplace was already much more structurally separate from the home and there were fewer family enterprises.

Immigration affected ideas of family life in various ways, as different groups settled in different styles of family life and household. The Caribbean-sponsored migration to provide workers for London transport and the National Health Service tended to encourage young adults to migrate separately. Lord Scarman reported from American sociology when he argued that fatherless families in Brixton in 1981 had helped create social disorder among young black men; arranged marriage and dowry systems in some South Asian families were seen as creating an unusually strong reliance on the family. The state intervened to redefine eligibility for settlement and provide quotas by introducing the concept of 'patriality' and removing rights from commonwealth citizens in the Immigration Act of 1971. Family members were allowed to follow migrants, but in restricted numbers, and the state's commitment to family was limited as far as migrants were concerned.

Family remained the place where fortunes were to some extent made or prevented as life chances continued to reflect birth not educational achievement.[23] Emotional economies replaced political economies, as popular versions of social and psychological theory were spread through magazines and the universal provision, for example, of *Family Doctor* pamphlets about babies given to all new mothers when their child was born. Ideals of normative child development became widespread through both commercial and governmental accounts. The Newsons in Nottingham showed that these changes were well underway in *Patterns of Infant Care* in 1965, and *Four Years Old in an Urban Community* in 1968, both published by Penguin, and reaching quite large numbers of readers through journalism and other popular exposition.[24] The study of the children in Douglas's *The Home and the School* located social development firmly in the household.[25] All were based on the assumption that class affects patterns of behaviour but not in simple ways. My own research on discipline in British families shows variation within a general greater democracy and increasingly limited paternal authority.[26]

The greatest difficulty in this model of the changing European family is in locating the institutions of civil society – the concept is a complicated one. As an analytical space it is one which includes academic research where people

[23] Blanden and Gregg 2004. [24] Newson and Newson 1965, 1968.
[25] Douglas 1972. [26] Thom 2009.

look at the activities of voluntary bodies. Britain has a long and strong tradition of youth organisations, which provide alternative places for integration, but they became much less significant in Britain after the early 1970s, competing weakly with commercial pleasures. It is difficult to know how to assess the various histories of youth styles like those of mods, skinheads, punk music, rave culture. All are associated with specific drugs from alcohol to ecstasy and might have offered areas of loyalty and friendship which replaced some of the family activities of the age of austerity. Certainly, they represented a diffusion of power and a challenge to some of the normative assumptions of family sociology, which had difficulty dealing with youth as opposed to children. For adults, such new cultural forms were much less likely to develop into anything either critical or constructive. There remained in British culture a variety of leisure pursuits which were pursued independently of family life by adult men – snooker, fishing, various sports, the pub. For women, the divide between the affluent and the educated took young women who went to university further away from home and household before they had children but returned them to domesticity to some extent afterwards. The sociology of Basil Bernstein and others, asking why equal educational opportunity had failed to abolish inequality, reflected a notion of working-class deficit through linguistic impoverishment, which the community studies contradicted.[27] The studies of social mobility of the 1960s looked to the same processes but by concentrating only on boys missed one of the major changes of the period.[28] Feminism both reflected and created change in the period and it is arguable that most of the changes in post-war Britain reflect far more change in women's lives than in men's.

During the period approximately between 1965 and 1973, British society thus became one in which civil society institutions were, much less than in the 1940s, mutually reinforcing sites of integrative citizenship but increasingly pulling against both family and certain parts of the state. They operated in a variety of different ways. Demand for nursery places, continuing support for abortion law reform, equal opportunities and equal pay tended to be based upon a notion of supporting family rather than challenging it, using women's importance in the lives of their children to mobilise. Some questions of sexual politics around normative sexuality pulled away from family towards individualism; it also divided men from women and challenged male hegemony. Predominantly, though, the feminist impulse was itself matrifocal, as it emphasised women's needs and demands including those of mothers – for example, for improved maternal health, maternity care and childcare provision while feminism challenged norms of male behaviour in wider society as much as demanding a change in female manners.

[27] Bernstein 1971. [28] Halsey, Heath and Ridge 1980.

III

Three major forces for change in thinking about British families have been feminism, social science and popular history. All flowered in the period in Britain after 1968. Feminism had a long history in which the state had been both friend and foe to women. This ambivalence persisted in the approach to political change seen in the women's liberation movement, which emphasised self-transformation through consciousness-raising groups and independent organisation around six demands. These demands included abortion and contraception, childcare and equal opportunities; and some argued that emotional work was labour as well, vital to family support just as paid employment was to economic maintenance.[29] The 'Wages for housework' campaign took this even further, seeing payment as the source of male power and autonomy and all household activity as in need of negotiated conditions and fair wages. This kind of feminism saw family life as the main source of women's dissatisfaction with the world as it was and that women needed to escape some of its burdens. However, many feminists in practice wanted to transform family life, not leave it altogether, and the practical consequences of much agitation were mostly about opportunities in employment, equal pay and greater access to education. Reproductive rights were increasingly seen as legitimate demands for all women where feminism allied itself to ideas of self-help in health. In this period the contraceptive pill and other reproductive technologies meant that women could control when and how often they gave birth. Studies of contraception in this period indicate that the pattern of the period before 1964 – that contraception was mostly a mutual marital decision – became less common and women chose and organised their method themselves.[30] Legislation helped but the use of oral contraception was not created by it, and the decision to provide free contraception on the National Health Service owed as much to eugenists, anxious to encourage reproduction in general and to improve female health, as it did to feminist demands. What feminism did do was to limit shame and prudery by encouraging a liberation of thinking about the body.

Feminists argued very strongly for childcare provision but were less successful in creating a wider support for the political demand. Most local authorities provided nurseries for young children but not in sufficient numbers to enable women to expect a place if they needed to work. The war nurseries had been unpopular partly because they had been staffed and run on an assumption that only needy or delinquent mothers would put their children into institutional care, partly because they had had high rates of colds and influenza and partly because war work had been uncongenial.[31] The nurseries of the 1960s were

[29] Coote and Campbell 1982.

[30] Fisher 2000; Szreter and Fisher 2003, 2010; Cook 2004.

[31] Riley 1983a.

more attractive places where mothers were increasingly able to come in when leaving their child and where the nursery nurses were trained to see themselves as creating development rather than redeeming slum children. However, good-quality public childcare with a ratio of one member of staff for three babies or five toddlers was expensive, and although employment rates were high in the 1960s there was no labour shortage, so the political will to see this demand as a priority was lacking. Again, feminism's effects were more about the attitudes and aspirations of women themselves, who no longer felt it necessary to choose between having children or a successful career. A maternalist, pro-natalist welfare state as in the Scandinavian countries had never managed to develop the idea of state sponsorship of parenthood to any great extent and there was little demand for paternity leave or larger numbers of nurseries to stimulate the birth rate.

The main effect of feminism was in the creation of a large group of educated and ambitious women who began to penetrate the elite institutions of Britain, not in a new way but in new quantities. The civil service, teaching, law and medicine all saw larger numbers of women entrants. The interdependence of state and civil society is shown by the way in which these workers often found themselves in public sector work. The expansion of universities helped to sustain a growing professional middle class and helped, to some extent, to undermine the one group in British society for whom family remains central – the aristocracy. Feminism was helping to broaden meritocracy, though not to make it dominant.

The last effect of feminism was to demand full equality in the home. The effect of campaigns against domestic violence and patriarchal attitudes was slow but steady and extensive. Refuges for battered women, campaigns against pornography, rape counselling and self-help groups, demands for more sympathetic policing turned the family into an object of concern, a place of risk and danger rather than a place of safety. Language itself was called into question by the recognition of the implicit inequality in labelling. Probably the main way these questions of cultural politics and police power were most questioned was through the media and the teaching profession. But change was evident in the way in which fathers began to participate in childcare and domestic work as time budget studies showed in the 1980s.[32] Change was also evident in the policing and prosecution of sex workers and the handling of rape and domestic violence.

The social sciences provided the second area where attitudes to family were questioned and changed. Penguin Publishing was one of the central forces for this change in the 1970s, producing large numbers of texts reproducing the findings of academic studies in readable and accessible cheap paperbacks.

[32] Berthoud and Gershuny 2000.

Some of these, like the community study of family life in the East End by Willmott and Young or the Newsons' accounts of childcare practices, sold in very large quantities. Donald Winnicott, John Bowlby and Susan Isaacs popularised psychological thinking about the family and psychoanalysis. These were probably just as important as the more liberal attitudes of Dr Benjamin Spock in his childcare manual, *Baby and Child Care*, which first appeared in Britain in 1953. These were books that carried a powerful argument about the dangers of repression and restriction and the importance of parental attentiveness to a child's needs. The academic studies were also conveyed through the burgeoning market in magazines for women, which reported on research findings. For example, the National Childcare Trust, which helped to transform hospital births in Britain, came into being as a result of an article in a women's magazine which inspired some women to organise to support each other and learn the methods of natural childbirth. Breast feeding on demand replaced the Truby King model when timed feeds were provided at regular intervals to prevent 'spoiling' the child. As feminist scholars of the time noted, this science of childcare saw the caretaker as the mother but the political result was more to encourage greater recognition for maternity and support for it.

Jacques Donzelot's argument that the mother provides the route through which the regulatory complex enters and divides the family ignores the way in which women's position improved in the family as a result of paying family life more attention.[33] It also ignores the interactive nature of people's deployment of the ideas of social scientists. Studies of parental discipline of feeding and weaning habits, sleep patterns and play show a diversity of practice and demonstrate quite clearly what theorists of governmentality ignore, which is that people do not always do what books tell them to do. Harry Hendrick has argued that feminism has been limiting for children because it encouraged women to work outside the home, but he ignores the way in which rising affluence, falling hours of work, social science and feminism combined to ensure that both parents spent more time with their children.[34] He also points out that monitoring, surveying of children has increased intervention by regulatory bodies without encouraging citizenship rights except as an afterthought. But this history of children losing a vanished golden age of constant parental attention is worth mentioning as it is one of the historical arguments that keeps coming back.

The third area of civil society which has had an impact on thinking about the family is popular history itself. As the political demands of feminism and the findings of social science fed slowly into popular culture and professional practice it remained also affected by ideas based upon historical accounts.

[33] Donzelot 1979. [34] Hendrick 1997, p. 4.

Genealogy only became a major popular leisure pursuit after the popular historical series *Who Do You Think You Are?* began to air on television, but the idea of the family as a history was already embedded in the practice of schools and adult education. British feminism was always remarkably historical in its account of origins and causes. Sheila Rowbotham used history to explain the dynamics of women's situation in her *Woman's Consciousness, Man's World*, and in her *Hidden from History* she tried to recover a lost history of women's political organisation and activism.[35] British social sciences were also prone to narratives of change as explanations of cause with short sections of historical stage setting in most works of sociology. The history of the family was one of the main ways in which people developed an account of historical change. The fiction of happy families of the past was replaced by a history of misery and deprivation from which grew a welfare state and modernity. History is one of the ways in which British people think about society and their own histories. Family and its relationships and activities was at the heart of such popular history.

When the makers of the television programme which tracks famous people's ancestry began their series they intended to illustrate a theme in each programme. They planned to start with industry, then look at medicine and transport. What they found again and again was movement and diversity, both immigration and travel around the country. Large numbers of these celebrities' ancestors had fled religious or racial persecution. They also found stories of appalling deprivation from the early years of the twentieth century which tended to emphasise a progressive and Whiggish history of change brought about by social improvement. In these histories the coming of the welfare state features again and again as the moment of transformation when a family was at last able to thrive. Thinking historically also led to substantial amounts of history 'from below' where ordinary citizens were asked to narrate their memories. Again, this tradition was not new but the volume of it was and its presence in public discussion raised questions about upbringing and about relationships, which caused a greater strength of feeling about collective responsibilities for the welfare of others. The political consequences were ambiguous, as might be expected, as popular history can be used either to say how much better things were in the past or to say that governments have done a good job in removing some of the evils of the past.

An implicit history of progressive social change creating modern families is part of the fictions which people watch and observe. Family romance remains a major category of popular fiction. The era which has been most used to provide such historical fictions is the Second World War. One of the reasons for

[35] Rowbotham 1973a, 1973b.

this might well be that most of these novels, plays and films are written by and for women and provide a dramatically neat way of exploring ideas of change and transformation for women as well as men. But it also shows nostalgia for a past when people looked after each other and there was no crime. Politically, it probably diminished in impact during the years of the third shift I want to outline.

The British welfare state was, like that of Italy, founded upon the notion of the male family wage and the assumption of full male employment. The married woman's stamp and different national insurance for work under sixteen hours both helped to sustain a segmented labour market. Economic downturn in 1973 and the rise of male unemployment and public spending cuts began the long reversal of the mutual support of family, civil society and state, undermined cultural optimism about public sector institutions as supports for family and created what many have called, with varying degrees of disapproval, the privatisation of the family.

IV

The third turning point is difficult to locate precisely. I could call it Thatcherism and it has long roots overlapping with my second period of change from 1967 to 1973. In 1985 on 11 November in her speech to the Lord Mayor's Banquet, Margaret Thatcher said

> natural authority starts in the home, in the family. And beyond the family, it runs through school, church, work – and our many institutions. But some parents opt out of their duty to their children. Just as some teachers ignore the need to educate their pupils in the obligations of citizenship. And some neighbours just don't want to know.[36]

In the 1990s, negotiation replaced obligation with a new calculus of risk. Janet Finch in 1989 saw this process continuing in a new risk society where the family is one of the ways in which risk is managed.[37] The 'democratic' family is characterised by 'equality, mutual respect, autonomy, decision-making through communication and freedom of violence' wrote Anthony Giddens[38] in arguing for a revival of the voluntary sector – which sounds pretty much like Paul Ginsborg's version of civil society. But the intellectual and historical problem here is that families are not only places of strength and decency and civility and such social forces cannot be maintained against ineluctable forces such as the housing and labour markets. The rise of unemployment and the continuing decay of traditional industrial areas meant that aspirations to an egalitarian and democratic family life, both within the household and among the wider family

[36] Thatcher 2010, speech to Lord Mayor's Banquet 1985; cf. Durham 1991.
[37] Finch 1989a. [38] Giddens 1998.

in the society, were much harder to fulfil for those whose economic life was hard after the 1980s, while those who were affluent lived in a society in which the state increasingly withdrew from anything other than providing a safety net. Esping-Andersen has seen Britain increasingly as the minimal welfare state of the American model rather than the interventionist egalitarian welfare state of the Swedish type.[39] The question of how far the state promotes equality rather than preventing damage remains politically contentious.

How far did the state influence these patterns of childcare and family dependence? Rhetoric remained firmly based on an idea of the family as the building block of society. It remained largely untouched by feminist critiques of the 1970s and 80s in which the family became seen as a site of oppression, of danger and of potential for harm. Mary Mackintosh and Michele Barrett gave a critique of marriage and female dependence in their book *The Anti-Social Family* where women were urged to get out of the family and its damaging limitations on their fulfilment.[40] But criticisms of the family were more widely felt in discussing campaigns against domestic violence, which led to the foundation of refuges for battered women, originally voluntary, administered by supporters' collectives rather than by the state; to improved practice in rape policing; and to the defence of birth control and abortion, again seen as part of civil society rather than in the conventions of political parties or the actions of governments. Marriage and parenthood were seen as less desirable sole aspirations for women. Domestic labour was called into question, and its real costs brought to public view.[41] Girls' socialisation was criticised and the school studies of these processes anatomised and criticised the contrast in popular language between the 'drag' who was prudish and sexually inactive and the 'slag' who aimed to please men by being sexually active but lost respect by doing so.[42] The majority of new jobs were in areas where women predominated, the public sector, offices and shops, so increased education, training and full employment meant that the labour market probably changed women's lives more than family rhetorics or feminist campaigning itself.

Some deplored this change. The death of the family has been more worried about in the USA but Conservative politicians have reiteratively emphasised the crucial importance of marriage for preventing what they see as deterioration. Sir Keith Joseph in 1974, in a speech at Edgbaston, famously argued that

> the balance of our population, our human stock is threatened. A recent article in Poverty, published by the Child Poverty Action Group, showed that a high and rising proportion of children are being born to mothers least fitted to bring children into the world and

[39] Esping-Andersen 1990. [40] Mackinhosh and Barrett 1982.

[41] Although recent studies have shown little change in the domestic division of labour except in relation to childcare. See Gershuny and Sullivan 2003.

[42] Lees 1997.

bring them up. They are born to mothers who were first pregnant in adolescence in social classes 4 and 5. Many of these girls are unmarried, many are deserted or divorced or soon will be. Some are of low intelligence, most of low educational attainment. They are unlikely to be able to give children the stable emotional background, the consistent combination of love and firmness which are more important than riches. They are producing problem children, the future unmarried mothers ... single parents, from classes 4 and 5, are now producing a third of all births. A high proportion of these births are a tragedy for the mother, the child and for us ... Yet what shall we do? If we do nothing, the nation moves towards degeneration, however much resources we pour into preventative work and the over-burdened educational system. It is all the more serious when we think of the loss of people with talent and initiative through emigration as our semi-socialism deprives them of adequate opportunities, rewards and satisfactions.[43]

He had identified a historic change, which was that Britain did have a relatively high rate of teenage unmarried motherhood, and he saw the problem as being that such mothers were a reservoir of social problems. This was in fact exactly the same argument as used by eugenists in the 1930s about the 'social problem group' and by Victorians about the residuum. The belief that social problems lay in a small group of the population passing on poor qualities which were inherited was not new, but the suggestion that this group was female only was, as was the emphasis on the inheritance of these qualities directly. This speech was criticised but it demonstrated a revival of ideas of social control which contradicted neo-liberalism in the market.

Was marriage in decline? Single parents were just more than 5 per cent of parents of young children in 1971, more than 10 per cent in 1981 and more than 20 per cent of children were living with a lone parent in the 1991 census. Most of these were people who had been made single by desertion or divorce or widowhood rather than by choice. One of the ways in which change occurred in the possibility of marriage under Thatcher after 1983 was the sale of council houses, the introduction of internal markets in public services and the abolition of the Greater London Council. These changes meant that the chance of a new household for a new family were diminished as commercial building for rent was at a low level and what was built was not designed for the poor. Housing associations did to some extent provide for low incomes and charities continued to provide for the homeless but the extensive provision of the post-war welfare state which allowed young people to set up house independently gradually vanished or was sold off. Many young women who became pregnant young were thus encouraged to remain in the parental home. The relationship between citizen, state and public administration altered. Administrative costs in the health service for example doubled from 3 to 6 per cent. The state cushion of family life for poor families got thinner as a result.

[43] Thatcher 2010, 19 October 1974.

However, the family remained the main site of childcare, which continued to be seen as the preserve of mothers, and family members remained the main provider of support for working mothers. Britain has not followed the Scandinavian countries in parental leave provision and protection of mothers' work entitlement. It was even slower to recognise the change in family support needed to deal with dependent elders. The provision of childcare and old age homes has become increasingly the preserve of private investment, not state provision. Part of this is the result of simple demographic change. There are more older people and they are living longer, placing growing demands on state welfare. Under Thatcher, however, the growth in unemployment, which reached 3 million at its peak, cost substantially in benefits to support people during unemployment and in tax revenue foregone. Individuals were to be responsible for supporting themselves and the family was more addressed in rhetoric than supported practically. Control of juvenile misbehaviour with the idea of the short, sharp shock being imported from the USA for delinquents increased the level of surveillance for young people outside the home.

V

Cultural change led to new ideals of affection and relationship which included family life but created what Beck and Beck-Gernsheim call *The Normal Chaos of Love*.[44] The demand for markets created a problem of mobility in advanced capitalism and the family became more and more a virtual reality, kept together through the internet and telephone across continents and countries. Family remained a place where ideas about morality and responsibility were played out, but where economics and material constraints remained far more significant than ideology. Pierre Bourdieu wrote eloquently on the family as a site of socialisation where cultural capital is created and maintained but the state increasingly disengaged from the family in terms of constructing equality or nurturing citizenship. Bourdieu saw the problem of the family as being one in which market forces divided family members from each other. In particular, he saw the family as a site of competing needs for consumption. He saw the market increasingly being able to

> *call into question any and all collective structures* that could serve as an obstacle to the logic of the pure market: the nation, whose space to manoeuvre continually decreases; work groups, for example through the individualisation of salaries and of careers as a function of individual competences, with the consequent atomisation of workers; collectives for the defence of the rights of workers, unions, associations, cooperatives; even the family, which loses part of its control over consumption through the constitution of markets by age groups.[45]

[44] Beck and Beck-Gernsheim 1995. [45] Bourdieu 1998.

This view oddly echoed that of the right wing commentators who feared the death of the family. But Bourdieu saw family as the last smallest collective in a hostile individualist capitalist world. In Britain, government intervention moved towards reducing the state's activity in constructing citizenship or sharing out resources. In 1981 the Child Support Agency was set up, to return the financial responsibility for children to both biological parents, especially for those children supported on state benefits, a prime example of the privatisation of the family.

The transformation of intimacy was another argument about changing family patterns coming out of Anglophone sociology this time, rather than the European derivatives of Marx and Durkheim, who saw the family as both reproducing capitalism but also saving people from its worst effects. Marriage, said Giddens, was a relationship between democratic equals, reflecting what he calls 'plastic sexuality'.[46] Neither state nor labour market affected people's intentions and beliefs about fulfilment through close intimate relationships. One of the obvious problems of this argument was that the emotional dependence of childhood is nothing like the emotional interdependence of adults. Historically, Britain saw a steep rise in cohabitation before or instead of marriage, and the state recognising this through the benefits and taxation system as well as the practice of social work or medicine. Alternative families were, it was argued in the 90s, to replace conventional families. The state was enlisted to prevent this happening.

This argument says much about the sexuality of young affluent adults but it is inadequate to describe the overwhelming discursive dominance of conventional courtship, romance and familial cohabitation seen in popular music, in romantic fictions in books, films and plays; the celebration of Valentine's Day which first became big business in the 1980s; and the development of marriage type arrangements in the form of civil partnership introduced in 2004. Gay couples have been able to adopt children since the law changed in 2002. Thus, the model of adult carers in small units remains the same, but has been detached from sexual choices.

It remains the case that the majority of children are brought up in family households. Politically, British culture remains committed to marriage as the preferred choice for child rearing. However, the state did, briefly, try to resist innovation, and the development of non-standard families. In 1983 the *Daily Mail* attacked Haringey council for having a copy of *Jenny Lives with Eric and Martin*, a children's book in which a girl lives with her father and his male partner, in a school library; the result was a clause in the Local Government Act 1987, section 28, preventing councils promoting homosexuality or 'pretended family forms'. The clause was in fact hardly deployed at all.

[46] Giddens 1992.

Sexuality remained a cause of some government action in the propaganda around sexually transmitted disease. In 1981 the first AIDS case was identified in the UK; in 1987 the 'Don't die of ignorance' leaflet was sent to all households in the country, accompanied by opaque advertising showing ice floes breaking up. Civil society was seen by some to have become endangered by permissiveness and libertinism and to some extent the strengths of the concept can be seen in reflecting upon the political debates about public health. But, in practice, the most effective campaigns were those mounted by voluntary groups such as the Terence Higgins Trust which sought to encourage safe sex and to support people who had been infected. The commercial sector produced effective advertising campaigns aimed at young people. The Wellcome Trust (a philanthropic foundation) took over a survey of sexual behaviour when the government's Economic and Social Research Council was discouraged from funding it, which reported on a sample of some 20,000 adults in 1994 and concluded that Britain had a long history of multiple sexual cultures with a minority of Britons being monogamous or celibate, another minority having multiple, frequent sexual encounters and the majority in-between having serially monogamous relationships.[47]

The family has been supported by the state through legislation and through regulation. Cultural practice emphasises the value of family as a place of refuge and protection. But the relationship the other way around is harder to chart in the British context. Certainly, Britain remained an unequal society despite successive programmes designed to encourage some social mobility, like the expansion of nursery and university education.[48] But it is family in the wider sense of social circumstance leading to privileged education and cultural capital that increases the influence of some of the leading families. The idea that the family or kin are privileged as motors of political affiliation, sources of criminal activities or problems of democracy seems historically inappropriate in the British context. The 1907 special places scheme and the assisted places of the 11+ from 1938 to 1965 gave young people of humble background the chance to rise through education into the middle class and sponsored social mobility. After 1957, through the A level system and university grants, this social mobility increased for the few who benefited. However, while the civil service, medicine, law and engineering remain the destinations of people educated in this way, success in big business has much less association with the education system or meritocracy at all.[49] Britain retains an assumption of meritocratic independence in state functionaries, which makes an explanation based on amoral familism unhelpful in thinking about the history of British politics. The presumption that private interest is the main motor of political

[47] Wellings et al. 1994. [48] Blanden and Gregg 2004; Iannelli and Paterson 2006.
[49] Halsey, Heath and Ridge 1980; Nicholas 1999.

interventions became more widespread in the 1980s and was parodied by satirists and cartoonists but still with a sense of shock that the Victorian conventions of an 'ideal type' bureaucracy had been jeopardised. In other words the kind of study of familial connection and advantage described for Italy can only really be seen in the activities of press barons and football club owners rather than in all the institutions of British life. It is the market that is privileged and that is not necessarily much associated with family values. There is one exception to this picture which is the major British family supported by the tax payer – the royal family. This kin group has remained an object of sentimental public attachment but less as a unit and more as a metaphor for the variety of relationships and the complexity of modernity. When the ex-wife of the Prince of Wales died in a car crash in Paris in 1997 the family was juxtaposed and contrasted to the popular heroine and found wanting, which suggests that it no longer remains untouched as an icon or model of family life. Diana's funeral became a popular event observed by one third of the British people on television.[50] The monarchy thus remains a way in which people think through nepotism, family relationships and the public–private divide with a particular intensity in Britain, compared even to other European monarchies, but it does not demonstrate a particular power to the family as a source of moral or political authority.

Margaret Thatcher, debating with Paul Johnson, editor of the *New Statesman*, on the BBC radio programme *Woman's Hour* in 1970, summed up the limits of state power in explaining why she had voted for the Abortion Act despite deploring the permissive society.

> I think people are asking for – Parliament – for legislation to uphold standards until such time as everyone can exercise the amount of self-discipline that they reject things that you and I would reject. Homosexual offences and abortion, of course, are part of the Permissive Society, but only a very small part. I think what the average woman would really mean by it is rather more – a good deal more sexual licence now, fear of one's children going on drugs. Often how exactly does one guide one's teenage son and daughter as to how they should behave in this kind of society? How when it comes along to your argument with regard to abortion, for example, I do think that this happens to be not the cause of the phrase Permissive Society at all, it is just perhaps one – a single one of its features. I myself voted for the Abortion Act because I happen to think that one of the worst things anyone can do in this world is to bring an unwanted child into it. It starts with such a tremendous handicap.[51]

The contrast to Joseph's later speech was clear. She talks about what people should do with their own children, not what society should do about familial errors. However, it has also become evident in discussing family responsibilities that a more punitive concept of the family as the place of control

[50] Thomas 2002. [51] Thatcher 2010, 9 April 1970.

has become much more dominant with the development of the Anti-Social Behaviour Order – the ASBO – under the Crime and Disorder Act of 1998 as the way of returning the obligation of control to the family since most of these orders were issued to young people. Once subject to such an order the individual is required to avoid the offending behaviour and, in practice, the individual's family is responsible for enforcing it.

Political associations based around family life and support for family have long histories. Many of them came out of the new Liberal period of social imperialism before the First World War or just after it from the family welfare association to Soldiers, Sailors and Airmen, forerunners of the British Legion. The interwar years saw a large number of such associations, often aiming at specific constituencies, like the Council for the Unmarried Mother and her Child in 1927 or the Workers Birth Control Group. They were particularly strong among women, from the Women's Institute (which started on a Canadian model to encourage housewives to economise during the First World War) to the *Housebound Housewives Register*, as it was first called, which began in 1960, then becoming the *National Housewives' Register*, and in 1987 the *National Women's Register*.[52] These voluntary bodies created a substantial area of activity monitoring the state's performance of its tasks, raising money for unfunded groups and doing research into social questions. However, they do not represent a separate or distinctive place of political critique on government, as in France or Spain, as many members of these groups are also members of political parties and many initiatives combine the resources of charity or pressure group in partnership with the state.

In 2003 the minister for children, young people and families published a pamphlet about government plans for improving the life chances of all children called *Every Child Matters*. The central innovation of this document was to encourage people to exploit grandparents in support of children. The question about policing the family raised by Donzelot remains cogent because it is not always clear that the state has the capacity to support without intervening and potentially allowing the fragile family to lose its emotional bonds. The government policy on children tends to emphasise child delinquency rather than entitlement although the state has returned to instruction in citizenship.

Britain's history shows a continuing tension between the ideas or sentiments about the family and the state's support for a free market. Although politics reflected increased importance of an ideal of family life, particularly in supporting women, and increased representation of women's needs and demands, the state provided less support for dependent citizens against the impact of a commercial culture. Family remains central to the production of new generations and families remain crucial to individual happiness. However, the brute

[52] Gordon and Doughan 2001.

facts of the market in housing and labour are as important as the actions of the state. The idea that the relationship works the other way around, that family ideology has an effect upon the state, seems difficult to demonstrate in this British example. Fiona Williams's call for an ethos of care, in whatever family form it takes, being recognised by government was applauded by the then minister for work and pensions but has not been recognised by legislative action.[53] It seems likely that family obligations for dependent elders will require some public recognition of the people who do the work. The use of the idea of family as a demonstration of good intentions and political virtue has become stronger as the mass media have provided opportunities for such political rhetoric conveyed in the form of sound bites. But such rhetorics seem increasingly unimportant in the processes of cultural change which are rarely dependent on the actions of any one national government at all.

53 Williams 2004.

3 France

Sarah Howard

I

Every year, the French president officiates at a ceremony to confer the Republic's Médaille de la famille française upon those who have brought up a large number of children. The decoration has been awarded annually since 1920; it was especially feted by Marshal Pétain during the Vichy period. There are several categories of medal: bronze medals for those with four or five children, silver for six or seven children and gold for eight or more children.[1] The ceremony brings together politicians, family associations and families from around France; it receives a good deal of media attention and is the occasion for a reiteration of the state's commitment to families. In 2009, President Sarkozy used the event 'to reaffirm my attachment to family policy and my desire to support all families because they are the basis of our society'. He also celebrated France's high fertility rates, in particular the record number of births – the highest for thirty years.[2] The 2008–9 bumper crop of 834,000 French babies included little Maddox and Vivienne, born in the Var in August 2008. The twin's parents were the Hollywood stars, Brad Pitt and Angelina Jolie. Despite having six children, Ms Jolie was not eligible for nomination to the silver family medal – her children do not have French nationality. However, the large family's residency in France did mean that it was entitled to substantial family benefits, an integral element of the family policies of which the president so proudly spoke. According to *Libération*, the Pitt–Jolie entitlement amounted to 1,750 euros per month, almost certainly a useful addition to the couple's alleged annual earnings of 35 million euros.[3] Although it is not clear that the family ever claimed the benefits to

[1] The Médaille de la famille française was created by decree in 1920, to honour French mothers who had brought up a large family. It was altered in 1983 to include fathers or anyone else who had brought up children. The name was shortened to Médaille de la famille and now includes parents, even if they are not French, so long as their children have French nationality.

[2] Speech dated 13 February 2009. See www.elysee.fr/documents/index.php?mode=cview&press_id=2332&cat_id=7&lang=fr, accessed 5 November 2009.

[3] *Libération*, 27 August 2008.

which they were entitled, the affair illuminated the French state's seemingly generous and universal family policy.[4]

As the Pitt–Jolie affair demonstrates, the French state treats families with munificence and favours a universal approach to many family benefits. With a generous array of social, fiscal and educational policies, the state encourages families to populate France with bonny bouncing babies; indeed, France now has one of Western Europe's highest fertility levels with 2.02 children per woman in 2008, representing a regular rise from 1.66 in 1994.[5] This demographic imperative remains at the heart of French state intervention in family life and in some ways it helps to explain the family's important place in national consciousness, its high symbolic value and centrality to political discourse, state planning, fiscal and legislative endeavour.

This chapter examines the relationships that bind the French state, families and the groups that lie in-between. It assesses the extent to which the state overwhelms other groupings in its decisions on family policy and whether the French-style corporatist system precludes debate and disagreement over the way that the state deals with families. The chapter pays particular attention to the legislation that governs and shapes French families, examining whether family legislation has broken with the strictures of the past to reflect contemporary social change. It then goes on to discuss France's vaunted family policy, its historical imperatives and contemporary limits. Questioning whether French family policy is quite so benevolent as social commentators often claim, it analyses the degree to which policy favours the wealthy and the middle class at the expense of the poor and the young, tracing its roots back to the demographic and moral fears of the late nineteenth century and the Vichy regime. It looks at France's obsession with population and its reliance upon universal family policies and examines whether these historic imperatives hamper attempts to tackle family poverty and social exclusion.

In many ways, therefore, the chapter is quite consciously a tale of two cities. Recent works touching upon French families have focused exclusively upon social policy.[6] This gives the impression that, for better or for worse, French families are overwhelmingly influenced by a powerful state. The chapter seeks to nuance such a view by considering the full extent of state involvement in family life which goes far beyond its already extensive social policies. In this way, the chapter questions some widely held assumptions about the relationship between families and the state in France. Could it be the case that families are less affected by the state's seemingly stringent administrative

[4] Nadine Morano, the family minister, denied that the family had accepted the allowances to which they were entitled. See *Daily Telegraph*, 24 August 2008; *De Telegraaf*, 20 August 2008.

[5] This compares with 1.3 in Germany, 1.4 in Italy or 1.5 in Spain. Mermet 2009, p. 134.

[6] Chauvière and Sassier 2000; Commaille, Strobel and Villac 2002; Damon 2008; Godet and Sullerot 2009; Lefebvre and Méda 2006; Messu 1992; Smith 2004; Thélot and Villac 1998.

pressure, legal requirements and control than by its popular and generous family policy? For if France's family policy is as successful as its supporters claim, how can it be that so many French families suffer from high levels of poverty, social exclusion and live on housing estates blighted by unemployment, social unrest and problems in integrating immigrant communities? If French legislation and family administration is as constraining as its detractors suggest, how can we explain the kaleidoscopic diversity of modern French family units and couples?

II

The family plays an important symbolic role within French society and this shapes widespread consent for the state's far-reaching family policy. In a recent study, 75 per cent of French people said it was the most important thing in their life; even amongst those who were single or childless, the proportion was over 60 per cent.[7] French society is therefore highly committed to the idea of family; 99 per cent of people agree it has 'an important role' and 87 per cent agree that it has 'a very important role'.[8]

The state reflects these prevalent views and surrounds families with its own symbolism. This symbolism has not always been linked to Republican values. President Sarkozy discovered this to his cost when he proclaimed in 2010: 'I believe in family, I believe in work'; the statement was criticised for its echo, unconscious or otherwise, of Vichy's motto 'Travail, patrie, famille'.[9] The French state's interest in families means that it holds a unique role as the crossroad between public and private spheres. French families seem to accept that the state should be concerned with them; certainly this has been the case for over a century. Yet, the European Union's directorate of social affairs did not create a unit in charge of European family policy, because several member states objected that this would encroach upon a private domain. When the French complained, their state's traditional pro-natalist policy was identified as an unnecessary intrusion into family life. French government family advisers reacted with incomprehension, arguing that 'Of course family is a private affair, but because of the children and numerous external issues it involves, it also inevitably becomes a public affair.'[10]

French families are public in so far as the state sees them as being essential building blocks of society. Viewing families in this way means that the state can justify extensive family intervention through legislation, social policy and fiscality. State intervention in families occurs on several levels. The state uses legislation to regulate families, take account of their evolution and

[7] Houseaux 2003, p. 27. [8] Mermet 2009, p. 163. [9] *Le Parisien*, 6 January 2010.
[10] Godet and Sullerot 2009, p. 17.

the ways that social change impacts upon them. In this, families are viewed as the privileged arena for policies to promote equality, in particular gender equality, but also children's rights and conciliation between domestic and professional roles.[11] The state also plays an important role in family social policy. Family social security and fiscal policies traditionally encourage population growth through the promotion of horizontal equality that aims to reduce the social and financial inequity experienced by large families. In this, the state is supported by several official bodies linked to family policy and demographic research such as Institut national d'études démographiques (INED) and the Haut conseil de la population et de la famille. In recent years, the state has also introduced targeted or means-tested 'solidarity' policies to reduce the impact of social exclusion, poverty and/or disability for some families.

Yet the family is also a deeply private sphere subject to social changes over which the state does not always have much control. French families have changed dramatically over the past forty years. Contemporary family life takes multiple forms. There is now a clear distinction between married life and the life of a couple, two notions that were previously closely linked. Today, people largely make their own decisions about how to share a common life, with or without the constraints of marriage, same-sex relationships or even cohabitation. Couples, married or not, have new and wide-ranging expectations centred around personal fulfilment and autonomy, rather than social expectation, self-sacrifice or total fusion of the couple.[12] More often than before, couples and families break up and recompose in new configurations. The tradition of 'les Catherinettes', when women still unmarried at the age of 25 celebrated St Catherine's Day and were gently reminded of their anomalous nature, has totally disappeared.[13] The number of single people has grown to over 10 million; often it is alternated with periods in a couple.[14] Moreover, planned maternity has transformed the fertility calendar of women. The average age for the first child has increased from 26.8 years old in 1980 to 29.9 years old in 2008. By 2008, half of all new-borns had a mother aged 28 years old or over (25 per cent in 1977) and more children are born to women over 40 (3.8 per cent) than to women under 20.[15] Yet, French society remains highly positive about the changes to contemporary family life; only one in four of the population identifies them with a general decline in society and 42 per cent of these pessimists are over 75 years old.[16]

Between the family and the state, there are several intermediate groupings with varying functions and differing levels of influence and independence. Intermediate groupings have a role in representing the opinion and desires of

[11] Godet and Sullerot 2009, p. 10. [12] Dortier 2002, p. 66. [13] Dortier 2002, p. 3.
[14] Maurin 2009, p. 47; Mermet 2009, p. 118.
[15] Maurin 2009, p. 23; Mermet 2009, p. 134. [16] Mermet 2009, p. 135.

families to the state and assisting it in the establishment of family policies and legislation. The organisations that are primarily concerned with family social policy are far larger and better funded than the lobby groups that focus on legislative change. However, in practice, those groups interested in family social policy tend to defend the social policy status quo whilst the more radical special interest lobby groups seek legislative reform.

France is alone amongst its European neighbours in the fundamental role played by its national family association, the Union national des familles françaises (UNAF). The organisation is based upon the diverse Catholic and Republican family defence organisations that grew during the late nineteenth century. These were organised by Vichy into a unified structure to enable interpenetration between the associations and the state.[17] Vichy's corporatist conception was maintained at the Liberation with the establishment (or rebaptism) of UNAF. The organisation remains at once internal and external to the administration-political apparatus. As well as being the official representative of all French families, it is also a 'social partner', recognised and supported by the state and centrally financed through the social security system.[18] UNAF gives opinions on family policy, but it also accomplishes some indirect state missions such as childcare, illiteracy training and family mediation and is involved in the management of the state's social insurance agencies, known as Caisses.[19]

UNAF is proud of its pluralism. It federates over 7,500 groups, which represent nearly 1 million of France's 15 million families. As well as a hundred regional unions, it also comprises eight national family movements including Catholic, Protestant, secular and rural families and trade union based family groups. The federation also includes many smaller associations defending specific sorts of families such as disabled, adoptive, single parent and recipients of the national family medal.[20] However, the UNAF family does not quite reflect contemporary France. Rural and Catholic members recently disapproved of the proposed membership of the Association des parents et futurs parents gays et lesbiens (APGL).[21] In addition, UNAF's membership list shows little specific representation for those families who are increasingly important to public policy – unemployed, immigrant, ethnically mixed families or families living on problem housing estates. The main Muslim family organisation, the Union des familles musulmanes (UFM), is only integrated to UNAF within the Protestant family national movement.[22] This seems hard to justify on a doctrinal level, but

[17] The Loi Gounot of 29 December 1942. See Jackson 2003, pp. 330–1.

[18] Hassenteufel and Martin 1997. [19] Ancellin 1997.

[20] www.unaf.fr, accessed 5 November 2009; Commaille, Strobel and Villac 2002, pp. 38–40; Minonzio 2006.

[21] www.apgl.fr, accessed 5 November 2009.

[22] www.unaf.fr/article.php3?id_article=2333. Also see www.ufm.org, accessed 5 November 2009.

it is even more surprising given that, whilst France has 1 million Protestants, its Muslim population is now estimated at up to 5 million.

Whilst UNAF has an important role to play in the conception and delivery of France's family social policy, its composition and close links to the state mean that it cannot implicate itself in controversial social change without offending some of its members, neither can it fully represent those families who still need to lobby the state for particular recognition or specific benefits. Both despite and because of its supposed diversity, UNAF's official position is quite unanimous. It favours a global family policy, focusing on elements upon which its various members can agree, such as benefit increases, family allowances on public transport and family-based consideration in housing, health, environment and employment policies and employment.[23]

Other intermediate bodies with an interest in family matters are relatively silent in France for a number of reasons. France's secular Republicanism means that the public role of the religions is constrained. The state guarantees freedom of conscience, but it neither funds nor supports any religion. The 1905 separation of church and state dissolved public religious establishments, replacing them with cultural associations that could benefit from private donations, but receive no state support.[24] This provision continues to deprive religions of the official funding that allows other associations to offer family services such as nurseries or youth clubs.[25]

However, some religious family groups are incorporated into UNAF and can comment on families through this semi-official body. Despite the frequent hostility between church and state since the late nineteenth century, 'pro-natalism' has always offered at least one common objective, albeit for different reasons. Given the shared interest in population growth and family welfare, the state can be certain that, whilst religious bodies might disagree on legislative reform that reflects or shapes social change, they will always consent to a generous and universal family social policy to encourage family life.

Trade unions also have an interest in family issues. They have been involved in lobbying the state over specific policies such as the 1998 reduction in the working week (Réduction du temps de travail; RTT).[26] The thirty-five-hour week, unions argued, gave families more time to spend together. However, it also reduced opportunities for poorer workers to engage in lucrative overtime work.[27] Trade unions are also integrated into the French corporatist family structure. They have a role in UNAF and, together with employers (and UNAF itself), they are involved in the administrative councils of the state's social insurance agencies. In terms of family social policy, the main concern of trade

[23] www.unaf.fr, accessed 5 November 2010; Hassenteufel and Martin 1997, pp. 15–20.

[24] Larkin 1974.

[25] In 2004, Nicolas Sarkozy himself proposed revisiting the issue of state funding for religions. See Sarkozy 2004.

[26] Godet and Sullerot 2009, pp. 147–50. [27] Smith 2004, pp. 212–13.

unions, like the other major groupings, is protecting the status quo and this makes them reluctant to lobby for substantive change.

Employers contribute to family policy in several ways. Like trade unions they are involved in the administrative councils of the state's social insurance agencies. Their employer contributions support most of French family policy; these account for 65.5 per cent of total social security spending (29.6 per cent of GDP). In addition, the state has an ever-increasing reliance upon their private initiatives as they often offer informal help for employees and their children through workplace crèches, job-share schemes and the organisation of RTT.

Lobby groups also play a vital role between the state and families because, unlike family associations and trade unions, they are outside France's corporatist family structure. French lobby groups focus on specific issues that can be solved or at least debated in the legislative arena. Lobby groups can be small or large and they are increasingly highly specialised. Some are funded privately; others, if they are politically or religiously neutral and represent a 'general interest', receive state funds.[28]

Through the 1960s, groups such as the Mouvement démocratique féminin (MDF) and the Front de Libération féminine (MLF) worked with the Mouvement français de planning familial (MFPF) to influence legislative reforms concerning gender equality, particularly the legalisation of contraception and abortion.[29] Contemporary women's lobby groups deal with different issues such as domestic violence (SOS femmes) and the specific problems faced by women often from immigrant backgrounds, stemming from strict religious values, honour killings and forced marriages (Ni putes ni soumises).[30] More recently, gay rights organisations such as ACT UP, APGL, SOS homophobie, Collectif contre l'homophobie and Gaylib have also been important mediators between state and families, influencing thinking on homosexuality, homophobia and gay parenting issues. Although lobby groups have been very successful, particularly in inspiring and shaping legislative reform, they have gradually tended to be integrated into the state's embrace, either through state funding or involvement in government. This was particularly the case with the women's movement after the election of François Mitterrand. It has continued under President Sarkozy, who gave ministerial posts to lobby group leaders such as Fadela Amara of Ni putes ni soumises.[31] This might bring lobby groups into the centre of state power, but, to an extent, it also limits their radicalism, particularly their willingness

[28] Huteau 2006, pp. 12–15. [29] Duchen 1994, pp. 173–4.
[30] www.sosfemmes.com and www.niputesnisoumises.com, accessed 5 November 2009; Amara and Zappi 2003.
[31] Amar 2009.

to criticise the state's family social policy unless it has a direct bearing upon their particular area of concern.

III

From cradle to grave, the French state reaches far into family lives. It was not for nothing that Richard Cobb said:

> I was lucky enough not to have been born in France, for I would have given my poor parents endless troubles if I had been … I got married in France – a frustrating and formidable process, not unlike a game of snakes and ladders. And I hope I do not die in France, for that would be a cruel trick to play on those who had to dispose of my remains … France is … the most difficult country in the world to be born in, to marry in, to die in, to be cremated in.[32]

French family life is governed by an astonishing trail of official paperwork and legal documents from the *livret de famille*, given to all families on their wedding day, to the various *état civil* documents that accompany major life events such as births, marriages and deaths. Some elements of state control over families can seem overtly constraining. For example, a registrar can inform the authorities if parents try to give their new-born a 'harmful' name and a religious minister can be prosecuted if he officiates at a religious marriage ceremony for a couple before the mayor has married them in the compulsory town hall civil ceremony.[33] Until 2007, couples planning to marry had to undergo prenuptial medical checks inherited from Vichy.[34] In other ways, the state seems to hold powers over families that seem extraordinarily far-reaching, such as the President's exclusive power to permit posthumous marriages or marriages between close relatives.[35]

Yet, however pernickety the French state might be, in the legislative arena where the crossover of public and private spheres in families is most pronounced, it uses its official power to reflect, rather than shape, social change. French law governs many aspects of family life, but it has attempted to do so by taking account of the diverse social changes that have affected French families in the past decade or so, particularly the growing desire for autonomy and liberalisation from traditional patterns of behaviour.[36] Within an increasingly fluid society, which is less and less governed by traditional codes, legislation has become ever more vital as a way of managing social relationships.[37] The

[32] Cobb 1998, pp. 44–5. [33] Brisson 2004, pp. 104 and 226; Parquet 2009, p. 58.
[34] Brisson 2004, p. 104.
[35] Posthumous marriage was introduced in 1959. Fenouillet 2008, p. 39. See, for example, 'La compagnon de l'adjudant Devez dépose une demande de mariage posthume', *Le Figaro*, 9 September 2008.
[36] Commaille 1998, p. 240. [37] Dortier 2002, pp. 243–53.

new and rapidly changing configurations of French families, together with the impact of scientific advances in genetics and medically assisted reproduction, requires that legislation is frequently updated. In order to be assured of social consent and to respond to the evolution of public opinion, it needs to be the subject of political and public debate. Cobb's image of a fusty bureaucratic state might strike a chord with foreigners who have suffered at the hands of the French administration, but it obfuscates the dynamism of a legislative background that, in most spheres, has attempted to balance private life, public opinion and state interest.

Over the past forty years, in common with the rest of Europe, French society has been marked by a rapid and concerted change in gender roles. In turn, this has had a profound impact on family life. Women have taken a steadily larger public role as their participation in the workforce has increased from 34 per cent in 1961 to 47 per cent in 2007.[38] Most women are financially independent before marriage. Increasingly, decisions are taken together; two out of three couples have a joint bank account.[39] These changes have been translated into the gradual extension of equality both within couples and within French law.

The process of reflecting the changing social status of women began with the reform of marriage laws in 1965, inspired by widespread social change and women's lobby groups. For the first time, women gained the power to manage their own goods and finances or to take on a job without the consent of their husband. Within the family itself, the husband no longer exercised sole decision-making powers.[40] The extension of gender equality into families continued with legal reforms in 1970 replacing the concept of 'paternal power' with 'joint parental authority' over children.[41] Perhaps most significant was the 1975 law permitting abortion (which was extended in 2001).[42] Domestic violence is also increasingly recognised, although the process has been slow; marital rape was only recognised by the Court of Appeal in 1990.[43] However, criminal laws dealing with violent partners or ex-partners were reinforced in 1992 and 2006, services and campaigns to help abused partners have been established and the issue was named as France's 'grande cause nationale' for 2010.[44] French family legislation has continually shown itself willing to reflect growing equality, most recently in 2002 when the automatic attribution of the father's surname to children was ended. Parents can now reach their own decision on a child's surname, either the paternal or maternal surname can be chosen, or else the two can be used in hyphenated form (alphabetically if there is a disagreement).[45]

[38] Maurin 2009, p. 60. [39] Mermet 2009, p. 122. [40] Fenouillet 2008, p. 85.
[41] Fenouillet 2008, p. 87. [42] Kedward 2005, pp. 456–7.
[43] Hirigoyen 2006; Millet 2005; Souffron 2007.
[44] *Le Monde*, 25 November 2009. [45] Brisson 2004, p. 226.

In the same way, family legislation has taken account of the increasing fragility of couples.[46] As society has come to accept relationship breakdown, so legislation has followed and attempted to regulate an ever-more individualised sphere. Before 1975, the only divorce available to couples involved proving unreasonable behaviour. In order to respond to social change, no-fault divorce was introduced in 1975.[47] Divorces multiplied by 3.2 between 1975 and 2009, rising from 40,000 per year to over 130,000 per year. This is equivalent to one divorce for two marriages, putting France within the EU average.[48]

The evolution of French divorce law clearly suggests that the state does not railroad public opinion in order to force unpopular decisions on society. In 1998, when the Ministry of Justice undertook a study to revise the 1975 divorce laws, its proposals met with such public consternation that they were substantially altered. The public would not accept the proposal of abolishing divorces with fault (which still account for 46 per cent of French divorces).[49] Neither would it countenance the introduction of fast-track divorce procedures 'divorce sur declaration conjointe', agreed without recourse to a judge. The reformed law, finally passed in 2004, maintained both no-fault and unreasonable behaviour divorces, but it streamlined the procedure and introduced greater degrees of family mediation.[50]

Whilst French law has incorporated new attitudes on divorce, it has also adapted to new varieties of couples. Of the French population, 70 per cent live with a partner, but since the 1960s increasing numbers have been unmarried. By 2005, 3.4 million couples (one in five) lived together without being married, twice as high as in 1990. The practice of cohabitation is widespread and socially acceptable; nine out of ten couples cohabit before marriage (compared with one in ten in 1965); even amongst practising Catholics, 75 per cent cohabit.[51]

The French state has therefore responded to widespread change in regulating new forms of partnership. Until 1999, cohabiting couples (*concubins*) were not defined by law, only by jurisprudence.[52] The 1999 law gave cohabitation a clear definition in the Civil Code as a couple defined by 'stability' and 'continuity'. The requirement for gender difference that had previously been part of the jurisprudence was also abolished.[53] Although cohabitation is now defined in the Civil Code, it is not governed by any specific body of laws and remains very different from marriage. Although cohabitees can claim family benefits and social security together, to all intents and purposes French law treats them as single people. They have none of the duties that define French

[46] Chaumier 1999, pp. 20–5; Dortier 2002, pp. 41–42; de Singly 1993, pp. 12–15; Godet and Sullerot 2009, p. 88.
[47] Fenouillet 2008, pp. 218–20. [48] Sardon 2005. [49] Parquet 2009, p. 84.
[50] Fenouillet 2008, p. 129. [51] Mermet 2009, p. 117. [52] Fenouillet 2008, pp. 211–14.
[53] Fenouillet 2008; Parquet 2009, pp. 75–7.

marriage – faithfulness, mutual help, common life – and few of the rights of married couples linked to inheritance or property.[54] Although adoption remains illegal for cohabitees as a couple, it is accepted for each of them as individuals. Whilst the law endeavours to maintain a distinction between marriage and cohabitation, it has been willing to enhance protection for cohabitees. In 2001, a law ensured that the surviving member retained the right to continue living in the common abode.[55] The state has also been willing to respond to a practical need: a certificate of cohabitation (*certificat de vie commune*) was introduced in 2000; it could be used to ease claims for social security, family benefits and family transport reductions.[56]

In November 1999, a form of common union falling between marriage and cohabitation was introduced into French law; at the time, only four other countries had this type of civil union (Denmark, Norway, Sweden and the Netherlands). French civil partnerships (*Pacte civile de solidarité*), known as *Pacs* offered two partners (including same-sex partners) a contract establishing a shared life.[57] The legislative drive originated with the gay rights movement and its lobby groups. The law was deeply controversial; a previous attempt to introduce a civil union had failed in 1992 when deputies had brandished bibles in the National Assembly.[58] The partisans of the *Pacs*, notably the Justice Minister, Elisabeth Guigou, tried to build consent by arguing that the *Pacs* was not equivalent to gay marriage.[59] The initial legislation consciously constructed the *Pacs* in a way that was very different from marriage. Presented as a simple contract to organise a shared life, the *Pacs* was open to all couples. It offered certain fiscal advantages (after three years), a reduction in inheritance duties and some rights over property leases and common social security cover. Unlike marriage (or cohabitation), it simply entailed 'duty of mutual and material aid' and the contract could be made with a registrar without need for ceremony or prior publicity.[60] Nevertheless, this was always at heart a law about committed couples; married people could not have a *Pacs*, neither was it possible to undertake a *Pacs* with a member of one's own family.

Once the initial controversy over the *Pacs* had subsided and it had gradually been normalised, the *Pacs* underwent substantial reforms in 2006 and 2007 which increased its similarity to marriage. The duties of partners were reinforced to include the same 'duty of common life and mutual assistance' as married couples. In addition, a *Pacs* now required prior publicity, similar to marriage bans, and immediate fiscal advantages accrued from the official formalisation of a *Pacs*. The existence of a *Pacs* could now be taken into account

[54] Brisson 2004, pp. 129–31; Fenouillet 2008, p. 215. [55] Fenouillet 2008, p. 211.
[56] Brisson 2004, p. 129. [57] Commaille, Strobel and Villac 2002, p. 69.
[58] *Libération*, 16 November 2009. [59] Journal official 1998, pp. 6239–79.
[60] Fenouillet 2008, pp. 234–7.

for nationality issues and work papers and it offered some inheritance rights to the surviving member of the couple.[61]

There are still some differences between a *Pacs* and marriage; unlike marriage it does not entail duties related to faithfulness, to children of partners or mutual responsibility for debts, neither does it confer adoption rights.[62] A *Pacs* is easier and faster to dissolve than a marriage.[63] However, the state has managed the *Pacs* issue well, gradually shaping public opinion and tolerance as the *Pacs* itself evolves.[64] The controversy has largely disappeared and the *Pacs* has risen in popularity and social acceptance, particularly since its reform. The number of *Pacs* increased from 25,000 in 2002 to 147,000 in 2009. Whereas in 2003 there were nine times as many marriages as *Pacs*, by 2009 there were only twice as many marriages. The *Pacs* also enjoys far lower break-up rates than marriages, with only 13 per cent of *Pacs* being dissolved.[65] Paradoxically, the number of same-sex couples undertaking a *Pacs* has collapsed from 42 per cent in 1999 to 6 per cent in 2008. For Patrick Bloch, one of the deputies involved with supporting the original law, 'the best thing is that straight people have appropriated the *Pacs*. This is a great Republican law which benefits everyone.'[66]

In order to deal with widespread changes in family structures, legislation has increasingly focused upon children. In 2000, 73 per cent of French families were traditional and 'nuclear', 18 per cent were single parents and 10 per cent were so-called 'recomposed' families, comprising step-parents and/or children from previous relationships. Both recomposed and single parent families grew by 10 per cent during the 1990s and 2000s.[67] Just as the increasing fluidity of relationships impacts upon a child's legal status, so it affects the requirements of parenthood and relationships between children and their parents. In 1987 joint parental authority was extended to all children irrespective of whether or not their parents were married.[68] In 2002, the law took further account of the situation of children whose parents did not live together; the principle of shared parental authority was generalised, whatever the situation of the couple. The possibility of fixing a shared residence for the child was opened up, whether at one parent's home or both homes. This law also took into account the presence of a third party, usually a step-parent, in a child's life and softened the conditions and effects of delegating parental authority.[69]

Whilst the state has found it relatively easy to legislate for the social trends which began to affect families in the 1960s and 70s and secure general consent for reforms, the upheavals of the 1990s and 2000s have been more problematic

[61] Dibos-Lacroux 2007; Pillebout 2007. [62] *Le Point*, 23 December 2009.
[63] *Le Point*, 21 October 2009. [64] *Le Point*, 23 December 2009.
[65] Maurin 2006, p. 48; Mermet 2009, p. 114. [66] *Libération*, 16 November 2009.
[67] Godet and Sullerot 2009, p. 45. [68] Fenouillet 2008, pp. 416–18.
[69] Fenouillet 2008.

and controversial. This seems to suggest that the French state cannot quite decide what it wishes to achieve until it has widespread and durable evidence of what society feels is justifiable.

Rather than encouraging or discouraging certain types of families, French legislation has increasingly focused upon ensuring that all children are equal in the filiation bonds that they have to two parents. This is particularly important given that by 2008, 52 per cent of children were born to unmarried couples (the figure was 6 per cent in 1967).[70] The process has been surprisingly slow and difficult, proving controversial with the public at every stage of reform. Although French society accepts children born outside of marriage and treats them equally, it has been slower to accept that this equality needs to be enshrined in law. It is probable that this reluctance is related to the traditional inheritance rights enjoyed by legitimate children and the French tradition of 'le secret de famille'.[71] As early as 1972, illegitimate and legitimate children were granted equal rights and in 2001 they were given the same inheritance rights. However, it was only in July 2005 that a single unbreakable filiation replaced the legal distinction between the status of illegitimate and legitimate children, formally linking all children to their parents.[72] The proposal was so controversial that it was not even discussed and voted upon in parliament; instead it was signed directly into law by presidential ordinance.[73] The passing of this law and the controversy surrounding it offers an example of how, on occasions, the state has to force society to accept the consequences of social change.

The French state has also found it difficult to legislate in a way that reflects society's acceptance of genetic advances. It has particular problems in balancing a child's right to have filiation to two parents with the right of parents not to recognise their child when it is born. For the International Convention on the Rights of the Child, the child's right to know its origins is paramount: 'The child has, from its birth … the right to know its origins, maternal and paternal as far as possible.'[74] Yet, French society has always accepted that parents also have a right not to be identified with their child. This is particularly the case for the recognition of paternity; in France, unlike Sweden or Denmark, single mothers are not forced to give the father's name when registering a child's birth.[75] It remains illegal to use paternity tests without the permission of a family judge due to their potential to disrupt family life.[76] In addition, *Mater semper certa est* is not transcribed into French law. Following on from the traditional practice of abandoning new-borns to the church, the Vichy regime legislated for the mother's right to give birth anonymously ('accouchement sous X').[77] In such

[70] Maurin 2009, p. 37. [71] Dortier 2002, pp. 259–67. [72] Fenouillet 2008, p. 284.
[73] Fenouillet 2008, p. 285. [74] Godet and Sullerot 2009, p. 115.
[75] Godet and Sullerot 2009, p. 117. [76] *Le Monde*, 15 January 2005.
[77] Souty and Depont 1999, pp. 124–9.

cases, the mother agrees to give the child up for adoption immediately and both the maternal and paternal sections of the birth certificate are left blank.[78] There remains a degree of support for the principle of allowing women to give birth anonymously; indeed in July 2009, the French Court of Appeal upheld the right of a mother to give birth in this way over the wishes of her family to establish a link with the child.[79] In order to respond to the International Convention and its own increasing belief in double filiation, the state created the Conseil national pour l'accès aux origines personnelles in 2002. This attempted to ensure that all children, whether adopted or born anonymously, could access the identity of their natural parents, their health information and reasons for adoption; mothers who had given birth anonymously were encouraged, although not obliged, to leave their details in a sealed envelope with the Council.[80]

French uneasiness with issues surrounding the establishment of paternity and maternity has also led to problems in the way that the state regulates medically assisted reproduction, despite the fact that such procedures now account for over 6 per cent of French births.[81] IVF has been legal in France since 1972. During the 1990s, genetic advances and general confusion over their implications for children born of such procedures made further legislation necessary. In 1994, the anonymity of both sperm and egg donations was maintained, although any donations of either sperm or eggs had to be made by a donor in an established couple.[82] The child born of such a procedure had no legal right to be informed about this and he/she retained the filiation of the two birth parents with no reference to the donor. In response to popular opinion that any child born through artificial methods has to be assured of two stable parents, doctors can only treat stable heterosexual couples of an age to procreate who have an established medical need and have been in a relationship for at least two years. Both partners have to be alive, which precludes posthumous donations.[83]

The state has had particular difficulty in dealing with homosexual rights, where it finds itself split between the diverse expectations of civil society and the pressures of lobby groups. The state has therefore erred towards the conservative side of public opinion. Whilst homosexual relationships which are officially sanctioned, specifically cohabitation and civil partnerships, are widely accepted in France, the issues of homosexual marriage and adoption are more divisive. Still, over 54 per cent of French people claim to be in favour of homosexual marriage and 42 per cent support homosexual adoption. Opinions seem to split along political and generational lines. Two-thirds of over-sixties or people with right wing affiliations are opposed to homosexual marriage or

[78] Brisson 2004, pp. 186–7. [79] *Le Point*, 8 October 2009.
[80] Brisson 2004, p. 1987; Dortier 2002, pp. 273–81.
[81] Dortier 2002, pp. 273–9. [82] Fenouillet 2008, pp. 390–2.
[83] Parquet 2009, p. 158.

adoption. Amongst the 25–34 year old age group and left wing voters, 77 per cent support homosexual marriage, but the figures drop to 66 per cent of left wing voters and 59 per cent of young people who are in favour of homosexual adoption.[84] This is not, however, a massive social rejection.

Whilst the state's civil partnerships offer official recognition of homosexual relationships, they are general contracts which are just as popular with heterosexuals. Homosexual marriage remains illegal. Militant mayors such as Noel Mamère who have carried out marriage ceremonies for same-sex couples have been severely sanctioned.[85] French laws on assisted births are particularly unfavourable to homosexual couples. Unlike most other Western European countries, only heterosexuals can access such procedures and surrogacy remains illegal.[86] Most controversial is the continued prohibition of homosexual adoption in France. Homosexual adoption remains illegal, primarily due to the state's reluctance to dismiss the views of a substantial proportion of the population. The reticence also comes from the highest levels of the state, including the president himself. During the 2007 presidential campaign, Sarkozy promised 'not to legalise marriage or adoption for same-sex couples'.[87] Essentially, adoption remains reserved for married couples or single people. This means that the only way for a homosexual couple to adopt is to pretend to be single. France's failure to legalise homosexual adoption was condemned for discrimination on grounds of sexual orientation by the European Court of Human Rights in January 2008 and there have been several related challenges in the French courts.[88] Despite this, Sarkozy's spokesman, Luc Chatel, repeated his pledge in late 2009: 'We are not favourable to the adoption of children by homosexual couples.'[89] For APGL, which points out that 35,000 children in France are currently being brought up by homosexuals, this is 'l'homophobie de l'état'.[90]

Despite its continuing reticence over homosexual rights and medically assisted reproduction, the French state's legislative reforms demonstrate that it is not quite the fusty bureaucracy that it might, at first glance, appear to the outsider. The raft of legislation relating to families enacted over the past forty years has, for the most part, enshrined revolutionary social change into law with maximal social consent. There are few examples of the state railroading public opinion into accepting unpopular changes to the most intimate spheres of life. If the state has had difficulties in legislating for the most recent

[84] *Metro/opinionway*, January 2008, quoted by Mermet 2009, p. 125.
[85] *Le Point*, 21 April 2009; *Le Point*, 31 December 2009.
[86] See www.apgl.fr/documents/brochure_APGL.pdf, accessed 5 November 2009.
[87] Ibid.
[88] *Le Point*, 10 November 2009; *Le Monde*, 10 November 2009; *Le Monde*, 11 November 2009.
[89] *Le Point*, 10 November 2009.
[90] Ibid. See also www.apgl.fr/documents/brochure_APGL.pdf, accessed 9 November 2009.

upheavals to affect families, such as genetics and single-sex relationships and adoption, the example of the *Pacs* shows that legislative evolution is possible if public opinion is given time to catch up. Of course law making is ultimately state driven; indeed, offering a clear legal framework within which families can operate is increasingly important to the efficient functioning of society as traditional social and cultural norms dissolve. However, the French experience in formulating family law seems to demonstrate that, when the state and society work together, families can evolve gently within a widely accepted legislative framework.

IV

In the legislative arena, state reforms have responded to the needs, opinions and evolution of civil society and individual families together with the media and special interest groups. Legal reforms have, to an extent, framed and helped to build consensus around social change. Such openness has only been possible because, in its family legislation, the state's view of families has not primarily been predicated upon historical models or established traditions. However, this has not been the case with family social policy, another key area where the state and families meet. The state's role in family social policy has traditionally been so large that it has engulfed those groups, family associations such as UNAF and its associated groups, religious groupings and trade unions, with an interest in family policy, binding them tightly into the grip of a French-style corporatism. What is more, in its thinking on family social policy, the state has remained loyal to its demographic preoccupations and its traditional concepts of Republican universalism; both have been assured of wide approval in French society.

The state's highly developed and popular family social policy reaches far into family life and is at the centre of national consensus politics. This 'remarkable family policy, desired by General de Gaulle and theorised by Alfred Sauvy sixty years ago … created a climate favourable to the arrival of children and applied universally to all families'.[91] It is usually ascribed to the immediate post-Liberation period and Charles de Gaulle's view that 'if the French people don't multiply, then France can be nothing more than a great light which is being extinguished'.[92] Yet, as Timothy Smith points out: 'The roots of French family policy do not lie in some peculiarly French ideal of social justice or solidarity between the generations. Rather, they extend deep into the nation's past, to its 130-year-old collective concern over a rapidly falling birth rate and the dire military, cultural, and even racial consequences of this.'[93] Placed

[91] Declaration of de Gaulle at the Assemblée consultative, 2 March 1945.
[92] Godet and Sullerot 2009, p. 7. [93] Smith 2004, p. 208.

within its historical context, France's current family social policy is therefore a unique cocktail based upon nineteenth-century discourses of moralism and national decline, shaken up with some interwar pro-natalism, decorated by the organisational reforms of a family-friendly totalitarian state and served up in a Republican glass which still shines with the optimism of the Liberation.

If 'demography haunts the political culture of France',[94] it is due to the trauma of France's precipitous nineteenth-century population decline.[95] Between 1800 and 1900, fertility rates fell by 42 per cent, giving France Europe's lowest birth rate. From being the second most populous country in Europe in 1800, France had dropped to fifth place by 1900.[96] Across the political spectrum, Catholic conservatives, Republican radicals and socialists all agreed upon the need to encourage population growth and improve the moral health of French families.[97] State efforts at encouraging births and improving public health were supplemented by the private initiatives of employers who introduced extra payments for workers with families and began insurance schemes for sickness and retirement.

As France's demographic situation worsened during the interwar period, official interest in families grew. Legislation in 1920 and 1923 made abortion and contraception illegal. Throughout the period, the state regularly discussed ways of strengthening the family.[98] Family benefits (*allocations familiales*) were introduced and they increased according to the number of children. In 1938, the Code de la famille inscribed a litany of pro-natalist measures into French law, increasing family allowances for the third and subsequent child and dropping benefits for the first child. The Code paid mothers to stay at home and wrote off state loans to young peasant couples with five or more children. It hardened the 1920 law against abortion and punishments for advertising contraception; it also offered funds to combat alcoholism and sexually transmitted diseases.[99] Behind the Code lay a new state-financed Haute comité de la population with demographic experts such as Alfred Sauvy. Whilst the language of the code was traditional, it was highly reformist, vastly increasing public expenditure and laying out the path to the welfare state.

Little changed under Vichy; its very motto was 'Travail, patrie, famille'. Family was central to Marshal Pétain's National Revolution. The defeat was widely seen to underline the demographic lessons of 'too few children'.[100] Motherhood was reasserted as a national duty, reinforced by a 1942 law

[94] Rosental 2003, p. 367.

[95] Biraben and Dupâquier 1981; Ogden and Huss 1982, pp. 283–98; Rosental 2003, p. 367; Spengler 1979; Winter 1980, p. 189.

[96] Fine and Sangoï 1991; Gégot 1989; Le Bras and Todd 1981; Mitchell 1979, pp. 4–8; Wrigley 1985.

[97] Pick 1989. [98] Boverat 1924.

[99] Howard 2006, pp. 196–202. [100] Jackson 2004, pp. 30–3.

making abortion 'une crime contre la famille française' and a capital offence, under which one woman and one man were guillotined in 1943 and a further fourteen were condemned to life imprisonment.[101] Mother's Day was elevated into a national festival and laws strengthened the Médaille de la famille française, established in 1920.[102] In many ways, Vichy also continued the slow path towards France's post-war welfare state with the introduction of new state provision for pre- and post-natal care, the extension of social security and fiscal benefits and the encouragement of federated family associations.

Seen in this light, the family policy enshrined after Liberation is inherently characterised by continuity. De Gaulle's policy was guided by the state-financed INED, a new name for the interwar Haute comité de la population.[103] Its first director was Alfred Sauvy, whose prominent service for Vichy was quickly and conveniently forgotten. The family associations, federated under Vichy, became the UNAF and were incorporated into the administrative councils of the social security offices. De Gaulle and Sauvy imbued family policy with the optimism of national renewal, obscuring its origins in nineteenth-century discourses of national decline and the authoritarianism of Vichy.

Family social policy, designed to assuage French demographic concerns, was at the basis of the newly created social security system. Key family social benefits – family allowances, pre-natal allowances and early childhood allowances – were introduced. They have characterised French family policy ever since. Fiscal reforms aimed to ensure that the tax system encouraged families. In 1945 a tax break ('quotient familial') was instituted making income tax proportionate to the size of the family unit. Family tax breaks were highly pronatalist; indeed until 1953, couples were penalised if they did not have a child within three years of marriage.

V

Contemporary French family policy, like the general social policy from which it derives, is often feted as an example of enlightened and progressive thinking. Foreign commentators, particularly in the United States, often point to the French example as the benchmark by which to measure successful family policy.[104] Until recently, the model was widely defended in France and many groups still endorse its fundamental principles and the state's intervention in family life.[105] Although French policy has a chequered past, the contemporary

101 Pollard 2000, pp. 191–204.

102 The award of a bronze medal was made to mothers with French nationality who had five legitimate children living simultaneously, silver was awarded to those with eight children and gold for ten children.

103 Rosental 2003.

104 Bergman 1996; Kamerman et al. 2003.

105 Ramaux et al. 2006.

problem is that it has not demonstrated any marked propensity for evolution. As Patrick Krasensky and Pierre Zimmer argue, it is governed by 'three Ps – precaution, protection and preservation'.[106] One might add another P – that of population – for family policy still retains its traditional overt concern with demography and an allied interest in promoting the symbolism of the family. The historical legacy also means that France has an atavistic incapacity to jettison universal models.[107] Certainly in recent years, there has been a rapid growth in vertically redistributive measures and an increased interest in targeted and means-tested policies. However, there are real problems with the way that such targeted measures have been introduced, operated and funded; they remain highly controversial and are widely condemned for eroding France's traditional universalist family social policies.

Over the past thirty years, despite a healthy French birth rate, politicians, demographers and intellectuals have continued to talk about demography to an extent unheard of in the rest of Europe. Now that French fertility levels are amongst the highest in Europe, the logic behind the demographic debate is to encourage generational renewal and offset the effects of an ageing population, particularly the cost of providing pensions which falls upon those of working age. In 1980, a very elderly Alfred Sauvy was still promoting higher birth rates and complaining about the selfishness of an older generation who had failed to have enough children to provide for their pensions.[108] Similar concerns shaped political discourse at the highest level of the French state in the late twentieth century. François Mitterrand bemoaned 'a France impoverished of children' whilst his prime minister, Michel Rocard, declared that 'most Western states are in the process of killing themselves ... by demographics without even realising it'.[109] The last French president to be overtly concerned with demography was President Chirac for whom: 'Any drop in birth-rates sows the seeds of a fall in our competitiveness.'[110] In contrast, President Sarkozy has never used explicit pro-natalist language. In February 2009, his proposals to replace the universal Carte des familles nombreuses with 'more socially just schemes' led to widespread protests.[111]

Yet whilst French presidents, Gaullist and socialist, alike have spoken in favour of family policy and population increase, they have also been quietly cutting family spending. In contemporary France, the whole image of a generous and universal family policy has become a chimera. Spending on family policy in France has declined dramatically since the 1970s. As a proportion of

[106] Krasensky and Zimmer 2005. [107] D'Iribarne 2006; Julliard 2005.

[108] Sauvy 1980, p. 45. [109] Mitterrand 1988, p. 12. Quoted in Dumond 1991, p. 9.

[110] Godet and Sullerot 2009, p. 54.

[111] This is a state-funded card available to families with three or more children which offers discounts on a range of services, particularly train travel. See *Les Échos*, 11 April 2008; *Libération*, 9 April 2008.

the total social security spending, the family branch has declined from between 45 and 50 per cent in the early 1950s to 27 per cent in 1962 and to 9 per cent in 2002. This is no longer the golden era of the 1950s, when a working-class family of four with one wage-earner saw income double as a result of 'the world's most generous family policy'.[112]

Contemporary France has new expensive social priorities such as retirement pensions, healthcare and unemployment benefits. It also has issues that family social policy has failed to address which, like its deprived suburbs, are quite literally burning. The traditional weight of universal family social policy means-that France has a deeply held suspicion of targeted and means-tested benefits. The primary justification for universal benefits is the historical pro-natalist drive of the French state which means that families with children themselves represent a group with special needs whatever their social position or income. Universal policies reduce inequality between families with and without children; irrespective of income a family's standard of living drops by 10 per cent with each child.[113] In addition, it is suggested that universal benefits are more faithful to France's Republican ideals because they link together all of society in a spirit of mutual aid.[114] In contrast, means testing is seen as stigmatising and unfair. Opponents argue that it could fracture society by dividing beneficiaries from those who fund them. This would mean that those who finance social payments without deriving any benefit from them would rationally want to limit welfare and this could affect their political choices; ultimately spending on the poor would diminish as politicians are induced to cut welfare spending. For Julien Damon, the ultimate consequences of extending means testing could bring about an apocalyptic scenario where social protection collapses until it is only available for a tiny group of the most marginal.[115]

Universal family benefits are so important in French national symbolism that politicians cannot openly question them without invoking mass discontent, as Nicolas Sarkozy discovered with his proposed reform of the Carte des familles nombreuses. Prime Minister Alain Juppé learned a similar lesson when his plan for fundamental reforms to the social security system led to a wave of strikes which paralysed the country in 1995.[116] So did Prime Minister Lionel Jospin, who hastily shelved his proposal to cut tax breaks for the richest families in 1997–8 after widespread street protests and demonstrations.[117]

The increasing importance of targeted policies has therefore been a creeping by-product of cost cutting, rather than being motivated by any clear aim to help the poorest and most marginal in society. Means testing family benefits

[112] Hochard 1961, pp. 22, 175; Pedersen 1993, pp. 391–2; Smith 2004, p. 204.
[113] Godet and Sullerot 2009, pp. 8, 238; Math 2004a.
[114] Godet and Sullerot 2009, p. 231. [115] Godet and Sullerot 2009, p. 236.
[116] Béroud and Mouriaux 1997; Touraine et al. 1996. [117] Smith 2004, p. 206.

remains highly controversial in France. Such benefits are particularly important in housing payments and poverty relief, but neither are classed as family benefits because they include households without children. Since 1998, the family social insurance organisations fund the poorest through the Revenu minimum d'insertion (now called the Revenu de solidarité active) which offers a basic standard of living. In addition, poorer families receive extra help with the expenses of school-age children; those with more than three children receive the *complément familial*.[118] The state has shown itself willing to tailor some family benefits to social change and specific needs, particularly when public pressure or lobby groups have intervened. The universal allowance for single parent families was instituted in the 1970s to respond to their specific needs. Some single parent families qualify for extra support if they have been widowed or abandoned.[119] The state has also developed benefits for families with disabled children, both to help pay for their special needs or to compensate parents who have to abandon or interrupt their work to care for a sick or disabled child.[120]

France's need to reorient family spending has never been properly debated. This means that family social policy and public opinion concerning it have scarcely evolved. France's family social policy is no longer fit for purpose. France's expensive social policy has not protected it against high levels of poverty amongst society's most vulnerable families and widespread social exclusion. France might have lower levels of child poverty than other countries, but in 2003 it still had 1 million children living in poverty and 1.3 million working poor (of whom 1 million are women).[121] By 2005, when mass suburban rioting broke out, France had the highest rates of youth unemployment in Europe at 20 per cent nationally and up to 40 per cent on its housing estates.[122]

Traditional French distaste for means testing has resulted in a family policy that often seems disproportionately favourable to the well off, particularly in the realm of taxation. There are few parallels in Europe to compare with France's fiscal advantages to wealthy families. These advantages are a uniquely toxic combination of pro-natalism and social engineering in that they encourage certain (primarily middle-class) families to have more children. Family tax breaks are also extremely expensive for the state; in 2000 they were estimated to cost 6.1 billion euros and to account for 50 per cent of payments from France's main family policy fund.[123] Demographic preoccupations mean that income tax (and local tax) is calculated according to the household, not the individual; its total

[118] Allocation de rentée scolaire.
[119] Allocation de soutien familial and allocation de parent isolé.
[120] Allocation d'éducation spéciale and allocation de présence parentale.
[121] Godet and Sullerot 2009, p. 235; Smith 2004, pp. 210–11.
[122] *The Economist*, 12 November 2005.
[123] Commaille, Strobel and Villac 2002, p. 18; Thélot and Villac 1998.

revenue is divided by the number of mouths to feed. The 'quotient familial' makes income tax even more pro-natalist. Since the Liberation, it has reduced income tax for large families (with three children and above) in proportion to the number of children in a household.[124] The 'quotient familial' might encourage large families, but it primarily encourages rich large families by offering the biggest advantages to those with the highest taxable income.[125]

Universal family social benefits are the most expensive area of French family policy, accounting for 23.2 billion euros in 2000. An additional cost for the state is that family benefits are not included in income tax assessment; again this boosts the help that they offer to the richest. The key benefits aim to compensate for the expenses linked to children (until their twentieth birthday). They include the traditional and universal *allocation familiale* which retains its original pro-natalist drive as it is only paid from the birth of the second child.

France's family spending also includes generous spending to help parents after maternity and through early childhood, particularly with childcare requirements.[126] Perhaps as a mark of the successful pro-natalist policy, spending on these benefits has increased dramatically over the past decade or so to 7.4 billion euros. In its maternity and childhood benefits, the French state has attempted to move away from the normative assumptions of its historic policies predicated upon stay-at-home mums supported by a single wage-earning husband. However, as a function of the state's encouragement of larger families, benefits still offer substantial help for mothers of several children who decide to give up work. The *allocation parentale d'éducation* pays half the minimum wage to mothers of two or more children who interrupt their career. The benefit was recently successfully challenged for gender discrimination.[127] Those who choose to stay in work can benefit from generous childcare payments which offer a wide range of alternatives. Parents can choose between universal free crèche places or payments for home-based childcare or the employment of a nanny at home.[128]

Some French retirement pensions are also an integral part of the state's family policy and, rather ironically, its pro-natalism. Since Vichy, the state has traditionally offered its gratitude to parents through generous supplementary retirement benefits for people who have brought up a minimum of three children. These benefits, which now cost 10.4 billion euros per year, are supposed to compensate for the fact that bringing up a large family often forces a parent (usually the mother) to stop work or at the very least cut down on working

124 Commaille, Strobel and Villac 2002, p. 18.
125 One for each adult, half for each of the first two children and one for each subsequent child.
126 Allocations de naissance et pour le jeune enfant.
127 Commaille, Strobel and Villac 2002, pp. 16–17.
128 Allocation de garde d'enfant à domicile, aide à la famille pour l'emploi d'une assistante maternelle agréée.

hours with a resulting loss of pension contributions. Retirement pensions are therefore increased by 5 to 10 per cent on a graduated scale according to the number of children; extra annuities are offered to women who have cut down their working time or simply stayed at home with their children. In some civil service occupations, women with three or more children who have paid fifteen years of contributions can take early retirement without a minimum age.[129]

Of course, as well as taking money away from the young working families whose social security contributions fund them, these benefits discriminate against old age pensioners without children, who are often the poorest and least supported in society. The high mortality rates amongst old people in the summer 2003 heat wave were largely interpreted as the symptom of an uncaring society. Families were criticised for leaving their aged relatives alone whilst they went on holiday, but little publicity was given to the fact that most of the dead were in fact pensioners without close family. These people were doubly disadvantaged – not only did they have no children to care for them but the state also punished them financially for their failure to increase the French population.

French commentators have argued that generous pension provision fits the univeralist model because it encourages intergenerational solidarity as money flows within families from the old to the young.[130] Certainly, 8 billion euros did flow within family generations in the 1990s, but only half of young people received financial support from their families and they tended to be middle class. Paradoxically, the generosity of French provision has meant that since the 1980s French social policy has worked to the detriment of the young, who have been unable to benefit from the same full employment and wage bargaining powers of their parents.[131] The cost of French social policy, particularly pensions, falls disproportionately on the young and the poor due to fixed social security contributions, up to 20 or 30 per cent, taken directly from salaries to fund benefits that they will not necessarily receive; the level of contributions far outweighs the benefits for all but the largest families.[132] The state offers little encouragement to the young; its minimal welfare payments – Revenu de solidarité active (RSA) – are only available to over twenty-fives. Financial insecurity forces most French young people to put off forming their own family; one in four lives at home until the age of thirty. For most, a stable adult life with marriage, children and a job only commences between 30 and 35 years old.[133]

In this way, France's universal family social policy diverts resources away from those families and individuals in greatest need to help the richest in society, particularly if they have large families. As Pierre Manent argues: 'The

[129] Bonnet and Chambaz 2000; CNAF 2004b, p. 4.
[130] Attias-Fonfut 1995; Minonzio and Pagis 2009. [131] Chauvel 2000, p. 388.
[132] Smith 2004, p. 207. [133] Maurin 2009, pp. 99–105; Mermet 2009, pp. 150–1.

French system is very protective of those who already have something and very hard on those who don't … state charity quickly finds its limits.'[134] The family branch of social policy still accounts for higher spending than the branches dealing with unemployment benefits and social exclusion.[135]

The conflated effects of youth poverty and social exclusion became clear in the widespread rioting which swept France's housing estates in November and December 2005.[136] The estates had larger families and more young people than the national average; in La Rose-des-vents near Aulnay, 35.6 per cent of families had over three children (the figure was only 11.6 per cent for the Paris region as a whole).[137] Whilst the state had encouraged large families, it had done nothing to solve chronic unemployment, particularly youth unemployment. The deprivation on the estates was worsened by poor state provision of educational and sporting facilities. Local groups and associations had reduced their activities due to cuts in state associative funding.[138] The religious associations, particularly mosques, that could have supplemented the provision of child care and youth activities received no official funding.[139] Social workers complained that this meant that the largest mosques were often funded by foreign fundamentalist religious groups which pressurised women and young girls to conform to traditional religious family structures.[140] France's state secularism means that it is unable to target state provision at immigrant groups in ways that respond to their ethnic and religious requirements. Neither can the state undertake any form of ethnic monitoring to assess the level of social exclusion experienced by immigrant families.[141]

Politicians turned to the family as a potential solution to the rioting, despite the fact that its normative family policy was responsible for many of the problems. On 14 November 2005, President Chirac spoke of the importance of parental authority saying that 'families must take up their responsibilities'.[142] In a reverse form of targeted family policy, his interior minister, Nicolas Sarkozy, suggested that families of rioters should lose their right to family benefits. Family associations such as UNAF reacted with anger saying that 'universal family benefits were created to recompense the cost of families, not as a certificate of achievement'.[143]

As the 2005 riots made clear, France's family social policy has failed to help the poorest and most marginalised families. The demographic goals, the

[134] *Le Monde*, 4–5 December 2005.

[135] The branch dealing with unemployment and social exclusion represents 7.4 per cent, compared with family (9 per cent), health (35.2 per cent) and pensions (44 per cent). CNAF 2004b, p. 5; CNAF 2004a, p. 2. Also www.france.travail.gouv.fr, accessed 9 November 2009.

[136] Merlin 1989, pp. 91–112. [137] *Le Monde*, 15 November 2005.

[138] *Le Figaro*, 8 November 2005. [139] Sarkozy 2004, p. 15.

[140] *Le Monde*, 8 November 2005; *Le Monde*, 18 November 2005.

[141] *Le Monde*, 18 November 2005. [142] *Le Monde*, 16 November 2005.

[143] *Libération*, 15 November 2005.

rhetoric of Republican universalism and secularism have obscured an atavistic, expensive, corporatist social policy which increasingly diverts help from those who need it most. Yet, at the same time, many French families do benefit from the state's generous and concerted family policy. This explains its widespread popularity and the general reluctance to damage any of the principles set out at the foundation of the French welfare state. The state continues to reward those who have contributed to population increase throughout their family life and beyond into retirement, it offers choice in childcare provision, and it tries to compensate for the cost of bringing up children at every social level.

An analysis of the relationships that bind the state, families and those groups who intervene between them offers a rather confused picture where preconceptions do not necessarily tell the whole story. The French state's stereotypical image as a weighty bureaucracy that buries families under a weight of administrative and legal regulations is not far from the reality. Yet the state's impact upon the legislative field demonstrates that in some respects it is often willing and able to be shaped by social change rather than dictating it. Legislative reform also shows that intermediate groups and wider social opinion have a role to play, both in pushing the state and also in stopping it from going too far and straying into territory which, like homosexual marriage and adoption, or medically assisted reproduction, has not yet achieved widespread social consent. At the same time, family social policy suggests that the French state has a traditional well-established agenda which it is unwilling to change despite evidence that the policy is no longer working properly. Yet, however much the family associations that intervene to encourage family social policy are discounted as stooges to the French state, the fact remains that there is also widespread social consent for France's traditional family social policy and that any attempt to meddle with it is greeted with demonstrations and social upheaval.

A crucial irony has therefore come to define the relationship between the French state and families. Both see each other as being critically important, yet at the same time their symbiotic relationship means that each has the propensity to stifle the other. It is clear that state policy limits family autonomy in various ways, from the names parents give their new-born children, to the ways in which citizens marry, cohabit or form civil partnerships. The state leaves little room for voluntary associations, political parties or trade unions to involve themselves with families outside its own corporatist structure. In its official failure to recognise religious identity and ethnicity, the French state also ignores a central preoccupation for many families, preventing religious organisations and their associated voluntary networks from transforming individual families into strong communities. Without the institutions of a robust civil society, families struggle with their young adults who, in the poorest areas, have little in the way of hope, employment or leisure. France's least well-off families suffer disproportionately from the state's 'family friendly' policies which reduce their earning capacity, trimming the working week and limiting access to overtime. The situation is exacerbated by generous family benefits, primarily attributed according to family size, rather than family wealth.

Yet at the same time families themselves also stifle the state in a variety of ways. For over a century, they have been led to believe that the essence of being a good citizen is being a good parent. Social policy has reinforced this belief, rewarding them for having large families and aiming to help them equally, irrespective of their income. If the weight of French historic family policy has infantilised families, it has also turned them into particularly difficult and irresponsible children. They invoke the traditions of Republican universalism, but only to prevent the state from limiting a generous family social policy from which they can benefit. No French government dares to cut universal family benefits for fear of the country grinding to a halt. For the state, rioting suburbs are still preferable to strike-bound cities. In the same way, a substantial proportion of French public opinion will not consent to homosexual rights unless they can, in some way, be turned to their own advantage. The *Pacs* has been widely accepted, because it can apply to everyone, whereas homosexual abortion or marriage is more problematic. All children have the right to two parents, but not if the parents want to keep their anonymity.

If the tradition and the popularity that characterise French family social policy are responsible for many of its contemporary failings, the consent that usually governs the relationship between the contemporary state and families offers grounds for optimism. The 2005 suburban riots offered indisputable evidence that traditional family policy, like the social policy within which it is rooted, has failed many families. Hopefully, this will persuade the state to rethink its reliance upon traditional approaches whilst obliging French society to realise that universal policies are not necessarily the fairest. It means that both the state and families need to stop their traditional 'folie à deux', and instead allow social change to dictate and rationalise family social policy in the same way that it has shaped legislation. For indeed, to paraphrase Charles de Gaulle, who can govern a country that has 246 types of family benefits?

4 Germany

Adam Tooze

In his programmatic essay of 1995 Paul Ginsborg sets out a choice to be made by those studying the modern European family and its relationship to politics.[1] The choice, he argued, is between a dichotomous model descending from Aristotle and a tripartite model deriving from Hegel. The Aristotelian model revolves around a set of binary divisions between oikos and polis, between household and political sphere, a set of distinctions that derive ultimately from Aristotle's dualistic description of man as a 'political animal', both political and animal, that is. This dualism, Ginsborg argues, is too simple to capture the complex position of the family in modernity. Instead, he prefers a Hegelian tripartite scheme, which distinguishes between family, civil society and state. The state is constituted by law, the family by a bond of love. The economy, relegated by Aristotle to the household, is assigned by Hegel to a third sphere of civil society. Ginsborg does not rest here. In keeping with modern usage he makes a further distinction. Whereas in Hegel the economy and associational life are intermingled in the sphere of civil society, Ginsborg removes the economy to its own sphere and defines civil society essentially as what Habermas has taught us to call the 'public sphere'. As Ginsborg makes clear, what is at stake in these differing models are fundamental conceptions of the social order. The way in which the relationships between the private sphere of the family and the public realm are conceptualised is fundamental to how we address the most basic questions of order and freedom.

One might quibble whether a model in which the economy has been removed from the primary triad of state, family and civil society can be described as truly Hegelian. But that is beside the point for present purposes. Ginsborg's histories of Italy since 1945 have amply demonstrated the utility of his tripartite schema.[2] Furthermore, one can only agree with Ginsborg's contention

The author would like to thank the contributors to the Cambridge Historical Society Conference of May 2008 for their feedback. He would also like to thank Justice Dieter Grimm, former member of the 1. Senate of the Bundesverfassungsgericht, Visiting Professor at Yale Law School, for his invaluable advice.

[1] Ginsborg 1995. [2] Ginsborg 1990, 2001.

that the triadic conception of the relationship between state, civil society and the family has been fundamental to the organisation of most West European societies in the modern period. Certainly, the reconstruction of West Germany in the era of the Cold War was organised around a vision of the social order much like that which Ginsborg describes for Italy.[3] The philosophy of Konrad Adenauer's economics minister Ludwig Erhard centred on the restructuring of the relationship between civil society on the one hand and a more tightly circumscribed state on the other. Mediating between state and market, the consuming household unit was an essential building block of the social market economy.[4] But for the post-war Christian Democratic parties the family was more than that. It was a source of warmth, stability, human relations in a broken world. Marriage was a bond sanctioned by the highest authority, a relationship to be protected by the state and not to be instrumentalised by politics, whether for purposes of ideological indoctrination, surveillance or national demographic priorities.

But the Hegelian tripartite model as Ginsborg applies it to the Italian case is not merely descriptive. It is critical. It frames Ginsborg's critique of the narrow familialism and corrupt clientelism, which have dogged Italy's history since 1945. The family has been the nuclear unit of the economy, the driving force behind Italy's dramatic economic development. But, as Ginsborg makes clear, in post-war Italy it has also stood in chronic tension with the demands of the law and the wider public sphere. In the age of Berlusconi what is at stake is nothing less than the rule of law, the bedrock of the Rechtsstaat. Such tensions of course exist everywhere to some degree. In Germany, as well, cases of corruption are unfortunately not rare. But, unlike in Italy, in the Federal Republic corruption remains a scandal. The Rechtsstaat is not in question. Whilst Italy languishes in sixty-third place, the fact that Germany ranks 'only' in fourteenth place in Transparency International's global survey of corruption is a cause for anxious public comment.[5]

But if the tension between the family and the rule of law has not been a fundamental feature of the recent history of Germany, there is nevertheless a sense common to both countries that the Christian Democratic model of family politics inherited from the post-war era has reached its limit. Over the last twenty years family policy has become one of the most hotly debated areas of German politics. In the 2002 election campaign Gerhard Schroeder as the head of the Red-Green coalition was the first chancellor ever to make family policy a central part of his personal election platform.[6] Schroeder's successor Angela

[3] Moeller 1993; Kuller 2004. [4] Carter 1997.

[5] The table for 2009 is at www.transparency.de/Tabellarisches-Ranking.1526.0.html, accessed 12 August 2009.

[6] Pinl 2001.

Merkel and her dynamic minister for family affairs Ursula von der Leyen have promised nothing less than a radical transformation of the state's relationship to the German family.

The driving force in the German debate about the family is demography. The problem of ageing common to all European societies is exacerbated in the German case by an exceptionally low rate of fertility. Earlier than in any other Western country, in 1972, centuries of demographic growth in Germany went into reverse. Ever since, the native-born population has been in decline. Since 2001 the issue has been discussed with remarkable breadth and intensity.[7] And there is a broad though by no means complete consensus on the basic cause of the problem.[8] German women seeking to resolve the contradictions between an unsupportive, conservative family policy, the demands of the workplace and their aspirations to greater education and equality have dramatically restricted their fertility. The average age of first pregnancy is now around 30. But the most important driver of Germany's low fertility is not the choice for one-child families, but the decision by an ever larger minority of women to have no children at all. Of those born in 1965, almost a third have remained childless.[9] Amongst university-educated women the percentage is considerably higher. Amongst professional women in their forties the share of the childless rises from 40 per cent amongst doctors and university-trained economists to 67 per cent amongst those working in PR.[10] In the second volume of his history of modern Italy, Ginsborg highlights very similar trends in Italy.[11] And there is reason to think that these common symptoms are indicative of problems inherent in the Christian Democratic model of family policy. Gøsta Esping-Andersen certainly groups Germany and Italy together in his category of conservative-familial welfare states.[12] Whilst Christian Democracy celebrated marriage and maternity, the rejection of the Fascist legacy barred any overt state support for natalism. There is an instructive contrast in this respect between West Germany where family policy revolved around the institution of marriage, and France, where policy targeted fertility directly.[13] At the same time, anti-socialism informed an approach to welfare founded on employment-based insurance rather than direct state provision. And deep-seated social conservatism and hostility to demands couched in feminist language led to a refusal to honour even basic constitutional commitments to gender equality. The result, despite Christian Democracy's ideological commitment to the family and maternalism, was a lop-sided tax, benefit and employment structure, which left women bearing a grossly disproportionate share of the burden of reproductive labour.

[7] For this particular dating by one of the most vigorous contributors to the debate, Herwig Birg, see 'Der Lange Bremsweg', in *F.A.Z.*, 4 March 2005, Nr 53 / Seite 37.

[8] Deutscher Bundestag, 7. Familienbericht (2005), Drucksache 16/1360.

[9] Birg 2001, p. 75. [10] Kirchhof 2006, p. 176. [11] Ginsborg 2001, pp. 68–93.

[12] Esping-Andersen 1999. [13] Kuller 2004, p. 14.

So Italy and Germany have much in common. The fascination of the German case is that since the 1990s, faced with what is viewed as an imminent demographic crisis, three powerful currents have converged to break open the Christian Democratic stalemate: the powerful process of social and cultural liberalisation set in motion in the 1960s and continuing into the present; the removal of Cold War taboos through the collapse of Communism and the absorption into the Federal Republic of Germany (FRG) of the radically different model of family policy developed by the Communist regime of East Germany; finally the emergence of a powerful strand of judicial activism, which has called the legislature to account for its flagrant failure to honour explicit constitutional commitments to the protection of the family and equal treatment of all citizens. The result is that over the last twenty years Germany has witnessed an unprecedentedly open-ended debate about demography and family policy, which has overturned the parameters of the post-war, Christian Democratic model.

And this in turn has conceptual implications. Given the centrality of demographic questions to the current German debate it would seem positively perverse not to make use of the insights provided by the diverse body of literature that addresses itself to what has come to be known as the biopolitical. This, however, takes us back to the fork in the intellectual road map outlined by Ginsborg in his 1995 article. The one thing that unifies the biopolitical literature is that it is rooted not in Hegel's tripartite distinction between family, state and civil society, preferred by Ginsborg, but in the dualistic Aristotelian model and its supercharged distinctions between the public and the private, the political and the natural.[14] Despite their many differences, an idea common to thinkers such as Hannah Arendt and Michel Foucault is that one of the central dynamics of modernity is the erasure of the Aristotelian distinction between the public and the private, the political sphere on the one hand and the biological and economic spheres of the household on the other.[15] Arendt in *The Human Condition* describes the emergence of 'the Social' as the site of this blurring.[16] In the realm of 'the Social', formerly private matters of procreation and household management are raised to the status of national political concern. On the other hand, politics is reduced to a bartering over family allowances and childcare vouchers. For Arendt this erasure of the fundamental Aristotelian distinctions has potentially drastic consequences for political freedom. As Ginsborg notes, the Platonic appeal to the family as a model of unity in contrast to the divisions of the political sphere, the temptation to erase distinctions against which Aristotle protested, is one of the fundamental inspirations of modern dictatorship.[17]

[14] Arendt 1958; Foucault 2008. [15] Dolan 2005. [16] Arendt 1958, pp. 38–49.
[17] Ginsborg 1995, p. 256; Ginsborg 2000.

And in the German case, it is of course tempting to make a straightforward juxtaposition along Cold War lines. On the one hand, there was West Germany with its constitution of liberty founded on the trinity of family, civil society and the law-bound state. On the other hand, there was the biopolitical totalitarian nightmare of Communist Eastern Germany, the German Democratic Republic (GDR), in which everything – law, love and private property – was collapsed into an amorphous totality, not a state properly speaking, but an amorphous regime of power with the Socialist Unity Party (Sozialistische Einheitspartei Deutschlands, SED) and its chairman at its apex. Even in May 1989 such Cold War stereotypes could be mobilised by the right wing of the Christian Democratic Party (CDU) against modest reform proposals mooted by Helmut Kohl's family minister Ursula Lehr.[18]

In practice, the biopolitical regime of the GDR fell far short of the totalitarian standard set by Maoist China with its one-child policy, state monitoring of menstrual cycles and widespread campaign of forced sterilisation.[19] But it was nevertheless amongst the most comprehensive and far-reaching ever seen in Europe. One can, after all, hardly ask for a more brutal and basic measure of population policy than the 'anti-fascist protective wall', which from 1961 containerised the population of the eastern state. Furthermore, the GDR was the first German state explicitly committed not only to the principle of gender equality, but to its realisation through the means of the state.[20] And because this was state socialism in the Stalinist mode, that equality was to manifest itself first and foremost through the universal enrolment of all women in the workforce. From the 1960s the GDR underpinned this with a dramatic expansion of female education at all levels. Unlike family policy in the West, the East German state's pursuit of biopolitical efficiency was radically consistent.[21] If one aimed to maximise both productive and reproductive output, it was essential for the burden of child rearing to be socialised. So from the early 1970s the GDR enormously expanded state-funded childcare, offering comprehensive cover for under-threes, kindergarten age children and pre- and after school facilities for those of school age. The regime trained tens of thousands of care workers according to a manual personally authorised by Margot Honecker and equipped thousands of facilities.[22] They thus ensured a comprehensive, not to say totalitarian, enmeshing of biological existence and family life with the priorities of the regime. By 1989 the difference in childcare enrolment and female labour market participation between West and East Germany was spectacular.[23]

[18] 'Nicht gewachsen', *Der Spiegel* 21/1989 22 May 1989, pp. 27–31.
[19] Greenhalgh 2003.
[20] Flockton, Kolinsky and Pritchard 2000; Kolinsky and Nickel 2003.
[21] Gerlach 1996. [22] Pritchard 2000. [23] Reyer and Kleine 1997.

Childcare provision FRG–GDR, percentage of age group covered

	1970	1980	1989
Nursery (0–3 years)			
FRG	1	1	2
GDR	29	61	80
Kindergarten			
FRG (vast majority half-time)	39	78	79
GDR	65	92	95
After school care			
FRG	2	4	4
GDR	47	75	81
Activity rate, women 16–60			
FRG	50	53	60
GDR	66	73	78

In retrospective estimates it appeared that the GDR had managed to socialise no less than 85 per cent of the total cost of child rearing; by comparison, in the early 1990s less than a quarter of the total costs of a child were covered by the West German state.[24] Not surprisingly, therefore, unlike in the West virtually all East German women had at least one child in their twenties and at the same time virtually all adult women worked. Of women born in the late 1950s no more than 7 per cent remained childless in the GDR, whereas the figure in the FRG exceeded 20 per cent already for these cohorts.[25] Whereas choices with regard to children became increasingly polarised in West Germany, the concentrated system of state intervention in the GDR created remarkably homogeneous biographies. With housing allocation directly linked to parenthood, half of all East German women had their first child by the age of 22. Early cohabitation was commonplace. There were few obstacles to divorce, more often than not initiated by the female partner.

Share of selected family types in population 16–65, GDR and FRG, 1990

	GDR	FRG
Couple, children <16, both full-time employed	32	3
Couple, no children, both full-time employed	12	6.5
Couple, children >16, both full-time employed	8	2.5
Couple, children <16, man full-time, woman not employed	7	14.5
Single, full-time employed	5	11
Couple, no children, both non-working	4	10.5

[24] Gerlach 2000a, p. 130. [25] Birg 2001, p. 75.

There is no question, therefore, that the GDR did manage to reshape its population in a most dramatic way.[26] But whilst it may be tempting to map conceptual schemes on to the fault lines of the Cold War – to assign Ginsborg's tripartite, Hegelian scheme to an analysis of West Germany, whilst reserving the Aristotelian nightmare of modern biopolitics for the study of the GDR – to do so would be to miss the point. If we take the theorists of biopolitics seriously then we cannot confine their critique only to the overtly dictatorial regimes. The point that Arendt, Foucault et al. were making was that this blurring of the public and private in the sphere of 'the Social' was a generic feature of modernity, silently underpinning liberal regimes as well as the more overtly dictatorial forms of polity. Christian Democratic West Germany may have had inhibitions about speaking the language of eugenics, but it was nevertheless the Federal Republic, founded as it was on the triumphant Deutschmark, that for Foucault served as the example par excellence of a regime based on the pure biopolitical logic of economic development.[27]

Furthermore, the notion of the emergence of biopolitics as the central arena of modernity need not necessarily be shaded in the bleak colours preferred by Arendt. Where Arendt saw the emergence of the realm of 'the Social' annihilating everything that might be authentically described as either politics or privacy, for Foucault the biopolitical arena offered a multiplication of possible sites of political contestation.[28] Indeed, it was precisely in the biopolitical sphere that two of the major emancipatory projects of modernity – socialism and feminism – were articulated. As Malcolm Bull has recently pointed out, it is no coincidence that another of the influential bodies of social theory recently to draw on the dualistic Aristotelian framework has been the 'capabilities approach' of Amartya Sen and Martha Nussbaum.[29] They think of themselves as updating the emancipatory promise of the young Marx.[30] And if to include this under the rubric of biopolitics seems far-fetched, it is worth recalling that Marx's vision of an unalienated existence was that of the full realisation of 'species being'. Another way of describing that same outcome was the transformation of politics from the exercise of power by one person over another to the administration of things. For Marx, thus, the full realisation of human nature was coupled to the end of politics. And one might add to Bull's remarkable map of convergence a further vector, which is that of feminist social theory, for which the intersection of the body and the political is an utterly indispensable reference point. Arendt herself acknowledged this rootedness of both Marxism and feminism in the biopolitical sphere in the following fabulously backhanded remark: 'The fact that the modern age emancipated the working classes and the women [sic] at nearly the same historical moment must certainly be counted

[26] Mayer and Schulze 2009. [27] Foucault 2004, pp. 41–212. [28] Dolan 2005.
[29] Bull 2007. [30] Nussbaum 1992, p. 175.

among the characteristics of an age which no longer believes that bodily functions and material concerns should be hidden.'[31]

Against this conceptual backdrop, this chapter revisits the choice offered by Ginsborg in his 1995 essay. In the era of the Cold War Ginsborg is surely right to insist that the conservative tripartite model of family politics espoused by Christian Democracy held at bay the more radical biopolitical impulses of modernity across much of Western Europe. With the end of the Cold War, however, these restraints have largely collapsed. In Germany at least, the fall of the Wall brought not the victory of the Christian Democratic model, but rather the lifting of those inhibitions which previously constrained the frank discussion of the underlying logic of modern family policy. The result has been to unleash a singularly wide-ranging debate squarely situated on the ambiguous terrain of the biopolitical.

Not surprisingly, immediately after reunification, triumphant voices in West Germany sought to discredit the GDR's system of family policy. Only a last-minute intervention by the Bundestag secured any financial support in the transition treaty for the elaborate and expensive childcare infrastructure in the eastern states.[32] The Bundestag enquiry into the Communist dictatorship denounced the GDR's comprehensive network of pre-school education as ideological manipulation. Right wingers called for the scrapping of the entire system. Left Freudians conjured up images of entire cohorts of authoritarian personalities scarred by Stalinist potty training. Early in 1993 Angela Merkel, then as youth minister a rising star in Kohl's cabinet, presided over a Koenigswinter conference at which these theses were given an influential airing.[33] In the anxious debate about teenaged criminals and skinheads in the new eastern states it was widely argued that their anomie derived from the deprivation of motherly love. Seizing on the apparent homogeneity of GDR life courses, West German sociologists managed to convince themselves that East German family patterns reflected conformist social pressures and a lack of self-reflexive individuation, which they contrasted to the supposedly pluralistic, post-industrial lifestyles of the West.

In fact, the evidence suggests the opposite. Rather than being the passive recipients of the imprint of the regime's biopolitical energies, East German women and men appear very consciously to have fashioned their biographies around both the opportunities and constraints that faced them.[34] Once the regime that had conditioned these choices began to disintegrate in the last months of 1989 they showed no sign whatsoever of any 'cultural lag'. On the contrary,

[31] Arendt 1958, p. 73.
[32] 'Fuehrungscharme gefragt', *Der Spiegel* 33/1990 13 August 1990, p. 16b.
[33] 'Hingehen und Zuhoeren', *Der Spiegel* 2/1993 11 January 1993, pp. 36–41.
[34] Trappe 1995.

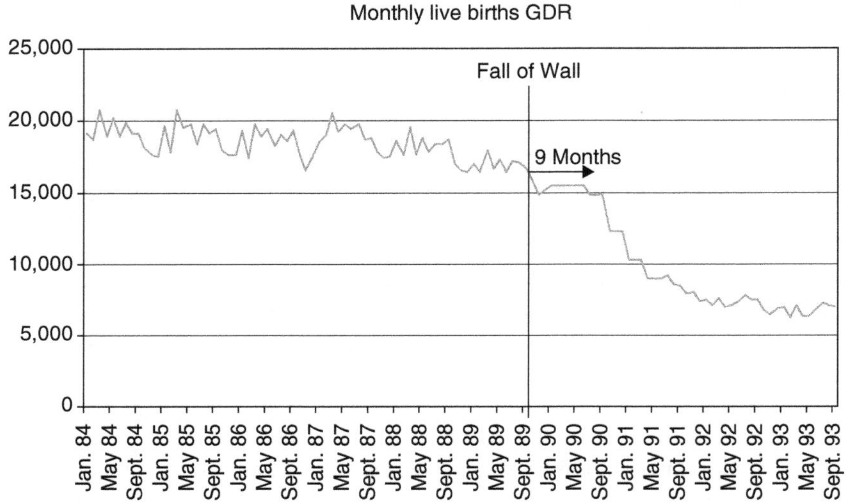

Figure 3
Sources: Monthly data from Statistisches Bundesamt, *Sonderreihe mit Beitraegen fuer das Gebiet der ehemaligen DDR* Heft 32 V (Berlin, 1999), and successive issues of *Wirtschaft und Statistik.*

their command of their fertility was nothing short of virtuoso.[35] Exactly nine months after the fall of the Wall, in the summer of 1990, the number of live births in what was destined soon to become the former GDR began to plunge. In the process of German unification demographic variables that we normally think of as belonging to the realm of the *longue durée* took on the properties of business-cycle indicators. The adjustment was so rapid that it is necessary to track fertility rates on a monthly time scale, as we do fluctuations in the stock market or the dole queue.

But again, one should be careful not to fall into the trap of imagining that the biopolitical logic operated only in a 'top down' manner, with causality running one way, from the state to the family. What is even more striking is how, despite the stark financial constraints facing regional governments in the East, grass-roots mobilisation has served to sustain key elements of the GDR's family policy regime. Under pressure from their constituents East German politicians recast elements of the GDR system in the rights-based language of the Western Rechtsstaat. Childcare was established as a legal right in many of the eastern states. By the mid-1990s opinion pollsters were finding that distinctive

[35] Kreyenfeld 2002; Niephaus 2003.

attitudes towards the issues of gender equality and childcare had become a symbol of East German identity.[36] The Christian Democratic administration of the south-eastern state of Thuringia was buffeted by an unprecedented popular mobilisation in defence of nursery and kindergarten provision.[37] Though large parts of the GDR's state-provided nursery system were dismantled in the course of the Wende, the percentage of East German children covered remained dramatically higher than in the West. If we combine the demographic data with the data for childcare provision it would seem as though a precarious kind of equilibrium was being maintained, in which, as the ability of their collective political institutions to sustain childcare dwindled, the East Germans shrank the number of children they produced.[38]

	West Germany			East Germany		
	1990	1994	1998	1990	1994	1998
Number of places 000						
Nursery (0–3)	38	47	59	353	103	109
Kindergarten	1,552	1,919	2,152	888	552	335
After school	128	146	179	818	285	271
Number of children						
0–3	2,144	2,143	2,095	626	250	298
3–6	1,981	2,251	2,110	785	473	253
6–10	2,565	2,846	3,027	930	833	569
Percentage cover						
Nursery (0–3)	2	2	3	56	41	37
Kindergarten	78	85	102	113	117	132
After school	5	5	6	88	34	48

With the GDR's family model proving surprisingly resilient, in the 1990s it was the contradictions and dysfunctionality of West Germany's model of family policy that came under the spotlight.[39] In 1994, the attempt to harmonise East and West German expectations with regard to childcare forced the Christian Democratic government to concede a legal right for West German families to a kindergarten place for all children over the age of 3. But little practical action followed. Impatient for assistance, a rash of parental self-help initiatives sprang up across major Western cities.[40] Between 1990 and 2002 the

[36] Schlegel 2000/2004.
[37] See the documentation at www.bessere-familienpolitik.de, accessed 6 January 2011.
[38] Hank, Tillmann and Wagner 2001; Kreyenfeld 2004.
[39] 'Glaubenskrieg ums Kind', *Der Spiegel* 9/2008 25 February 2008.
[40] 'Waldwichtel im Bauwagen', *Der Spiegel* 1/2002 30 December 2002.

number of autonomously organised childcare places for children under 3 rose in the state of Hesse from 4,000 to 20,000 and in Bavaria from a few thousand to 18,500. And since much of the Kindergarten movement had its roots in the radical urban sub-cultures of the 1970s it was only logical that it was the Red-Green coalition of 1998 that finally broke the West German deadlock.[41]

The Bundestag elections of 1998 delivered a parliament containing 30 per cent women deputies and appeared to mark a breakthrough for women in German politics.[42] The Red-Green coalition government headed by Gerhard Schroeder, whose widowed mother had supported him after the Second World War by working as a farm labourer, had five female members out of a cabinet of fifteen. Following the resolutions of the UN women's conference in Beijing in 1995 and the resolutions of the EC on gender mainstreaming, Schroeder's cabinet became the first West German government to commit itself explicitly to the promotion of women's work outside the home. As its first priority the Red-Green coalition attempted to impose a new gender equality law on private sector employers, only to find the powerful employers' associations insisting that there could be no real progress for women and mothers in the workplace unless the public authorities ensured the provision of more adequate childcare facilities.[43] In 2001, both the Social Democratic Party (SPD) at its Nuremberg party conference and the Red-Green coalition raised the question of increased female labour market participation backed by publicly provided childcare to the top of the political agenda.[44] Chancellor Schroeder took a leading role, denouncing the existing situation of childcare in West Germany as befitting a 'developing country'.

Returned to power on the back of a strong majority of women's votes, the Red-Green coalition finally attempted to address the acutely sensitive issue of national subsidies for local childcare infrastructure.[45] This produced criticism from left feminists who objected to the way in which a project of emancipation was being recast to meet the needs of the labour market.[46] But the main opposition, predictably enough, came from the Christian Democrats. In Germany's federal political system, the member states jealously guard their rights with regard to educational policy. The entrenched regional power bases of the Christian Democrats in West Germany and in particular their conservative 'sister party' the Christian Social Union (CSU), which dominates Bavarian politics, stood solidly against any dramatic action on childcare by a Red-Green national government.[47] To allow large-scale funding to be channelled directly

[41] Authors Collective 1970; Reyer and Kleine 1997.
[42] Mushaben 2004, pp. 183–4. [43] Maier 2005.
[44] Opielka 2002; *Der Spiegel* 4/2001 22 January 2001; 'Mehr Krippenplaetze' and 'Teuere Auszeit', *Der Spiegel* 46/2004 8 November 2004, p. 74.
[45] Gerlach 2004. [46] Jansen 2002.
[47] 'Kampf um die Krippen-Quote', *Der Spiegel* 45/2002 4 November 2002, p. 44.

from Berlin towards building new kindergarten and crèches in West Germany required nothing short of a constitutional compromise. Significantly, however, whilst the Bavarian CSU backed by elements in the Catholic church hierarchy continued to cling to the shibboleths of the Adenauer era, the national leadership of the Christian Democrats dominated by Angela Merkel, herself a childless East German science Ph.D., had already begun to shift position. Though the overtly feminist language of the Red-Green coalition would always be alien to the CDU and though their top priority was to provide tax breaks to middle-class households in which the mother opted out of paid employment, on the childcare issue there was to be no retreat to the stand pat conservatism of the Kohl era.

The result of the closely fought election of 2005 in which family issues were again unusually prominent, was a grand coalition of CDU and SPD headed by Merkel, who chose as her family minister the photogenic Western power-Frau Ursula von der Leyen. Apart from her c.v., which includes a successful family of seven children on top of degrees in both economics and medicine and time spent at the London School of Economics and Stanford, what recommended von der Leyen to the coalition was her willingness to continue the radical family policy agenda of Schroeder's government. With the majority of the national CDU behind her, von der Leyen has made herself into the figurehead of a national drive for the expansion of infant childcare. She surged to huge national popularity after announcing a target of 750,000 nursery places. In so doing, she courted vicious antagonism from the diehard conservative wing of her own party, but carried with her roughly two-thirds of the electorate.[48] Reversing earlier arguments about the disastrous effects of the GDR's extensive childcare provision, von der Leyen mobilised international research results, notably from the US, to argue that public childcare facilities had a crucial role particularly in supporting socially disadvantaged households, many of which of course were in the former GDR and amongst West Germany's Turkish minority.[49] In the spring of 2008 on behalf of the CDU–SPD grand coalition von der Leyen pushed through the Bundestag the Child Promotion Law (Kinderfoerderunggesetz). In an unprecedented break with Christian Democratic taboos, the law committed the West German government to providing childcare for 35 per cent of infants under the age of 3.

It is indicative of the changed terms of the debate twenty years after the Fall of the Wall that it was the Western states not the states of the former GDR that were held up as deficient. In the West in 2008 less than 10 per cent of children

[48] 'Kulturkampf um Kinder in der Union', www.spiegel.de/politik/deutschland/0,1518,466611,00.html, accessed 6 January 2011, and 'Gebaermaschinen-Schelte', www.spiegel.de/politik/deutschland/0,1518,468031,00.html, accessed 6 January 2011 and 'Familienkrach', *Der Spiegel* 9/2007 26 February 2007, p. 42; Rita Suessmuth in 'Ich habe geglaubt, dass die Union weiter ist', www.spiegel.de/politik/deutschland/0,1518,478935,00.html, accessed 6 January 2011.

[49] 'Glaubenskrieg ums Kind', *Der Spiegel* 9/2008 25 February 2008, p. 40.

under 3 have access to day-care. By 2013, 750,000 additional places are to be provided and from that date all children under the age of 3 are to have a legally mandated right to childcare. Childminders are to be brought within the system of state subsidy and paid at national rates. No less than 12 billion euros are to be invested in new childcare centres with the federal authorities providing a third of the costs. A continuing federal subsidy of 770 million euros towards the childcare system is to be financed by a permanent shift in the distribution of sales tax revenues between the federal coffers and the states. Controversially, those parents, overwhelmingly mothers, who choose not to take advantage of the system will be provided with off-setting federal subsidies. The CDU thus clings to elements of its traditional agenda of maternalism. But the overwhelming priority is clearly to free mothers for labour market participation and to bring Germany into line with what UNICEF in early 2008 proclaimed as the 'global childcare transition'.[50] Currently in the UNICEF's global comparison, Germany ranked just ahead of Italy and just behind the UK in the inadequacy of its childcare provision, whilst all three lagged far behind France and the Scandinavian leaders.

And Minister von der Leyen has made clear that she is banking on more than electoral support from the German population. In a remarkably literal fashion she seems to expect the example set by the East German population in 1989–90 to be followed in the West – this time in reverse. In response to the dramatic shift in the German state's attitudes towards the dilemmas of child rearing, she expects an immediate increase in the birth rate. In the spring of 2008 von der Leyen announced to a stunned press conference that she was staking the vindication of the government's new family policy on the latest batch of demographic data to be announced that summer.[51] And the numbers did indeed reveal 2007 to have been the best year for German births since reunification. But in seeking in this literal-minded fashion to provide direct empirical evidence for the success of her policies, von der Leyen has politicised Germany's demographic data to a quite unprecedented extent. Data that were once relegated to little noticed statistical year books are now being put out by the federal statistical office on a quarterly basis amidst a storm of media comment.[52] And each new publication poses a test of the government's openly natalist agenda. In the spring of 2009 von der Leyen found herself in an embarrassing situation when the federal statistical office first announced that the upward trend of 2007 had continued into 2008 reporting a figure of 690,000 births, only for this figure to undergo technical correction to 682,534. This was a minor and statistically insignificant adjustment. But it forced von der Leyen to abandon

[50] UNICEF 2008.
[51] www.spiegel.de/politik/deutschland/0,1518,547660,00.html, accessed 14 December 2009.
[52] www.spiegel.de/spiegel/print/d-66360385.html, accessed 6 January 2011.

her naive insistence on an upward trend. And in August 2009 her minute attention to the numbers came back to haunt her once more when the European Community released a study of European demographic performance which placed the number of live births in Germany at only 675,000. This produced an angry response from von der Leyen who accused the European Community of using out-of-date figures. The furore over a discrepancy of 0.07 per cent was not enough, however, to distract attention from the major finding of the EC survey. An enormous gap remains between Germany with a net population loss of 168,000 in 2008, Italy with a nearly static population and their far more dynamic neighbours, notably the UK and France where births exceeded deaths by 215,000 and 291,000 respectively.[53]

Placing Minister von der Leyen's activities at the centre of our analysis, we might arrive at the conclusion that family policy in Germany has morphed since 1990 from an arena dominated by fundamental value judgements into a strange new arena of technocratic, biopolitical fine-tuning. But this would be to underestimate the ideological heat that the topic is still capable of generating and it would fail to do justice to the radical strand of thinking introduced into the argument over the family by the German Constitutional Court.[54] The Bundesverfassungsgericht potentially occupies a position of power within the FRG akin to the US Supreme Court and in recent decades, believing itself to be acting in line with the undercurrent of public opinion, it has begun to flex its muscles in earnest on issues concerning family policy. Since 1990 in an unprecedented bout of judicial activism the court has delivered a series of rulings which have called into question the entire structure of the German fiscal system and welfare state in their relation to the family.[55] As its lever, the court has used provisions in the 1949 constitution for the special protection of the family, combined with the even more basic provision of the equality of treatment of all citizens. And it combines these with a more or less explicit biopolitical commitment, which requires the German state not only to abide by its formal constitutional obligations, but to secure the renewal of the German nation in a literal sense. Already in 1984, faced with the family-unfriendly pension reform plans of the Kohl government, the then president of the Constitutional Court, Wolfgang Zeidler, attracted attention with an interview given to the weekly *Der Spiegel* in which he made the extraordinary comment that 'in every wolf pack it counts as an obvious instinctual rule that the raising of the young is a priority task for all. But our highly organised and civilised state lacks even the understanding of a wolf pack.'[56] Though he was aligning himself with the Catholic church hierarchy in demanding better pensions for stay-at-home

[53] Data available from www.spiegel.de/media/0,4906,21309,00.pdf, accessed 9 December 2009.
[54] Gerlach 2000b. [55] Nees 2005.
[56] 'Die Laufen ins offene Messer', *Der Spiegel* 10 December 1984, www.spiegel.de/spiegel/print/d-13511243.html, accessed 6 January 2011.

mothers, Zeidler was a social democrat who took an aggressive view of redistributive justice.

In recent years the rhetoric has been hardly less dramatic, most notably perhaps from former Constitutional Court justice, judicial activist and sometime Merkel-adviser Paul Kirchhof. In an oft-cited speech Kirchhof asked the question: 'Do we wish to be a society dying at the workplace, or living vitally through its children?'[57] Expanding his argument, Kirchhof has drawn on the proposition by the German legal theorist and Constitutional Court judge Ernst Boeckenfoerde that a 'free and secularized state lives on preconditions which it cannot itself guarantee'. Freedom, therefore, is a wager.[58] Boeckenfoerde, who was heavily influenced by Carl Schmitt, was referring to the problem of securing civic virtue in a secular society. Kirchhof's concerns, by contrast, are more starkly biopolitical. Germany's current predicament highlights the fact that the reproduction of the state in the most basic biological sense also depends on the free choice by men and women to marry and procreate. Just as citizens may abdicate their right to vote, they may opt out of the biological reproduction of the body politic. Nor does Kirchhof shrink from the conclusion that decisive state action may be necessary to restore the proper balance and to save German society from the biological perils of freedom.[59]

But though Kirchhof, who served on the Second Senate of the Constitutional Court, is perhaps the most radical voice, the agenda of judicial activism on family policy was shared by many members of the court who did not necessarily subscribe to his brand of Catholic social conservatism. The first of the court's dramatic judgements was delivered in May 1990 by the First Senate and concerned tax allowances for families.[60] Against the backdrop of the massive financial demands of reunification, the Constitutional Court declared that the German state was responsible for securing a minimum income for all its citizens including children. To meet this target required either a huge increase in child benefits or the exemption of a large part of parental income from direct tax. Two years later in the summer of 1992 it was again the First Senate of the court that delivered the so-called Rubble Women (Truemmerfrauen) verdict. Truemmerfrauen are the iconic female figures, bereft of their menfolk, who rebuilt Germany in the immediate aftermath of the Second World War. After doing their bit amidst the ruins, many women in this cohort had withdrawn from the workplace to raise the young workers who sustained the economic miracle into the 1960s and continue to provide the contributions necessary to finance Germany's lavish, pay-as-you-go occupational pension system. In the

57 Kirchhof 2005.
58 Boeckenfoerde 1976, p. 60; www.taz.de/1/politik/bundestagswahl/artikel/1/%5Cfreiheit-ist-ansteckend%5C/, accessed 6 January 2011.
59 Kirchhof and Schmidt 2004.
60 Gerlach 2000b; Sans 2004.

1980s the Kohl government had made a first attempt to take account of the contribution made by these women, by allowing a minimum pension calculated on the basis of one year of child rearing per child. However, the inadequacy of this provision was made clear by the case brought before the Constitutional Court concerning a mother who had raised no less than ten children through the hard post-war years. In the early 1990s she was receiving a monthly pension of 347 DM whilst her offspring were paying a monthly total of 8,500 DM into the national pension pot. This, the judges opined, exposed a fundamental lack of equity in a welfare state, which socialised the risk of old age through the pension system and yet treated child rearing as a private cost. And it repeated this argumentation in 2001 with regard to the new system of long-term care insurance. In the 1950s, the German welfare state had left behind the once strictly enforced contributory insurance principle in favour of a far more generous pay-as-you-go system. This rested explicitly on an intergenerational bargain, which could only be secured through the succession of generations. The labour of child rearing was thus no less fundamental to the long-term viability of the system than financial contributions by paid members of the workforce. Since the benefits of the new care insurance system were to be paid independently of individual contributions, the court argued that those who had taken on the extra cost of rearing large families should be provided with adequate compensation through a reduction in their contribution liability.

Dissatisfied with the progress made in the 1990s, in November 1998, only weeks after the election of the Red-Green coalition government, the Second Senate of the court, with Kirchhof leading the way, delivered the most dramatic judgement to date. Extending its demands of the early 1990s, the court called for an even larger share of family income to be exempt from taxation and mandated that if no legislative action was taken in response, then as of 1 January 2002 taxation of this minimum income would be devoid of legal basis. Furthermore, as the Red-Green coalition began to formulate its new approach to reconciling the demands of work and family life, the court delivered a stunning judgement of its own. To meet the requirements of the constitution it was an obligation on the German state to ensure that parents had a 'truly free choice' between different modes of child rearing. Whether women chose to continue working and to make use of publicly provided childcare or whether they instead chose to leave the labour market temporarily, it was the state's responsibility to ensure that they suffered no material disadvantage, including any long-term damage to their career prospects.

If fully implemented, the judgements of the court since 1990 would involve redistribution between German households on a truly spectacular scale. The child benefit and tax threshold judgements alone, which effectively mandated the end of child poverty, were costed at 33 billion euros. The social insurance judgements were no less dramatic in their implications. And the implications of attempting to neutralise the effects of different choices with regard to child rearing in labour law would have been astonishingly far-reaching. Not surprisingly, despite the increasingly aggressive timeline set by the justices, successive German governments have struggled to comply with the court's full demands. Indeed the conflicts over 'family policy' have become so routine that they have prompted some commentators to speculate about an incipient constitutional crisis, as the court and the executive branch and legislature find themselves fundamentally at odds over the possibility of honouring the court's radical agenda.

Nor are the pro-family activists content merely with an ex post judicial rectification of family-unfriendly legislation. The systematic failure of the legislature properly to take into account the needs of families suggests, to some, the need for more fundamental constitutional change. Jochen Borchert, a vocal adviser to the CDU government of Hesse, for instance, has argued that, as the demographic and age balance in German society begins to shift, only electoral reform can ensure that the voices of families are properly heard.[61] Otherwise, since children are not entitled to vote, politicians are bound to listen to the people who are, namely the old and childless.[62] Given that what is at stake is nothing less than national extinction, the solution for this contradiction between family life and democracy is to call for a modification of the electoral system, to enfranchise all children at birth, to allow parents to exercise their children's votes until the age of 18 and thus to give households a voice in proportion to their true importance.[63] In the early 2000s the idea of Familienwahlrecht gathered considerable momentum, finding support amongst others from Roman Herzog, former president of the Constitutional Court and president of the Federal Republic itself, who since retirement has become an outspoken critic of an increasingly self-serving 'pensioners democracy'. To prevent the retired from holding working tax payers to ransom he suggested that serious consideration should be given to a radical lowering of the voting age.[64] The German Family Association (Familienverband) assembled a heavyweight memorandum on the issue which opened with a historical survey pointing out the very recent history of the now normal adult franchise. At every stage since 1871 the extension of voting rights to further groups of Germans had been dismissed as unimaginable radicalism.[65] Seen against this backdrop, enfranchising parents on behalf of their children was simply the next step in

[61] C. Rath, 'Freund der Familie', *Tageszeitung* 3 April 2001.
[62] Van Parijs 1998.
[63] Hessische Staatskanzlei 2003, p. 96.
[64] See Herzog warnt vor 'Rentner-Demokratie', www.spiegel.de/politik/deutschland/0,1518,546690,00.html, accessed 10 December 2009.
[65] www.deutscher-familienverband.de/fileadmin/DFV/Bund/Dokumente/aktionsleitfaden.pdf, accessed 10 December 2009.

the ongoing development of democracy. In September 2003, a motion to modify the constitution to allow family voting was put to the Bundestag, not by a maverick loner but by a substantial multiparty coalition of forty-seven deputies headed by the speaker of the Bundestag Wolfgang Tierse backed by Green and Liberal (FDP) deputies.[66] A similar motion was repeated in June 2008, again with cross-party backbench backing.[67]

The advocates of the family as the fundamental unit of an 'order of freedom' have thus injected a considerable new energy into one of the oldest causes of modern conservatism. But the terrain of the biopolitical remains nevertheless extremely ambiguous in political terms, as is revealed by an interesting new strand in the argument, which has the potential to turn the entire discussion on its head.

One of the most radical ideas to emerge from the debate that followed the election of 2002 was for the creation in Berlin of a new super-ministry. The incapacity of the political system to respond adequately to the challenges of national demography was parallel, it was argued, to its incapacity to respond to the emerging ecological challenge. The solution was a new ministry which would twin family and youth policy not with education or the economy, but with the environment.[68] A super-ministry for long-run biopolitical challenges should address itself to both. The very idea may seem far-fetched. But we should not be parochial. In the neo-Malthusian scenarios that haunt the Intergovernmental Panel on Climate Change or the United Nations Development Programme, it is already a matter of course to draw connections between demography, the question of women's education and the global problems of economic development and the environment. And it is very striking that the key buzzword in German family policy since 2003 has not been von der Leyen's growth-orientated boosterism, but the term *Nachhaltigkeit*, which translates into English as sustainability.[69]

However, the full implications of that term for family and population policy in Europe do not yet appear to be realised. At the climate change talks in Vienna in August 2007 a senior Chinese Foreign Ministry official announced to the world's press that China's coercive one-child policy had prevented the birth of 300 million children whose carbon output would have been 1.3 billion tons. This he pointed out was equivalent to the carbon produced by the 82 million inhabitants of the FRG.[70] In other words, if the nightmare of Kirchhof et al. came true and the irresponsible exercise of individual freedom by the

[66] 'Mehr Demokratie Wagen durch ein Wahlrecht von Geburt an', Deutscher Bundestag, 15. Wahlperiod Drucksache 15/1544 11 September 2003.

[67] www.sueddeutsche.de/politik/587/315478/text/, accessed 10 December 2009.

[68] Hessische Staatskanzlei 2003, p. 124.

[69] Deutscher Bundestag, 16. Wahlperiod Drucksache 16/1360; Ristau 2005.

[70] 'China says one-child policy helps protect climate', www.reuters.com/article/environmentNews/idUSL3047203920070830, accessed 6 January 2011.

affluent citizens of Germany led to their nation's biological extinction, it would have the same beneficial impact on the global environment as China's draconian biopolitical regime. In light of equations such as this, how long can it be before we find ourselves in the midst of a truly holistic discussion, in which the peculiar trajectory of the European family and its implications for demography are enmeshed with questions of resource use, environmental impact and economic equity on a global scale?

5 Ireland

Tony Fahey

I

One often finds analyses of the family and the state in historical and social scientific research but it is less common to see civil society included in the picture. This chapter explores what the addition of a civil society focus might bring to traditional analyses of the family–state relationship in Ireland and on that basis seeks to draw some conclusions about the value of the civil society concept as a tool for the examination of social and institutional change both in Ireland and in modern societies generally. Within the space available, it is not possible to deal with these issues comprehensively, even for Ireland. The approach adopted, rather, is to select two contrasting cases of civil society institutions in Ireland and examine them as illustrative instances of the different ways that civil society can play a role in the family–state relationship.

The first instance selected is the Catholic church, an obvious choice when it comes to questions of influence on either the family or the state in Ireland, but perhaps questionable as an example of a civil society institution. Scholars disagree on whether churches, especially those that play a hegemonic role in their societies, should be considered part of civil society.[1] Certainly, the Catholic church in its heyday in Ireland might be thought to have been too dominant and too resistant to active participation by the laity for it to be classed as a civil society institution. However, the focus of the present chapter is on the period since the 1960s, an era when the church lost its presiding role in Irish society and generated contrasting internal developments in response. On the one hand, among the Catholic laity in general, and indeed among many clergy and religious, the tendency was to accept and adapt to central aspects of the new liberal culture and in particular to move away from traditional Catholic teaching on questions of family and sexual morality (in the areas, for example, of contraception, sex outside marriage, divorce and homosexuality). This secularisation of family and sexual morality even among practising Catholics

[1] Malena 2008, p. 188.

was reflected also in a gradual though heavily contested liberalisation of the state's social legislation.

On the other hand, the contested nature of that liberalisation was evident in a conservative counter-reaction which emerged among well-organised Catholic lay groups. These originated on the fringes of the institutional church and in the 1980s and 1990s mounted a series of powerful campaigns in defence of the traditional Catholic cast to the state's social legislation. What is of interest here is the civil society character of this counter-movement. While the clergy and hierarchy played their part, a striking feature of the response was the degree to which it was powered by a number of small, highly effective Catholic lay groups who aggressively challenged the new, emerging liberal consensus. This was a time, in other words, when new, active civil society organisations emerged within Irish Catholicism and became powerful combatants in the culture wars over family and sexual life that were a defining feature of public discourse over this period. It thus provides one instance of what civil society can entail and of how the civil society–family–state triangle has evolved over the past half century in Ireland.

An equally revealing instance is provided by the second civil society institution examined in this chapter – the Gaelic Athletic Association (GAA). This very different case is drawn from the world of sport, an arena which is often overlooked in discussions of civil society and is given even less attention in accounts of the state–family relationship. Much sport in modern societies is big business. It is professional and commercial and belongs to the market, especially in the fields of mass entertainment and advertising, rather than to civil society. However, large parts of sport are founded on community-based, voluntary organisations which, as entities that exist apart from market, state and family, fit squarely within the realm of civil society. The GAA is selected as an example here because it is the largest sporting body in Ireland and exemplifies the community-based model of sports organisation to an exceptional degree.[2] In addition to the civil significance of the GAA, it is also relevant because, although it is a non-family institution, it has close relationships with family life. It has a major focus on sport for children, depends heavily on the contributions of time and effort by parents for its functioning at local level, and interacts closely with schools in promoting sport and physical activity among children. It thus can be interpreted as a civil society institution which, in part at least, is structured around the dimension of child rearing represented by children's sports, a dimension which, as we shall see later, is particularly significant for boys. If sport is often neglected in the analysis of civil society, the significance of sport for children and, through them for their families, is

[2] Delaney and Fahey 2005.

an aspect of sport often overlooked even by those who take an interest in the broader subject.

In recent years also, the third side of the civil society–family–state triangle has been added to this mixture as public policy has brought sport within its ambit. The government in Ireland commenced spending money on sport in the 1990s and now has a considerable annual budget for that purpose. A state sports body which administers much of the budget, the Irish Sports Council, has been in existence since 1999, and there is a government ministry with the word 'sport' in its title (the Department of Arts, Sport and Tourism). Although the GAA flourished for most of its history without public funding, in the past decade it has become a recipient of state spending on sport and hence some of its activities have become an arm of public policy. There is a certain fuzziness as to what that arm is intended to achieve, particularly between the public health concern with getting people to take exercise and the social capital concern with encouraging social participation and volunteering.[3] However, it is clear that part of the motivation relates to the developmental role of sport in regard to children and the community engagement it provides to families. Here, then, we have an instance where a civil society organisation is inserted into the family–state relationship and where the nature and significance of that insertion could be missed if we were not sufficiently inclusive in our understanding of what civil society entails.

The body of this chapter first considers the role of the Catholic church and of Catholic lay organisations in affecting the family–state relationship in Ireland in recent decades. We then turn to the GAA and examine its nature as an organisation and the role it plays in the family sphere through its focus on sport for children. The final section seeks to draw some conclusions from the two instances viewed together.

II

Catholic influence on the family and on state regulation of family life in Ireland prior to the watershed decade of the 1960s is well recognised, as is the disintegration of that influence in the space of a single generation from the 1970s onwards. The church's influence reached its peak in the period following the achievement of national independence in 1921. In these years, the church focused very much on family and sexuality as the core concerns of its moral teaching, and Irish people accepted that focus as legitimate. Under the government of the newly independent state in Ireland, the Catholic hierarchy had the opportunity to press its concerns on legislators. The result was that Ireland acquired a body of moral legislation in this period that reflected the prevailing

[3] Delaney and Fahey 2005.

Catholic ethos. A new censorship law in 1929 provided not only for the control of erotic literature but also defined as obscene any literature which provided information on or advocated 'unnatural' birth control methods. Legislation in 1935 banned the importation and sale of artificial contraceptives. The Public Dance Halls Act in the same year aimed to eliminate the threat to morals represented by unsupervised dances. The constitution adopted in 1937 strongly reflected Catholic social teaching in its provisions on marriage and the family: among other things, it prohibited the legalisation of divorce and assigned a special status to the role of women in the home.

The liberalising tide that swept over family and sexual culture in the entire Western world in the 1960s was initially slow to affect Ireland. In a survey of a national sample of Irish adults carried out in 1974, for example, 74 per cent of respondents agreed with the view that sex before marriage was always wrong,[4] an indication of how little impact the 'swinging sixties' had by then had on the majority of Irish people. Similarly, when the sociologist Betty Hilliard interviewed a sample of working-class mothers in Cork in 1975 she found that most of them were still strongly under the sway of Catholic teaching on family roles and sexuality, particularly in regard to contraception.[5] However, change was underway and was soon far-reaching in its effects. The belief that sex before marriage was wrong had melted away by the 1990s and the disappearance of the large Catholic family by the 1980s indicated the almost total disregard shown by then towards the Catholic prohibition of contraception.[6] When Betty Hilliard returned in the year 2000 to the same mothers that she had interviewed twenty-five years earlier, she found them angry and disillusioned at the domineering, unsupportive role the church had played in their lives as young women and antagonistic towards its teaching on family issues.

It would oversimplify the nature of change in family values and behaviour in Ireland to portray it as a straightforward displacement of Catholic belief by secular culture. The actual picture is more nuanced, if only because mainstream Catholic attitudes themselves changed quite extensively and became more diverse. This transformation is well exemplified by the church's changed approach to unmarried parenthood and, by implication, to pre-marital sex. Traditionally, unmarried mothers had been harshly treated in Catholic teaching and practice, reflecting the broader view of parenthood outside of marriage as the shameful consequence of sexual laxity.[7] By the late 1960s, this repressive approach was coming to be seen as unchristian and led to internal criticism within the church. In addition, the passage of the 1967 Abortion Act in Britain opened up new options for terminating pregnancies among Irish women and led to a view in Catholic circles that, compared to abortion, unmarried motherhood

[4] Nic Ghiolla Phádraig 1976. [5] Hilliard 2003.
[6] Fahey and Layte 2008. [7] Ferriter 2009.

was very much the lesser of two evils and should be treated much more supportively on that account. Furthermore, the 'shot-gun marriage' as a solution to pregnancy outside marriage also came to be seen as unacceptable, not only because marriages formed in such a way had a high risk of instability but also because the pressure on the couple often compromised the validity of the marriage in canon law, thus giving rise to subsequent nullity proceedings in church tribunals.

For all these reasons, the Catholic church, paradoxically, became one of the institutions in Ireland which contributed to the de-stigmatisation of unmarried motherhood. Pastoral policy changed in the 1970s so that face-saving marriages among young pregnant women were actively discouraged. The church began to promote the view that the couple should marry after the birth of the child if they still wished to rather than before. These changes took much of the force out of the church's traditional hostility towards pre-marital sex – it was impossible to promote a supportive attitude towards unmarried mothers and at the same time sustain the traditional total condemnation of sex before marriage. Indeed, it dissipated much of the traditional Catholic obsession with sexual purity as a key aspect of the moral life.

The consequence of these internal developments in Catholicism was that no major social force in post-1960s Ireland persisted with undiluted traditional attitudes to family or sexuality. The centre of gravity in public discussion of these fields shifted in a liberal direction, inside the Catholic church as well as outside it. While many aspects of change generated intense opposition, others slipped by unnoticed and the debates which did occur were framed in a more open and liberal context than had previously existed. These processes of change are difficult to track in detail and the precise timing and direction of shifts that occurred are difficult to explain. However, the dimensions of change that relate to public policy are more visible and symbolically more significant than those relating to private belief or behaviour, since changes in the law signal shifts in normative approbation on the part of the state in addition to any practical consequences they might have. It was for this reason that social and political conflict engendered by family change in Ireland focused on questions of public policy, and much of this conflict occurred within the realm of civil society.

The most important development in civil society acting on the side of change in this context was the growth of the women's movement.[8] Alongside the campaign for greater economic independence for women and the right to work on equal terms with men, a core issue for this movement was women's right to control their own fertility. Controversy on this topic had begun to build in Ireland from the late 1960s as groups of women radicalised by new feminist thinking challenged the legal prohibition on the importation or sale of contraception

[8] Connolly 2002.

then in place. On the opposing side, the papal encyclical *Humanae Vitae* reiterated the existing Catholic position and underpinned Catholic opposition to change.

The major breakthrough in this conflict emerged in 1973 in the form of a Supreme Court decision which struck down the legal ban on contraception then in place as unconstitutional.[9] The basis for this decision proved to be momentous, as it provided the stimulus for what subsequently emerged as a powerful counter-reaction by Catholic civil society groups. The case at issue was taken by Mary McGee, a 27-year-old married mother of four children who, against the backdrop of medical difficulties with her previous pregnancies, was advised by her doctor that a further pregnancy could threaten her health, if not her life. Contraceptive jelly which she ordered by mail from England as part of her efforts to avoid becoming pregnant on foot of this advice was impounded by Irish customs. It was her constitutional challenge to the legislation that empowered the customs authorities to act in this way that arrived before the Supreme Court. Constitutional law in Ireland in the years leading up to this event had placed a new emphasis on the protection of individual rights, partly on account of the international influence of American judicial interpretation in this area. In the event, it was precisely such a trend that was evident in the Supreme Court's judgement on Mrs McGee's case, as it ruled that she had a constitutional right to marital privacy which was interfered with by the legal ban on contraception and which therefore rendered that legislation unconstitutional.

The Court's decision on *McGee* posed the challenge for the political system of introducing new legislation on contraception, and political controversy surrounding various attempts in that direction rumbled on for almost two decades.[10] However, that issue was thrashed out in the legislature and in conflict at the party-political level and was only moderately affected by advocacy on the part of civil society groups. The more important civil society response was prompted by the possible implications of the *McGee* judgement for the law on abortion, for it was here that Catholic activists saw *McGee* both as an elemental threat and as an opportunity to respond with an ambitious blocking move that bypassed established party-political structures. The issue that concerned them was whether, in the manner of the American Supreme Court's decision in *Roe* v. *Wade*, the Irish courts would eventually rule that women had a right to abortion. This possibility did not seem entirely far-fetched, since the marital privacy principle on which *McGee* was based was not that far removed from the bodily privacy principle that underpinned *Roe* v. *Wade*. There seemed to be enough latitude in the personal rights clause in the Irish constitution for judicial interpretation to move in the latter direction. As debate on abortion

[9] Hug 1999, pp. 96–8. [10] Hug 1999.

unfolded during the 1970s, a number of influential lay Catholics came to the conclusion that such a risk was entirely real and that the only certain means to avoid it was to amend the constitution. The consequence was that, in April 1981, an *ad hoc* grouping which called itself the Pro-Life Amendment Campaign (PLAC) launched a campaign to insert a clause in the constitution which would give explicit protection to the right to life of the unborn.

The PLAC brought together a disparate array of small Catholic lay organisations, including the Society for the Protection of the Unborn Child, the League of Decency and Youth Alert. Leadership of the movement was dominated by medical and legal professionals, of whom William Binchy, a law professor in Trinity College, was an especially effective performer in public debate. Exploiting a period of political instability and knife-edge electoral competition between the major political parties (there were three general elections in 1981 and 1982), the PLAC succeeded in extracting a commitment from the incoming Fianna Fáil government in February 1982 that it would frame a suitable wording and call a national vote on a pro-life amendment to the constitution. In the event, the wording for the clause that was put forward for a national vote pledged the state to 'defend and vindicate ... the right to life of the unborn, ... with due regard to the right to life of the mother'.

Two aspects of the context in which the ensuing campaign on abortion developed are worth noting as they were significant for civil society mobilisation beyond the limits of this particular episode. One was the focus on constitutional law. The Irish constitution included a range of social provisions, such as the ban on divorce and protections for the integrity of the family, which served as a bulwark of conservativism in family life, but it also contained provisions on individual rights which, *pace* the American example, could be drawn on to move in a liberal direction. The sense of the constitution as an elemental ground of conflict between these two tendencies served to keep it at the centre of controversy in debates on the family for more than two decades following the McGee judgement in 1973. The second feature, which is connected to the first, was the requirement in Irish law for a national referendum to change the constitution. National referendums on the constitution amounted to direct appeals to the people on single issues, and when the issues in question related to matters of family and sexuality, they carried great emotional punch and had enormous mobilising potential. They provided rich opportunities for campaigning groups who sought to exert their influence outside the established party-political and legislative structures. Referendums were also intermittent, singular events and did not require the ongoing organisation or entanglement with the criss-crossing compromises of political life that faced political parties. The constitution therefore was not only substantively important in connection with family issues, it was also inviting in the potential for direct action it offered to civil society groups.

The launch of the pro-life amendment campaign unleashed what has been called a 'moral civil war' in Ireland such was the polarisation of opinion and intensity of feeling that the ensuing debate aroused.[11] Its divisiveness was all the more remarkable in that none of the major protagonists adopted a pro-abortion position. In the light of the depth of anti-abortion sentiment among the majority of Irish voters, the strategy of the anti-amendment side, rather, was to argue that the amendment was unnecessary, since abortion was already illegal, but to refrain from implying that women should have a right to choose to terminate pregnancies. Much of the controversy, therefore, focused not on the rights and wrongs of abortion but on the need for the amendment, the wording of it and how far it elevated concern for the unborn over the desire to protect women's health or to acknowledge the difficulties that women with crisis pregnancies faced.

The campaign resulted in what, in one sense, could be seen as a triumph for the PLAC, in that when the national vote was taken in September 1983, the amendment was supported by a majority of 66 per cent of those who voted. Its triumph was qualified by the lowness of the turnout, which was 56 per cent, and, in a country where disapproval of abortion was strong, by the considerable success of the anti-amendment forces in challenging the rationale for the amendment in the first place. The campaign helped liberal groups develop a voice and a degree of organisation that had previously been lacking. Yet the momentum clearly lay with Catholic civil society. Its organisations had dictated the direction of events, while the liberal side was merely reacting and seeking to hold the line against initiatives over which it had no control.

The period from the mid-1980s to the mid-1990s witnessed three further major confrontations in the battle over the constitution between Catholic and liberal civil society forces. The first of these, which occurred in 1986, was occasioned by a move on the part of the government of the day, led by Garrett FitzGerald, to remove the ban on divorce from the constitution. The remarkable aspect of the referendum which was held to decide this issue was the sharp shift in public opinion which defenders of the status quo succeeded in bringing about in the lead-up to the vote. In advance of the campaign, opinion polls had suggested that voters were broadly in favour of change,[12] but in the actual vote, they chose emphatically to keep things as they were – the vote yielded a two-to-one majority in favour of retaining the ban on divorce. The anti-divorce lobby, which was led by many of the same figures who had come to the fore in the abortion referendum, had mounted a campaign highlighting risks to children and to wives abandoned by errant husbands which was enough to sway a large number of waverers in the middle ground and bring them into the anti-divorce

[11] Ferriter 2009, p. 470. [12] Hug 1999, pp. 46–7.

camp – one estimate had it that 25 per cent of voters had changed their minds in the three weeks prior to the vote.[13] In some senses, this achievement was even more remarkable than the anti-abortion victory in 1983, since there was a degree of sympathy among voters for the idea of divorce that was entirely lacking in regard to abortion and that had to be negated and turned around in order to achieve the result that emerged.

If the referendums on abortion and divorce of the 1980s were a triumph for conservative Catholicism, those that followed in the 1990s were a different matter. They indicated that while Catholic civil society had won some initial battles it was nevertheless losing the longer war and indeed that its own social and political influence was quickly reaching its limit. Even in regard to abortion, the apparent solidity of sentiment in Ireland began to crack in the early 1990s. The turning point was the 'X' case which came before the Supreme Court in February 1992. This case related to a 15-year-old girl who had become pregnant as a result of rape by a neighbour and who had threatened suicide if she were compelled to bring the birth to term. In an improbable sequence of events, plans on her parents' part to obtain an abortion for her in Britain came before the High Court, which issued an order prohibiting that solution on the basis of the right to life of the unborn. This outcome caused widespread dismay, as it raised the prospect of an intrusive new form of policing of the intentions and actions of Irish women travelling abroad. Even anti-abortion activists were concerned as they recognised that the High Court order had the effect of dividing public opinion and fracturing the pro-life consensus which up to then had prevailed in the country.[14]

The parents in the 'X' case quickly responded by appealing to the Supreme Court. In a four-to-one majority decision, the Supreme Court overturned the High Court order and ruled that the girl in question was entitled to an abortion on the grounds that the pregnancy caused her to have suicidal intent and therefore constituted a threat to her life which, under the terms of the 1983 constitutional amendment, took precedence over the obligation to protect the life of the unborn. This decision had the effect of legalising abortion in Ireland in certain circumstances, a stunning outcome given that it was based on a pro-life clause in the constitution which had been intended to prevent just that eventuality. The Supreme Court did not rule definitively on two additional issues that had been thrown up by the 'X' case – whether women had the right to travel abroad to obtain an abortion (the 'right to travel') and whether agencies in Ireland had the right to provide information about foreign abortion services to Irish women with crisis pregnancies (the 'right to information').

[13] Hug 1999, p. 46. [14] Hug 1999, pp. 166–72.

Public response to the 'X' case was sympathetic to the plight of the girl at the centre of it and revealed a substantial body of support both for the Supreme Court's judgement on the substantive abortion issue and for a more nuanced approach to abortion in Irish law. On the other hand, anti-abortion activists reacted fiercely against the judgement and portrayed it as a betrayal of the spirit of the 1983 amendment. In the fevered atmosphere of public debate which followed, the government decided that the only politically feasible resolution was to put the issues to the people again. In consequence, a referendum was held in November 1992 which asked voters to decide on three proposed amendments to the constitution, one which in effect would overturn the Supreme Court's ruling in the 'X' case and two which would guarantee the rights to travel and the right to information in regard to foreign abortions. The resulting vote gave an indication of movement in Irish public opinion away from the anti-abortion certainties of the 1980s. It produced clear majorities against the amendment to overturn the 'X' case judgement, which meant that that judgement stood (and still stands), and in favour of the right to travel and the right to information.

The year 1992 is regarded by some as a turning point in the history of Catholic influence in Irish society, partly because the 'X' case and the referendums which followed revealed a waning Catholic influence over Irish public opinion on 'moral' issues but also partly because the first of the sexual scandals which were soon to engulf the church in Ireland came to light. This was the year that Eamonn Casey, the high-profile Catholic bishop of Galway, was exposed as having fathered a son seventeen years previously. In the light of later revelations about child abuse in the church, this offence seems reassuringly normal and human but at the time it shocked Irish Catholics. Other evidence suggests, however, that isolated individual cases such as that of Eamonn Casey, or indeed of the initially scattered instances of child abusers who were revealed among Catholic priests and religious, did not seriously affect Catholic popular belief and practice in the 1990s[15] and that it was only in more recent years, with the accumulation of more grotesque revelations, that more serious effects on the church's standing emerged.

Yet, as the 1990s progressed, it was becoming increasingly clear that Irish people in general, including practising Catholics, were paying less and less attention to Catholic doctrine on family issues and were finding a new moral basis for this area of their lives.[16] The final serious effort by conservative Catholic civil society to halt the effect of this trend on state legislation came in 1995, when the government launched another attempt to remove the ban on divorce from the constitution and scheduled a referendum for November of that year to decide the issue. Conscious that Irish voters were still concerned

[15] Fahey, Hayes and Sinnott 2006, pp. 54–6. [16] Fahey 1999; Inglis 1998.

about what they saw as the social evils of 'easy' divorce, the government in advance of the referendum framed a divorce bill that was quite restrictive by international standards in that couples had to be separated for four years before they could apply for divorce. As they cast their ballots in the referendum, voters therefore knew not just what they were being asked to get rid of (the ban on divorce) but also the full details of what they were being invited to opt for. Again, opinion polls in advance of the referendum suggested that the tide of opinion was moving in favour of change but, in another repeat of past events, Catholic organisations mounted a strong campaign highlighting the negative consequences of divorce for children and women. The outcome was a knife-edge decision. The 'yes' side won but only by the narrowest of margins – the majority in favour of change was a bare 50.28 per cent.

Narrow though the victory was, the acceptance of divorce in the 1995 referendum was decisive and had the effect of bringing controversy about divorce in Ireland to a definitive end. The legislation published in advance of the referendum was enacted and came into force in 1997, at which point the topic disappeared off the political agenda and has not reappeared since. However, it was not just divorce that faded from view. Rather, the 1995 referendum proved to be the last of the battles about moral issues that had animated public debate and caused turbulence in political life over the previous two decades. One could say that it marked a certain culmination of the gender and sexual revolutions in Irish life, following which values and attitudes in these areas have settled down into something like a new liberal consensus. While that consensus is considerably more conservative in Ireland than in many other countries, nevertheless it is radically different from the Catholic-dominated consensus that had existed up to the 1960s. It is now relatively stable following the rapid change that occurred between the 1970s and the 1990s.

Equally significant, the 1995 referendum on divorce marked the end of Catholic civil society as a force in Irish politics. There has been no recurrence since then of the kinds of campaigns that Catholic activists had been so effective in mounting since the first abortion referendum of the early 1980s. While the demise of their influence was part of a broad social and cultural change that has no single explanation, there was one specific factor that is worth highlighting. This is the centrality of the constitutional referendum to the *modus operandi* of the organisations involved. As mentioned earlier, the direct appeals to the people which referendums represented had possibilities which Catholic civil society exploited to outstanding effect in the abortion and divorce referendums of 1983 and 1986. However, the very different outcomes of the parallel referendums of the 1990s revealed that, in a context where the tide of public opinion was moving in a liberal direction, referendums were a gamble in which the odds were stacked against defenders of the status quo: victory was only temporary but defeat was permanent. Thus, the win achieved by Catholic civil society in the divorce referendum of 1986 was not enough to rule out a re-run of the same question nine years later, whereas the loss in the referendum in that re-run in 1995 was enough to take the issue permanently off the agenda.

However, before seeking to draw any further general lessons on civil society and the family from these events, we turn next to the quite different instance represented by sport as an arena for civil society and by the particular instance of the GAA.

III

Social scientific interest in sport has tended to arise more under the heading of 'social capital' than of civil society, though clearly there is overlap between the two. The most influential text in this regard is Robert Putnam's *Bowling Alone: The Collapse and Revival of American Community* (2000), which seeks to show that forms of social engagement, ranging from informal neighbourly connections to participation in civil society, have weakened in the United States since the 1950s. The image of the solitary bowler which Putnam alludes to in the title of his book is presented as the epitome of this decline. According to Putnam's data, men's participation in ten-pin bowling leagues peaked in the 1960s at over 80 league members per 1,000 men; by 2000, that figure had fallen to 20 per 1,000 (women's participation peaked in the late 1970s but subsequently fell at the same rate as men's).[17]

One aspect of Putnam's argument is very much in tune with a theme of the present chapter, namely that sport is significant beyond its leisure and recreation functions in that it embodies types of informal sociability and formal organisation that are important to the smooth operation of society. However, another aspect – the assertion that the social engagement represented by sports participation and similar activities is in long-term decline – is at odds with the argument presented here and therefore is worth a second look. On this question, Putnam himself acknowledges that the 'bowling alone' metaphor for social disengagement is not the whole story, nor indeed that it is entirely valid even as a representation of what happened in American sport (and Putnam is to be credited for assiduously assembling data which pose many difficulties for the thrust of his own theses on these issues). In the case of bowling, for example, according to Putnam, while *league* bowling has plummeted in recent decades, informal participation in bowling has increased, so that by the late 1990s 'more Americans were bowling than ever before'. He also accepts that 'only poetic license authorises my description of non-league bowling as "bowling alone"' since informal groups dominate in present-day bowling. As he therefore points out, 'the fact that participation in bowling has held more

[17] Putnam 2000, p. 112.

or less steady in recent years actually represents an exception to the general diminishment of informal ties'.[18]

The difficulty for Putnam's argument is that other aspects of sport are also exceptions, and here again his own data are sufficient to suggest this. Some case could be made from these data that, taking all forms of playing of sport together, where some have expanded and others declined, the overall trend in active playing of sport has been slightly downward. However, there is no doubt about the trend in *attendance* at sports events, which has been sharply and unambiguously upwards.[19] Attendance at major league events in baseball, football, basketball, hockey and NASCAR auto racing almost doubled between the 1960s and the late 1990s, rising from about 380 per 1,000 of US population in 1960 to about 720 per 1,000 in the late 1990s.[20] Putnam deals with this exception to his disengagement thesis by dismissing its significance: he interprets attendance at sports events as 'passive spectatorship' that has little social value compared to the 'active participation' represented by playing a sport. Anyone who has experienced the heart-stopping, adrenaline-pumping experience that spectating at sports events can amount to, not to speak of the collective identity that crowds of supporters can generate, will not be persuaded.

In any event, all I wish to note here is that even in the United States, *contra* the influential thesis propounded by Putnam, sport is one arena where popular participation seems to have remained strong and, if we count attendance at sports events as a form of participation, where it may even have grown sharply over recent decades. It is in this context that the picture of sport in Ireland may seem less surprising, for here the undoubted pattern has been one of long-term expansion. This has occurred not just in the form that is most obvious, namely as television entertainment focused on professional sport, but also in popular participation. One recent estimate has calculated that active sports participation in Ireland is some two-thirds higher among the current generation of young adults than it was among present older people when they were in young adulthood.[21] Growth has occurred because of both a widening array of sports that are available to people and stability or growth in traditional sports. Some popular sports today, such as aerobics and swimming, have limited social content in that people engage in them alone, but others have evolved a strong, community-based organisational and social infrastructure, which in turn require a large input of voluntary effort. According to some measures, volunteering for sport is the dominant form of volunteering in Ireland, while other data place it below volunteering for social and charitable work.[22]

[18] Putnam 2000, pp. 112, 113. [19] Putnam 2000, pp. 109–11.
[20] Putnam 2000, p. 114. [21] Lunn and Layte 2008.
[22] CSO 2007; NESF 2003, p. 63; Ruddle and Mulvihill 1999, pp. 64–5.

It is in connection with social and organisational aspects of sport that the GAA is of special relevance to our concerns in this chapter. It is by far the largest sports body in Ireland and is the strongest representative of the voluntarist, community-based model of sports organisation. Its dominance arises not so much among players – more people play soccer and golf than GAA games (which consist of Gaelic football and hurling, with slightly different versions played by men and women). Rather, it stands out in the Irish social landscape because of its organisational strength. This strength is evident especially in its local club network. In 2008, it had over 2,600 clubs on the island of Ireland, of which some 2,000 were in the Republic and over 400 in Northern Ireland.[23] It had an additional 291 clubs overseas, which are supported by the Irish diaspora, mainly in Britain and North America.[24] These clubs engage more than just players: the GAA is unique among Irish sports organisations in having almost twice as many members as active players.[25] A survey in 2003 found that it accounted for 40 per cent of all sports volunteering in Ireland (compared to 17 per cent for soccer, the next largest sport for which people volunteer), 29 per cent of all sports club memberships (the next largest category being aerobics and fitness clubs with 20 per cent of memberships) and 60 per cent of all attendances at sports events (soccer came second here too with 16 per cent of attendances).[26] The organisation has a democratic governance structure and, while it has a core professional management body at national level, the bulk of its activity remains amateur and voluntary. For 2004, the GAA reported that it had over 20,000 active playing teams[27] (a team would normally have 15 players on the field, plus 3–4 substitutes). It has long had a policy of acquiring and developing its own playing fields and facilities and now has an extensive physical infrastructure at club, county and national level. In 2004, the combined value of its physical assets was loosely estimated at €3 billion, which would average out at something over €1 million per club.[28] The GAA rebuilt its national stadium – Croke Park – between 1992 and 2005 at a cost of €260 million. Gate receipts and other income from the use of Croke Park, along with €110 million in state grants, meant that the debt on that development was close to being paid off by the time it was completed.[29] The popularity of its games as spectator sports is indicated by the level of attendance at inter-county championship games held during the summer months. Total attendances at these games in 2007 amounted to 1.6 million, which amounted to a four-fold increase over the level of attendances recorded fifty years earlier.[30]

[23] GAA 2008.
[24] For an account of the GAA in one Irish community abroad, see Darby 2005.
[25] Delaney and Fahey 2005. [26] Delaney and Fahey 2005.
[27] GAA 2005, p. 24. [28] GAA 2004, p. 22. [29] GAA 2005, p. 57.
[30] GAA 1971; GAA 2007.

The size and strength of the GAA as a sports organisation is not the only aspect of its unusual character and gives an incomplete indication of its significance in Irish life. The most notable of its other features is the wide range of social and cultural objectives it sets itself, over and above its activities in sport. The Association was founded in 1884 as part of the wider Gaelic revival movement.[31] Its objectives were overtly nationalistic and embraced the promotion of Irish language and culture as well as of 'national pastimes'. It allied itself closely with the Catholic church, the Catholic parish became the spatial unit on which clubs were based, and it considered that its role was to help construct the Irish nation as well as to organise sports. The nationalist ethos of the GAA has evolved in recent decades, particularly in regard to what some see as a move from an exclusive, ethnic nationalist mentality to a more open form of 'civic nationalism' – and in Northern Ireland to the present day, the GAA's identity as a nationalist organisation is still a significant feature of its social role.[32]

Alongside its nationalism, the GAA has also espoused a strong community ethos. It is particularly strong in rural Ireland but part of its recent growth is due to its success in rooting itself in new urban and suburban communities.[33] This in turn reflects a strategy adopted in the 1970s to make clubs into community and social centres and to put in place a long-term programme of development of club premises.[34] Today, the GAA defines its mission in sporting, cultural, community development and national identity terms. An internal strategic review carried out in 2001 stated that its vision was 'to use the national games to build a sense of local community identity and national *tir ghrá* [love of country] within Irish communities everywhere', and added that further essential tenets were its community basis, volunteer ethos and amateur status. It has also recently adopted a 'strategy for inclusion and integration' aimed at integrating new immigrant communities into its activities and thus into Irish life.[35]

From the perspective of this chapter, a key feature of the GAA is the degree to which it is an organisation for children and families. While the annual inter-county and inter-club competitions for senior players are what attract public attention and generate much of the GAA's revenue, sport for children and the work needed to sustain it are what constitute the bulk of activity at local level. Indeed, one might argue that the real foundation of the GAA as a community organisation at local level is the triangular relationship it has built up between families, clubs and schools in providing opportunities for children

[31] For a standard history of the GAA, see de Búrca 1999; see also www.gaa.ie/page/about_the_gaa.html (accessed January 2010).

[32] Bairner 2005; Hassan 2005.

[33] On the role of the GAA in new suburbia generally, see Corcoran, Gray and Peillon 2008; on the social class profile of sports in Ireland, including the GAA, see Lunn 2007.

[34] De Búrca 1999, pp. 207–8.

[35] GAA 2002, pp. 14, 78–81; GAA 2009.

to participate in organised sport. A telling contrast here is with soccer, which is the most popular playing sport among young men and has attracted a huge spectating public in Ireland in the form of a television audience for the professional sport. Soccer in Ireland is nonetheless weakly organised at community level: its local club network is patchy and poorly endowed with facilities and its main national organisation, the Football Association of Ireland, is more concerned with the professional sport than with fostering either popular participation or community clubs.[36] The case of soccer in Ireland demonstrates that there is no necessary connection between, on the one hand, the commercial importance of a sport in televisual or commercial terms, or even its appeal to young players, and on the other hand its presence as an organised force in local civil society. Rather, as the case of the GAA demonstrates, while televisual appeal, commercial sponsorship and the revenue from gate receipts all help, it requires much more to create a sporting organisation that reaches right down into the daily lives of local communities.

The issue for us here is the significance of children and families in that process of community engagement and thus in the construction of sport as an element of civil society – and the prominence of these mechanisms in the success of the GAA. Some two-thirds of the GAA's active teams are under-age, and the provision of back-up for those teams is a major impetus for the large volume of volunteering and attendances at sports events which the GAA generates. Among adults who volunteered for sport in Ireland in 2003, one third of males and almost six out of ten females gave as one of the reasons for volunteering that their own children were involved, while among those who had given up volunteering one of the most commonly cited reasons was that their children had become older.[37] When it comes to attendance at sports events, our usual image may be of big crowds at major games with much television coverage. But a large share of attendance takes place in the more humble circumstances of the local park or club with children's teams on the field of play. Data on sport in Ireland for 2003 suggest that about one third of attendances by adults at sports events was accounted for by under-18 events and, as one might expect, by far the most common reason adults attended these events was that their own children were playing.[38] These patterns are highly gendered: males constitute the majority of the players, the club members, the volunteers and the spectators, but women appear in surprising numbers among the volunteers and spectators even for what are mainly male sports. The main reason is that they are there to cheer on their own sons, and perhaps also to provide transport and take turns in washing the team kit afterwards – humble tasks, perhaps, but essential to the operation of community sports clubs.

[36] Delaney and Fahey 2005. [37] Delaney and Fahey 2005, pp. 29–30.
[38] Delaney and Fahey 2005, pp. 43–5.

Part of the underlying reality here is that contact team sports such as GAA games, soccer and rugby are played mainly by children and the local community aspect of these sports overlaps to a great degree with the world of children. Data for Ireland suggest that between seven and eight out of every ten children take part in sport and that the vast majority of them do so with great enthusiasm and enjoyment,[39] a level of sporting activity for which there is no parallel in adulthood. Participation peaks in the early teenage years, it begins to drop off from around the age of 16 years, particularly among girls, and drops off further as teenagers leave second-level schooling.[40] The field then drops down to smaller groups of adult enthusiasts, from whom are drawn the tiny minority that become the focus of mass spectator attention. For sports with a professional layer at the top, the children's version of these sports is the nursery that supplies the professional game with new talent, but for sports with a strong community focus, the children's layer can be an end in itself and indeed is often a major part of the rationale for existence of the local sports organisation.

Another underlying feature is the linkage between children's sports and schools, and in the Irish case, especially in regard to the GAA, that linkage also embraces local clubs. In Ireland, the physical education (PE) slot in the school curriculum is the official means by which children are drawn into physical exercise. In practice the more intense and more enthusiastic participation takes place in sports that are organised by teachers in the school but outside of the official school timetable. That is paralleled by a high level of participation among schoolchildren in club sports outside the school and by a certain level of interaction between clubs and schools. A study in 2005 found that, in addition to activity in PE, some 70 per cent of pupils in second-level schools in Ireland played sport either in school or in clubs outside the school, and in many cases both. For boys, these activities were dominated by GAA games, while these games were less important but still significant to some degree for girls.[41] A long-standing symbiosis between the GAA and schools had in the past seen the direction of support run from the schools to the GAA – male teachers in the schools were the recruiting agents and early induction arm that brought children to the organisation. However, with the feminisation of the teaching profession, the crowding of the school day with new extra-curricular activities, and widespread shortcomings in the adequacy of school facilities for sport, the direction of support has tended to reverse – clubs now help the schools to provide sport for children. The most common type of support is use of club facilities, particularly playing pitches – and the majority of principals in Irish

[39] Fahey, Delaney and Gannon 2005.
[40] Fahey, Delaney and Gannon 2005; Lunn and Layte 2007.
[41] Fahey, Delaney and Gannon 2005, pp. 22–5.

schools report that they obtain at least some support for sport in their schools in this way.[42] In the Dublin area in recent years, GAA clubs have gone a step further in that they have begun to employ paid sports development officers whose main job is to go into schools and provide direct coaching and organisational support for GAA games. Initially, this activity was funded out of club resources (for example, the profits from the club bar) but the advent of state funding has meant that clubs now have more secure income streams which they can use either singly or in cooperation to hire the necessary staff.

IV

This chapter set out to examine what insights into the family–state relationship could be gained by taking account of the additional dimension represented by civil society. It sought to do so not by looking at this question in a general way but by focusing on two instances of civil society institutions – those connected with the Catholic laity and with the organisation of sport – where it was possible to identify significant but very different forms of interaction with the family, the state and the linkages between those domains. In now seeking to identify what we have learned by looking at these two instances together, the first point to highlight is simply that both of these quite different institutional arenas have a place in the analysis of civil society and indeed are significant even when the focus is on the role of civil society in the family–state relationship. They certainly consist of institutional forms that exist apart from state, market and family but yet have a socially significant presence. They also entail collective action around shared interests, purposes and values. They thus tick many of the boxes that are at the core of the notion of civil society. It is self-evident that the campaigns of Catholic civil society groups on the 'moral' clauses of the constitution were significant for the state–family relationship, and were widely viewed as such in their day. It is less obvious that the GAA was also relevant to the same broad territory, but the contention in this chapter has been that one needs a different perspective, particularly one that appreciates children's interest in sport, the developmental role it plays in their lives and the response it evokes from parents and schools in order to understand how this is so. Clearly, Catholic civil society and the GAA relate to very different aspects of family life and the state's role in the family, but that is simply a consequence of how multifaceted this field is. Indeed, part of the value of looking at the GAA in this context is the reminder it provides that families work on many levels, that the state has many different kinds of role in how they work and that the range of civil society institution that can contribute to their functioning is broader than we might at first think. The very diversity of the two instances we have looked

[42] Fahey, Delaney and Gannon 2005, pp. 44, 61.

at here could thus be taken less as an indication of incoherence in the concept of civil society than of the richness of the social field it refers to. Indeed, one might argue that scholars who study civil society should worry not that the field is too broad but that they may easily overlook instances with real civil significance that can be missed if the concept is interpreted too selectively.

Having said that these two institutional arenas can be validly and usefully brought together under the label of civil society, one must also acknowledge the different levels at which they operate. Catholic civil society in the period we examine was focused on the law, particularly on constitutional law, and made use of the national referendum in order to appeal directly to the people in a number of attempts to block the liberalising tide in certain areas of family and sexual life. It relied on the campaigning activity of small but highly organised groups in order to 'sell' a message on highly charged topics to the Irish electorate, topics that are widely viewed as fundamental to human well-being. It thereby became a prominent actor in the politics of the family in this period and through that in national politics generally. It left its mark on the history of state–family relations, at least temporarily, though as time passes the traces of its influence are steadily fading away.

The GAA, on the other hand, has virtually nothing to do with formal politics (save in regard to lobbying for public money) and is a national body built on a combination of a strong organisational skeleton and a large and inclusive but loose membership. It is a service provider and a cultivator of both individual and collective self-expression rather than an advocacy movement. Its core activities evoke strong passions and commitment from many people, both players and supporters, yet belong to the realm of recreation rather than the workaday world. They are therefore easy to dismiss. Historians and social commentators usually overlook them, and in analyses of big social movements they often fail to register. Yet one could argue that the GAA and organisations like it embody social processes that have fundamental social significance. The recent upsurge of scholarly interest in 'social capital' indicates that this may be so and has produced evidence on how the everyday, low-level social interactions that are generated by community sports organisations are necessary in a well-functioning society. Here we have emphasised the importance of these processes for children and their families and for aspects of public policy that are concerned with child development and family life. A significant feature of the GAA's role in these areas is that it has grown and expanded in that role in recent decades and is showing no sign of fading away. Contrary to those who might argue that social capital or civil society is in decline in the modern world, it provides an instance where old local community-based institutions can adapt to social change and find a new vitality in an urbanised, globalised context.

6 Italy

Paul Ginsborg

I

In March 2008, the government of Romano Prodi, which for two years had been dependent upon a fragile coalition of centre-left parties, fell from power. New national elections in the spring resulted in Silvio Berlusconi's third term in office, this time with a very comfortable parliamentary majority. The crisis of Prodi's government was thus an important turning point in Italian politics and its dynamics are of considerable relevance to the themes of this chapter. The politician principally responsible for the crisis was a local power broker and Catholic politician, Clemente Mastella, a corpulent but energetic figure with darting eyes and a certain natural cunning. Mastella can with safety be called an archetypical figure of the European south. His party, strongly rooted in one southern region only, Campania, had polled just 1.4 per cent of the national vote. However, this had been sufficient, thanks to the system of proportional representation in operation at the time, to give him power of veto over Prodi's unwieldy coalition government. Indeed, so important was Mastella to Prodi that he was nothing less than minister of justice.

The crisis had broken in January 2008, when various of Mastella's closest political collaborators were arrested and accused of distorting normal administrative practice by means of corruption, extortion and intimidation. His wife, Sandra Lonardo Mastella, whose political career Mastella had assiduously cultivated, was placed under house arrest. The details of the accusations evoke long-standing practices in the Italian state. Basically, Mastella ran his party as a sort of family fiefdom, exchanging favours and services with a vast *clientela*, controlling local and regional sub-contracting, and placing his men in key positions of local society. At the head of the fiefdom was Mastella, his wife, the father of Mastella's son-in-law, Carlo Camilleri, and the regional secretary of his party, Andrea Fantini.

Here it is possible only to mention briefly one area of their activity – the appointment of senior doctors in local hospitals. Hospitals have always been revelatory institutions with regard to the deep structures of the Italian Republic. In this case, the police's telephone tapping revealed a dramatic picture of pressures, menaces and total disregard for the professional qualities and qualifications of the doctors in question. The director general of the Caserta hospital, Gigi Annunziata, had shown alarming signs of autonomy in the appointment of consultants. Mastella is recorded as saying on the telephone: 'I can't understand if Gigi Annunziata is one of ours or not. He's just given the job of principal gynaecologist to the brother of a politician from *Forza Italia* [Berlusconi's party]. But haven't *we* got any gynaecologists?' Mastella's wife, Sandra, was rather less delicate: 'As far as I'm concerned he [Annunziata] is dead. And he is for my husband as well. Steer clear of him in future.'[1]

The power of family connections, the system of *raccomandazioni*, the absence of any meritocratic or transparent principles of selection, the infighting between clans masquerading as parties – these are all elements that come to the fore. I shall return to some of them later.

Faced with the judicial onslaught upon his party and his family – twenty-three persons were put under investigation and four were held in prison – Mastella resigned as minister of justice. In dramatic tones he announced: 'I have been forced to choose between politics and my family. I choose my family.' On this point, rather disconcertingly, he received messages of solidarity from all parts of the chamber of deputies. But Mastella also announced that he was withdrawing his support from the Prodi government. In his opinion, Prodi should have made light of the separation of powers and protected 'his' minister of justice from the magistrates' enquiries. When he did not, Prodi found himself without a majority and fell from power.

From this description it is easy to present a stereotypical portrayal of Italian politics as little more than a vast network of nepotist and clientelist practice. To do so would be a mistake. The Mastella story is of considerable relevance for the nexus of relations to be analysed here, but Italian public life is not just made up of Mastellas. There are consistent minorities who are appalled by the long-standing political culture revealed by such episodes. Indeed, one of the reasons that makes the Italian Republic so fascinating is that there is a constant tug-of-war between what is and what ought to be, between the law and its flouting, between democracy and its enemies.

II

I must begin by stepping back from Italian society and politics in order to place the Mastella story in a wider methodological and theoretical context.

[1] Bonini and Del Porto 2008. For the wider context of clientelist relations in the centre-left government of the Campania region since 1993, see Maugeri 2009. The recent Neapolitan garbage mountains grew out of this political humus.

The attempt to examine the connections, or lack of them, between individuals, families, civil society and the state is a rather unusual approach to contemporary history. While there are a plethora of studies which concentrate on *civil society–state* relations, and very many which treat of the relationship between *states and families* (above all in the discussion of welfare states), there are very few which deal with family–civil society relations, and even fewer which try to keep these multiple relations in the forefront of their explanatory apparatus of the history of a single country.[2]

At a theoretical level, Hegel's *Elements of the Philosophy of Right* (1821), especially paragraphs 158–81, offers the most suggestive treatment of this series of connections.[3] In particular, his moment of 'dissolution' (*Auflösung*), of transition from family to civil society, is as extraordinary as it is neglected in current debates on civil society. Hegel's transition is complex in nature. It bears the analytic weight of a triple-layered process: first, the negation in civil society of the previous ethicity of the family; secondly, the dismemberment of the family of origin as its children procreate and form new families of their own; finally, the entry of male heads of households into modern civil society. Naturally, neither this account of the meeting of family and civil society, nor Hegel's version of gender relations, are ones that we are likely to accept today. The same applies to his renowned definition of civil society as that which 'affords a spectacle of extravagance and misery as well as of the physical and ethical corruption common to both'.[4] Yet what makes Hegel unique is his invitation to concentrate on family–civil society relations, the intensity of the gaze that he brings to bear and his isolation of the moment when family and civil society come to *touch* each other. Few, if any, later thinkers return to these themes.[5]

No legacy is more contested than that of Hegel, and each of us selects that which seems most relevant, either to castigate or celebrate.[6] Perhaps, though, it is possible to agree on the power and fascination of his *methodological* invitation – to examine individuals in relation to a triad of social spheres (families, civil society and the state), and to render our enquiry into family–civil society

[2] For further elaboration of this point, see Ginsborg 1995.

[3] Hegel 1991. [4] Hegel 1991, p. 222, §185.

[5] Habermas 1989 famously ascribed a central role to bourgeois families in the creation of a European public sphere in the eighteenth century, but this role of prime importance gives way in the latter part of his work to a reductionist view of the modern role of families. The family is deprived of its major functions, it shrinks into a 'sphere of pseudo-privacy' and becomes little more than a 'community of consumers'. This demotion of the family and denial of its status as a subject of history is not easily acceptable as an account of historical developments in the twentieth century.

[6] In the recent series of volumes on European Civil Society, edited by Dieter Gosewinkel and Jürgen Kocka, it is interesting to note the widely divergent views of Hegel adopted first by Terrier and Wagner (2006, pp. 19–20) and then by Trägårdh (2007, pp. 12–14, 29–30).

relations at least equal in its intensity to those regarding the state and the family, and the state and civil society.

A further question deriving from Hegel concerns the shape of the chain of connections that we wish to establish. In *The Elements of the Philosophy of Right* the underlying direction, though subject to considerable dialectical turbulence, is linear and ascending. At the end of the work, from paragraph 257 onwards, the state makes its majestic entrance. It constitutes the force capable of reconciling the universal with the particular, and of resolving all previous contradictions. So nineteenth-century a view of the potential of human institutions is not an easy one to share. As David Runciman argues in chapter 1 of this book, it probably makes more sense to conceive of a chain of connections (individuals – families – civil society – state) in circular rather than linear terms, with no specific endpoint in view. Analytically, it is possible to enter the circle at any point, without necessarily beginning with the family, or conceiving of it as some sort of kernel from which will grow the great tree of state.

With regard to this chain of connections, the history of each democratic nation-state offers different variants, emphases and balances. In the sections that follow I intend to examine the constituent elements of the Italian case, looking first at individuals and families, then civil society and last the relations between families and states.

III

Peter Nichols, the veteran correspondent of *The Times* in Rome, described the Italian family in 1973 as 'the accredited masterpiece of Italian society over the centuries, the bulwark, the natural unit, the provider of all that the state denies, the semi-sacred group, the avenger and the rewarder'.[7] More soberly, in a BSA (British Social Attitudes) comparative social survey of 1989 of seven different countries – Britain, the USA, Australia, (West) Germany, Austria, Italy and Hungary – Italy emerged with a particularly distinctive pattern of family and personal relationships. Italian adults were much more likely to live close to their relatives – especially their parents – and to be in close and constant contact with each other. Indeed, the spatial and emotional proximity of Italian families is very marked indeed.[8]

At the centre of these families stands the mother, the provider of a constant flow of totalising care, directed primarily towards her child or children, but also towards her husband, her parents and often her husband's parents as well. Though there are regional differences, bilateral kinship relations are broadly

[7] Nichols 1973, p. 227.

[8] Finch 1989b; Ginsborg 2001, p. 331, diag. 8, 'Average distance from mother to place of residence of married children in Italy, 1989.'

the norm, with the central maternal figure serving as their lynch-pin. In the general context of a slowly dissolving patriarchal system,[9] Italian mothers are to an ever greater extent the voice of authority, especially with regard to children. Fathers, as in other European countries, have become more uncertain figures.[10]

The intensity of the mother–son relationship is especially marked. Those who have been brave enough to reflect upon the archetypes that lie at the heart of maternal behaviour in Italy have usually made reference to two figures in particular: the Virgin Mary and the Mediterranean *Grande Madre*. The Virgin Mary as the supreme example of purity, as the symbol of motherhood defined as humility, pain and sacrifice; the *Grande Madre*, in the words of the German Jungian psychoanalyst Ernst Bernhard, who practised for many years in Rome in the 1950s, as

> a mother who spoils her sons with the maximum of instinctiveness … but the more she spoils them, the more she makes them dependent upon her; and the more natural come to appear her own demands upon her sons, the more they come to feel tied to her. At this point the good mother, protective and nourishing, is transformed into her own negation.[11]

Of course, Italy is not the only country where family, or mothers, matter so much. The comparative survey just cited did not include any other southern European country, nor any Islamic ones. On the southern shores of the Mediterranean the Arab family, with its long endogamic traditions, first marriage between parallel cousins on the father's side of the family and now increasingly on the mother's side, offers an even stronger example of family cohesion and matricentric practices.[12]

Slowly, often with great difficulty and widespread racism, Italy is becoming a multicultural country. This is a very recent process by European standards, substantially covering the last thirty years. There are now some 4,500,000 immigrants with regular permits, around 7.5 per cent of the population. Each year some 40,000 foreigners become Italian citizens, a number far below the British or the French but significant nonetheless. The largest national groups of new citizens are Albanians and Moroccans.[13] Italy is thus moving away from a pattern of family culture and formation that had previously been extraordinarily homogeneous – in colour of skin, religion and even in language, as dialects declined.

During the sixty years of the Italian Republic much has changed in the structure of families. They have become much smaller, as in all of Europe, with the

[9] Therborn 2004. [10] Pietropolli Charmet 1995. [11] Bernhard 1969, p. 171.

[12] Rugh 1984, pp. 108ff.

[13] *La Repubblica*, 22 April 2010. For the overall number of regular immigrants, see Caritas/Migrantes 2009.

average number of members per household falling from 4 in 1951 to just 2.5 in 2007. To explain the extraordinary paradox of strong families and low fertility in Italy is a long and complicated business. Suffice it to say here that both modern and traditional forces have pushed couples into having fewer children. In modern terms, the spread of contraception and of legal abortion, the increasing, though still unsatisfactory, presence of women in the labour force and their higher levels of education have all played a crucial limiting role. So, too, have the uncertainties of putative fathers, who now measure their sense of achievement more in terms of work than in that of reproduction. The old imperatives for child rearing have disappeared, as have many of its temporal and spatial opportunities. Italian couples of all classes express a clear preference for families with two children but usually only manage to have one – the syndrome of *il bambino negato* – the 'missing child'.[14]

Some more traditional elements of Italian family culture also weigh heavily against high fertility rates. A very high percentage of Italian couples express the felt obligation to have children within marriage and in a stable work situation. Marriage thus comes late, and so does conception – reducing the chances of further births after a first child.[15] The negative gender balance within Italian families, with men continuing to contribute very little in terms of housework or childcare, acts as a further deterrent. Finally, after the unfortunate Fascist experience in eugenics, the Republican state has shown very limited interest in reproduction politics. Public support mechanisms cannot in any way compare with those in France and much of northern Europe.[16]

Italian families have thus become strikingly 'thinner' in numerical terms. But they are also 'longer', in at least two senses: first, they are now habitually composed of three generations, with a greatly increased number of grandparents actively present in daily life; secondly, young people leave the family home at a later age than anywhere else in Europe (Spain and Greece are not far behind). In the 1990s, Cavalli and De Lillo found that at the age of 29 nearly half of Italian sons and more than a quarter of daughters were still living at home.[17] Tri-generational dependency patterns, with the youngest generation having great difficulty in breaking free, both for emotional and economic motives, have become the order of the day.

These strong, even suffocating, modern Italian families give substance to the European-wide division suggested by the historical demographer David Reher – that between weak and strong family systems. In northern Europe it is

14 Guazzini 1987, p. 51.

15 The average age of Italian mothers at the birth of their first child rose from 25.7 years in 1961 to 29 years in 2003; ISTAT 2007.

16 Dalla Zuanna and Micheli 2004; Ipsen 1996 for Fascist demographic policies; Schizzerotto 2007, pp. 153–66, for men not helping in the home.

17 Cavalli and De Lillo 1993, pp. 211–13; Fernandez-Cordon 1997.

the individual who counts for more; in the Mediterranean it is the family. Over time, the 'strong' system of southern Europe has been distinguished principally by two elements: the greater longevity of families of origin and the higher degree of solidarity between generations.[18]

There was a moment in the Italian Republic's history when these dependency patterns appeared to be changing. The great internal migrations of the late 1950s and early 1960s – from countryside to city, from south to north – weakened spatial and emotional proximities and the links between generations. So too did Fordism and the new youth culture, with the possibilities they offered young people of economic independence and alternative lifestyles. Leone Diena, in his study of young Milanese workers, published in 1960, asserted boldly on the basis of his interviews that 'Almost never does the family seem to constitute an important factor in the life of the workers.'[19]

This brave new world failed to materialise. There was no automatic connection between industrialism and new family patterns, and in any case the Fordist era in Italy had a very compressed time-span. No sooner was Italy in it than it was out of it. The service and consumption economy of the last twenty years has instead been accompanied by strong continuities in family behaviour.

There is a last element worthy of attention. The structure of much of the Italian economy reflects and reinforces the family trends just described. Italian industrial districts – textiles at Prato and Carpi, furniture at Arquata, ceramics at Sassuolo, shoes at Vigevano – have attracted a great deal of international attention for their entrepreneurial vitality, their flair for design and export, and their capacity to occupy important niches in the world economy in the face of very stiff competition. The structure of the firms in these districts, and that of the many artisan and retail enterprises that still flourish in Italy, is essentially a family one. Even medium- and large-size firms, as a detailed study by the Bank of Italy in 1994 revealed, had by far the most concentrated and family-controlled structures of all those in the principal industrialised countries.[20]

To a significant extent, therefore, family and work overlie each other in Italy, and what you are in one you are also in the other. Especially from the 1980s onwards, a decade of considerable prosperity, the 'thin but long' families of the Italian self-employed have become centres of income, investment, consumption and entrepreneurship – *aziende-famiglie* as the Catholic sociologist Giuseppe De Rita called them, family and firm all rolled up in one.[21]

What does all this mean for the problem that principally concerns us here – the nature of the connections between family, civil society and the state? Let

[18] Reher 2004. His work is a further refinement of John Hajnal's, who first proposed a famous dividing line between Trieste and St Petersburg with regard to European family systems (Hajnal 1965).

[19] Diena 1960, p. 73.

[20] Barca et al. 1994, vol. I, p. 86, table 3.8, vol. II, pp. 94–101.

[21] De Rita 1988.

me begin with a negative judgement from a considerable authority. In an interview of 1990, Norberto Bobbio expressed the opinion that in Italy 'a quantity of energy, commitment and courage is squandered on the family, but little is left for society or for the state'.[22] This is not a judgement to which Bobbio ever returned in his writings. It is certainly an exaggeration, as we shall see when we consider Italian civil society, but it suggests an image that reoccurs in many different types of historical evidence – that of a dominant and all-embracing family sphere, which tends to dwarf other moments of association. The family firms which are so much the backbone of the Italian economy are formidable instruments of accumulation and of self-exploitation, often by means of extended kinship networks, but they are less good at establishing benign relations between families and civil society.[23]

Not by chance did Italian sociology, alone in Europe, have a serious and ongoing debate about 'familism', a term first coined by the American Edward Banfield in 1958. For Banfield 'amoral familism' was the prevailing attitude amongst the peasants he studied in 1957–8 at Chiaromonte, in Basilicata. The extreme backwardness of this village was caused, according to him, by 'the inability of the villagers to act together for their common good, or indeed, for any good transcending the immediate, material interest of the nuclear family'.[24]

Banfield, Pizzorno and others, all in different ways, were convinced that these attitudes, the fruits of extreme poverty, would disappear with modernisation. But 'familism', both as an academic concept and as a term in common usage, has had an obstinate tendency not to go away, and to extend its descriptive range to urban as well as rural realities. Behind this longevity of usage lies a particular relationship between interiors and exteriors. Social psychologists have noted how Italian families express defensive, cynical and even predatory attitudes to much of the outside world, towards the institutions of the state, towards those wider loyalties that transcend kinship or narrow local networks of friendship.[25] The Republic, for all its formal democracy, has done little to combat these tendencies – the case of Mastella

22 Bobbio 1990.

23 Sciolla 1997, pp. 45ff, presents evidence from European Values Systems Surveys which appears to point the other way, with strong attachment to the family in Italy being accompanied by strong civic culture. See also Bagnasco 2006, pp. 30–1.

24 Banfield 1958, p. 10. His 'predictive hypothesis' was that the villagers acted as if they were following this rule: 'Maximise the material, short-run advantage of the nuclear family; assume that all others will do likewise' (ibid., p. 83). The anthropologist Amalia Signorelli has rightly pointed out that both Banfield and many of his critics missed the crucial point that nuclear families in the Italian south, though neo-local in residential terms and autonomous in terms of income, were (and are) very often integrated into a complex and extended bilateral network system. The real family ethos is this extended one (Signorelli 2000, pp. 4–5).

25 Rosci 1994, p. 302.

is highly indicative, with family and clan interests penetrating deeply into regional and national government.

To what degree, then, is the Italian family 'a real school in the virtues of freedom', to use a famous phrase of John Stuart Mill's?[26] I would argue, on the basis of more than one anthropological study,[27] that families in Italy do have a strong sense of freedom, but it is very much 'negative' freedom – the freedom from interference, the desire to lead one's own life without restrictions imposed from above and without the state poking its unwelcome nose into family business.[28] The most significant modern Italian champion of liberty interpreted in this way is of course Silvio Berlusconi. In a speech of November 1998, he said: 'We cannot accept their desire to control everything, their invasion of our lives, their presumption to regulate all our activities.' And in January 2004, on the tenth anniversary of his decision to enter politics, he repeated: 'For us liberty is an individual right which precedes society and precedes the State … Better Fascism than the bureaucratic tyranny of the judiciary.'[29] I will return to the judiciary.

A final word about Catholic attitudes. The church contributed significantly over a great period of time to the formation of the family attitudes which I have been trying to describe. In 1891 Leo XII had warned in his Encyclical *Rerum Novarum*: 'It is a great and pernicious error to think that the state can interfere as it likes in the sanctuary of the family.'[30] In 1950 the *Enciclopedia Cattolica*, in its entry on 'family', stressed the primacy of family over civil society, a primacy that was both temporal – the family is a 'natural' association that precedes civil society – and ethical. Family duties were primarily internal, not external – indissolubility, piety and the education of children.[31]

However, if the predominant view of family–society relations is the one just described, it is also true that Catholic social teaching, especially from the late nineteenth century onwards, stressed the need for good Italian Catholics to be active in society. In the 1950s in particular, a missionary spirit prevailed in the church, whereby family and society were both to be saved from Communism by the active intervention of crusading Catholics. Pius XII, the 'family Pope' as he came to be called, was the great champion of this integrist view of the relationship between the church, family and society.

A permanent tension thus existed *within* the Catholic view of the family, and this was to take more than one form in the history of the Republic. On the one hand, the church tended to stress the family's internal values, its primacy

[26] Mill 1991, p. 510. [27] See, for example, Pitkin 1985.
[28] Here the connections to the past are very strong, with Leon Battista Alberti's advice to Florentine families in his *I libri della famiglia* (1433–40) enjoying an extraordinary resonance in contemporary Italian public debate. See, in English, Alberti 1969.
[29] Berlusconi 2000, p. 201; Ginsborg 2005, p. 176.
[30] *Enciclopedia Cattolica* 1952, pp. 994–5. [31] Goffi 1962, p. 265.

over society, the need to protect it from a hostile world and state. On the other, there was the desire to overcome the family's isolation, and put it in an active relationship to the church, to civil society and even, through the Christian Democrats, to the state.

IV

Few terms in modern politics are more frequently and loosely employed than civil society. I think I should make clear from the outset what I intend by the term. Its most common usage today is as a description of both an *analytical space* and an *associational practice*. As analytical space, civil society is a vast intermediate area between the private sphere, the economy and the state. Civil society relates to families, to markets and to government, but is separate from them. As associational practice, civil society is characterised by a myriad of voluntary organisations, circles, clubs, rank-and-file networks, and so on. Some of these may acquire great stability and international weight, such as Amnesty International or Greenpeace. Others, the majority, will have much briefer lives, formed at a local level in a moment of enthusiasm and general mobilisation but soon destined to disappear.[32]

However, civil society cannot be defined only in terms of analytical space and associational practice. It has always had strong *normative* content, though the precise nature of that content is bound to be modified from one generation to another. The historian Jürgen Kocka has argued convincingly that civil society's modern origins are in the European Enlightenment, and that the project of civil society, however variegated and developed over time, remains an Enlightenment one.[33] In contemporary terms it can be said to harbour specific ambitions within the general condition of modern democracy: to foster the diffusion of power rather than its concentration, to use peaceful rather than violent means, to work for gender equality and social equity, to build horizontal solidarities rather than vertical loyalties, to encourage tolerance and inclusion, to stimulate debate and autonomy of judgement rather than conformity and obedience.

What, then, is the specific configuration of Italian civil society and how does it relate to the structure and culture of Italian families described above?

The first point to make is a very long-term one, to do with the influence of clientelism upon Italian and indeed Mediterranean history. Clientelism in its original Roman form was a formal pact established between patron and client,

32 It has to be said that this is a very 'Continental' view of the nature of civil society. For the Anglo-Scottish tradition, which puts the emphasis much more on civil society as the institutional framework for effective government and legislation, without necessarily separating state and civil society, see Harris 2003.

33 Kocka 2004.

in which the client swore loyalty to his master, but received in return a series of legal guarantees as to the conduct of the patron on his behalf. In this vertical diadic relationship, power was unequally distributed between the two persons involved, but was not exclusively the prerogative of one or the other.[34]

Clientelism did not die with the end of the Roman Empire, but rather showed a remarkable ability to survive and adapt in the Mediterranean world, and not only there.[35] Though it is painful to have to admit it, clientelism is the dominant mode of social relations in contemporary Italian society. It is the very antithesis of modern civil society – the one based on vertical relations, the other on horizontal ones; the one on the concentration of power, the other on its diffusion, the one on patrons and patriarchs, the other on citizenship and gender equality. Clientelism may oil the wheels of society, inculcate devotion, even bring prosperity; but it never furthers democratic relations.

In the Republican era, it is distinguished by two features in particular: first, the benefits to be distributed are no longer primarily those of the private patron, but those of the state; secondly, the pattern of their distribution is not, as in ancient Rome, broadly in accordance with official legal norms, but in defiance of them. That is why Clemente Mastella ended up in such deep trouble.

A second point is geographical. Clientelism is ubiquitous in Italy, but civil society is not. Associationism has always been much weaker in the south than in the centre or north of the country. At the end of the nineteenth century workers' mutual aid societies flourished everywhere in the centre-north but hardly at all in the south. The same was true for Catholic associations in the same period. In the deep rural south, at Chiaromonte in 1958, Banfield found no associations at all, except for a club of card-playing *signori*, who can only with difficulty be called members of 'civil society', however that term is defined. In recent decades associationism has flourished in many regions of the south, but the historical legacy remains a heavy one.[36]

A third point regards ideology. In the first two decades of the Republic (1948–68), Italian civil society was very much divided on ideological lines. The political science of the time talked of two great sub-cultures, the Communist and Catholic, but the Communist presence, however original and interesting, was confined principally to the central regions of the country and must be judged ephemeral in comparison to the Catholic. 'What is civil society?' asked Pius XII in June 1940, in a famous Allocution to newly weds. It is certainly 'not formed of a conglomerate of individuals, sporadic beings who appear one moment and disappear the next. Rather it arises from the economic sharing and

[34] See, for example, Deniaux 1993.
[35] For a global survey, see Eisenstadt and Roniger 1984. A recent and useful collection of essays is in Piattoni 2001.
[36] Trigilia 1995.

moral solidarities of families which, by passing on from generation to generation the precious inheritance of the same ideal, the same civilisation, the same religion, ensure the cohesion and continuity of social ties.'[37]

The two sub-cultures presented rather different attitudes towards authority. The Communists, often against the advice of their more prudent leaders, contested authority, led strikes and generally, though not always, sought collective solutions to individual or family problems. Theirs was a party-dominated idea of civil society. The church, on the other hand, preached the virtues of submission and docility, inviting families to seek mediated and individual, not 'mass', solutions to their problems. The whole tradition of the propitious invocation of the Madonna and of the Saints was the long-standing religious practice upon which modern clientelist practices were founded.[38]

There was a moment in the history of the church, and indeed of Italian society, when it appeared that things were going in a different direction. Just as in the mid-60s, with mass emigration from country to city, from south to north, family ties appeared to be loosening up, so in the wake of the pontificate of John XXIII (1958–63), it appeared that the church was changing in a direction that would foster the growth of a democratic civil society. The 1960s was a period of great religious ferment and change. The deliberations of the second Vatican Council, the preaching of radical priests like Don Milani and Padre Balducci, the founding of grass-roots Catholic communities in which participants lived with great simplicity, all seemed to offer a different version of the relations between the church, Catholic families and civil society.

The late 60s and early 70s were also an unparalleled moment of collective action in the history of the Republic. If the May events in Paris were the dramatic highpoint of 1968, the Italian movement was unusually long-lasting, earning for itself the epithet *il maggio strisciante*, the May that went on and on. Workers' councils, enjoying considerable power of control within factories, were instituted on a mass scale. By 1973 there were 16,000 councils and more than 150,000 shop-floor delegates, mainly metal and chemical workers.[39] So great was the pressure for change at that time that Norberto Bobbio noted 'an ascending power' which was spreading to 'various spheres of civil society'. He continued: 'Seen from this angle I believe that it is justified to talk of a genuine turning point in the evolution of democratic institutions which can be summed up in a simple formula: from the democratisation of the state to the democratisation of society.'[40]

It was not to be. The church gradually retrenched, the more radical aspects of the second Vatican Council were put to one side, and Paul VI set into action a gradual but distinct Restoration. Nor, with one or two exceptions which I

[37] *Insegnamenti pontifici* 1964, pp. 288–9. [38] Signorelli 1986, p. 155.
[39] Ginsborg 2006, p. 28. [40] Bobbio 1987, p. 55.

shall examine shortly, did the political parties use all the potential for reform of this particular historical moment.

Today, what is the relationship between civil society and families in Italy? If we return for a moment to Hegel's analytical categories, there is little that resembles a 'dissolution' of the family at its moment of contact with civil society, a subordinating of family interest and ethicity to those of civil society. On the other hand, a purely 'familist' approach, stressing the overarching importance of families to the exclusion of all else, misses much in modern Italian society.

The associations of civil society, in their modern and democratic expressions, are a considerable, though fluctuating, force. The 1980s and the 1990s were a period of slow growth but at the end of the century new elements came to the fore – the peace movement, the 'new global' youth movement organised in Italy into urban Social Forums (2002–6), the mobilisation of sections of the middle class against Berlusconi and in favour of the 1948 constitution. Today, if the Scandinavian countries are the heartlands of European civil society, with very high rates of participation in associations, Italy is not that far behind, especially in the centre and the north of the country.[41]

The recent CIVICUS *Global Survey of the State of Civil Society* (2007–8), if not quite what its title promises, has usefully tried to compare the strength of civil society in different nations. Using the four measuring rods of the general environment in which a specific civil society works, the values it holds, the structures it creates and its impact upon society as a whole, the Italian case emerges in positive terms, in fourth place of the forty-five nations examined.[42]

Italian civil society, as the CIVICUS survey points out, is not exactly the best structured or coordinated in Europe, but it is capable of extraordinarily powerful mobilisations – on peace, in defence of democracy, for civil and social rights. The willingness to take to the streets, to make one's voice heard, is a distinctly Italian quality, and the role of the Piazza in the civic history of the nation is an important one.[43] In September 2002 and again in December 2009, civil society organisations were able to mount massive protests of more than a million people against the *ad personam* laws in favour of the prime minister, passed by the second and third Berlusconi governments.

[41] It is notoriously difficult to measure the size and importance of different nations' civil societies, and we have to remember that merely belonging to an association is not enough – train spotting, as has often been said, is a pleasurable but not a civic activity. Nor is the accumulation of 'social capital' any automatic guarantee of the spread of civil society – the Mafia, as we shall see in a moment, is not short of social capital (nor economic capital for that matter), but is the opposite of civil society.

[42] Finn Heinrich 2007, pp. 209–17; Knight 2008, pp. 163–80.

[43] Isnenghi 1994.

It is as well to be clear what these mobilisations entail and what they do not. Although family groups are present at mass protests, it is above all individuals who compose civil society and participate in its initiatives. At the end of the day, these civil-society activists carry their experience home to be discussed in a wider family context, marked invariably by gender and generational differences. Sometimes Italian families express an extraordinary homogeneity of opinion. More often, families are battlegrounds where different opinions and actions are debated and contested, often in front of the television screen.[44]

Two final points are worth making, both sobering with regard to family–civil society relations. The first regards gender. Although many strides forward have been made in gender equality, with dramatic increases in women's education and the number of women graduates, Italy remains one of the European countries with the lowest female employment rate – that is, the number of employed women as a percentage of all those in work, little more than 30 per cent by the beginning of the new century. Women's work in Italy shows a marked tendency to tail off after childbirth, in contrast to Britain and Germany, where women return in great numbers to the workforce as their children grow up and leave home. Nor does Italy, unlike Holland or Britain, have any significant segment of part-time work for mothers with small children.[45] Many studies show the connections between women's education, work outside the home and membership of civil-society associations. Conversely, where a rigid male-dominated labour market excludes educated women, as in the south of Italy, there civil society is often weak and family loyalties unmediated. It is difficult to break out of this vicious circle.

A last consideration concerns the Mafia. For the Mafia there is no equilibrium to be sought between family, civil society and the state. Mafia 'families' are obviously neither pluralist nor democratic, but have their own value system of honour, shame and revenge. They seek to dictate terms to real families and to recruit young males from them. Often this puts the very close relationship between mothers and sons under unbearable strain. The Mafia boss Antonino Calderone told Pino Arlacchi:

> Women are uncontrollable if you touch their sons, because no greater love exists in the world. The link between mother and son is stronger than any other, more than that between wife and husband, between daughter and father, between sister and brother. The pain caused by losing a son is unbearable for a mother. If they kill her husband she may in the end accept … but if they kill her son …[46]

[44] Some excellent examples are in Comand and Santucci 1995.

[45] Malerba 1993, pp. 57–8.

[46] Arlacchi 1992, p. 165. For a deeper analysis of these relationships than is possible here, see Ginsborg 2001, pp. 197–9.

The history of the Mafia has its own periodisation in the Republican era. In the late 80s and early 90s, the state, largely in reaction to the confrontational actions of the Corleonesi and their killing in 1992 of the magistrates Giovanni Falcone and Paolo Borsellino, waged war on the Mafia and the other criminal organisations of the south. The initiative was supported by a burgeoning anti-Mafia civil society in Palermo and by parts of the local clergy – the Jesuits in particular. But during the Berlusconi era the state's advantage has gradually been eaten away. Now the dominion of criminal organisations is spreading ever more comprehensively all over the south and to parts of the north. Neo-liberal economic policies, which offer few opportunities of stable employment, when combined with the historic phenomenon of high unemployment rates in Campania, Calabria and Sicily, push many southern youth ineluctably towards criminal careers. Roberto Saviano's *Gomorra* is eloquent recent testimony to the way families are undone by a society over-run by barbarian values.[47]

V

In the Italian case the state cannot be said to make its entrance in majestic fashion, as in Hegel's *Elements of the Philosophy of Right*; nor does it hold out the promise of reconciling the particular with the universal. Rather, it expresses a deeply porous quality, conveying the sensation that its daily routines and values too often mirror and absorb those of society rather than distinguishing themselves from it.

Let me begin with the bureaucracy, the lynch-pin of the system. During the history of the post-war Republic a chasm separated the formal codes of behaviour of the public administration from its actual functioning. In formal terms, its actions are minutely regulated by administrative law, whose principal objective is to safeguard the citizen against the arbitrary power of bureaucracy. This is what has been called the 'justice-oriented' culture of Italian administration.[48] In reality, the habitual practice of the bureaucracy depends to a notable extent, even today, upon the exercise of discretionary power on the part of the functionary.

The key term 'discretion' does not in this case signify the necessary and desirable autonomy of action of the individual civil servant within a general framework of impartiality, but rather the performance of favours in response to particularistic pressure. The speeding-up and even the realisation of a bureaucratic act become dependent upon this sort of discretionary act, and the task of the citizen is to find the right levers to trigger the desired response. Not all citizens are equal or can exert equal pressure. Inducements to action vary, from

[47] Saviano 2006. [48] Dente 1989, pp. 147ff.

the use of relatives and friends to clientelistic networks, to outright corruption. As a result, a profoundly *deformed relationship* between citizen and state has come into being. The contrast between this and the Scandinavian attitudes described by Maria Ågren in chapter 8 of this book is very striking.[49]

Naturally, not all state transactions are of the same quality, and areas of efficiency and impartiality can certainly be found in parts of the Italian state. Simplified and automatic procedures on the Web have rendered more transparent many relations between state and citizen. It is also true that all modern administrations – not just the Italian one – function both on the basis of law and regulation, and also on personal contact and informal relations. However, it is the balance between these elements that is all-important. In the Italian case, the personal and the particular have too often outweighed and threatened to engulf the impersonal and the impartial.[50]

This historical legacy has profound importance for the modern relationship between families and the state. It has ensured that, in the vital process of *interiorisation* of codes of conduct in the public sphere, families have not been presented by the state with a constant and clear alternative to deep-rooted practices to be found in society, of which clientelism and nepotism are the most evident. Rather, the state presents an ambiguous attitude – formal condemnation (as in the case of Mastella) but substantial acquiescence. As a result, the state is often seen by families as neither impartial nor benevolent, but rather as a container of resources which they can hope to unlock – that is, if they are lucky and find the right keys.

In this process of 'particularising' the state, political parties have played an essential role. 'The state is there to be occupied' was a leitmotif of the first generation of Christian Democrats, and the party politicians of both right and left have never forgotten it.[51] In the early years of the Republic, the major parties boasted mass memberships and a real presence in society. They could argue, with some justification, that they were the political vehicles which channelled citizens' needs into the institutional sphere. More recently, however, both in Italy and in many other parts of Europe, parties' links with society have weakened and those with the state increased. Parties, to use Peter Mair's formula, have transformed themselves into 'semi-state agencies', increasingly using the state's resources to ensure their own survival while distributing jobs, favours and cash in return for political loyalty. These mechanisms are so developed that Italian democracy has rightly come to be defined as a *partitocrazia*.[52]

[49] See also the interesting comparison of Greece and Sweden in Papkostas (2001).
[50] Particularly useful in this context are Cassese and Franchini 1994; Melis 1996.
[51] Orfei 1976. [52] Scoppola 1989; Mair 1997, pp. 93–119.

Obviously, such a system does nothing for the possibility of democratic connections between families, civil society and the state. If we imagine the Italian state as a snakes and ladders board, families have understood that the ladders of political clientelism extend far up into the public sphere and that it is as well for one or more family members to be on them – the rewards are many and the snakes are few. Meanwhile civil society and political society eye each other with distrust: parties are anxious to minimise disturbance and to coopt rapidly the leaders that emerge from civil-society struggles; civil society demands that the parties clean up their act and devolve more power to citizens. The parties can boast great resources, deriving largely from the state, but they are in no way hegemonic. In all Italian surveys dedicated to measuring the degree of trust placed in various institutions (church, parliament, judiciary, etc.), parties regularly come out last, with abysmally low rating levels. Once again, it is possible to discern split attitudes, with families accepting the necessity of party-based clientelism at the same time as they despise it.[53]

Ideally, it would be desirable to examine different parts of the Italian state in this light. Here I must limit myself to just two, of neuralgic importance: the system of justice and that of welfare.

Claus Offe recently made the telling point that the 'Italian anomaly' is not Silvio Berlusconi himself, with his glaring conflict of interests and scarce respect for democracy, but rather the failure of the Italian judicial system to bring him to justice on any of the grave charges levied against him.[54] Bernard Tapie in France was a similar meteoric figure in the mid-1980s, Thaksin Shinawatra another in Thailand a decade later. Both were eventually brought to justice. Why has Berlusconi not gone the same way?

To answer this question is more complicated than may at first appear. One explanation that we must certainly bear in mind, the most obvious, is that he is innocent of all charges. A second regards the nature of proof. On 6 March 1991, the sum of $434,404 left the Credito Svizzero bank account at Chiasso of Berlusconi's holding company, Fininvest, transited fleetingly in Cesare Previti's 'Mercier' account in the Darier Hentsch bank in Geneva, and was then deposited in another secret bank account, this time of the Roman judge Renato Squillante. The purpose of the transfer was to corrupt Squillante and ensure his support in a number of key Roman trials, including the one concerning the ownership of Italy's biggest publishing house, Mondadori, which duly fell into Berlusconi's hands. The bank record of these transfers was one of the very

[53] Diamanti 2009. Compared to the trust ratings of the president of the Republic (70.3 per cent), the school system (57.5 per cent), the church (52.7 per cent), the European Union (49.3 per cent) and the judiciary (40.9 per cent), the banks scored 19.2 per cent, parliament 18.3 per cent and the parties just 8.6 per cent.

[54] At a workshop in the University of Sydney entitled 'Sceptics, Critics and Enemies of Democracy', coordinated by John Keane in October 2007.

few pieces of hard evidence that the prosecuting magistrates have ever had in the Berlusconi trials. It was sufficient to condemn the intermediary, the lawyer Cesare Previti, one of Berlusconi's closest advisers, to six years of imprisonment (which he never served).[55] But the key question was another: how could it be demonstrated that Berlusconi knew of the transfer? The answer was that it could not.

A third element of reply to Offe's observation brings us to the heart of the matter – the weakness, inefficiency and vulnerability of judicial power in the Republic. Berlusconi got off in more than one case because the statute of limitations came into play. Time had run out. And it had run out because an average twenty-seven months was necessary for a case heard under the penal code to reach a first level of judgement, another forty-eight if the case went to Appeal, and another fifty-four months if it went to the third and final level, the Corte di Cassazione.[56] As Berlusconi had no interest in rapid justice, it was easy enough to play for time until the guillotine dropped.

The conclusions are very clear: at the present time there are real difficulties in Italy in guaranteeing due process of law. In its place there reigns *l'incertezza della legge* – the law's uncertainty. Italian families have become resigned to the fact that redress of grievance is a very lengthy and unpredictable affair. This resignation, though, has increasingly been accompanied by growing cynicism towards the state, politics and even democracy. The state has failed in one of its most important legitimating duties, the provision of justice, and in so doing has increased perforce the desire for summary justice exercised, if need be, by a single strong and charismatic figure. Of those interviewed in a 1994 survey, 73.5 per cent agreed with the statement 'Italy today needs a strong man.'[57]

A second area of enquiry, more closely linked to the everyday life of families, is that of welfare. Traditionally in Italy social insurance was 'Bismarckian' in structure, occupationally based and restricted to certain categories of workers and white-collar employees. Healthcare, too, was segmented, with Catholic and private organisations co-existing alongside those of the state. At the end of the Second World War, Italy, unlike many other European countries, missed the opportunity to carry out a major overhaul of the system. Christian Democrat diffidence, reflecting the church's fear of losing its enormous influence in hospitals and other charitable institutions, was mainly responsible.[58]

Much time was lost, and it was only in the 1970s, again under the pressure of collective action, that Italy began to catch up. In 1978 a national health service

[55] Ferrarella 2003.
[56] These figures are for the year 1994 but little has changed since then; ISTAT 1995, pp. 214–16.
[57] Cesareo et al. 1995, pp. 314–15.
[58] For the fate of the D'Aragona commission's proposals for radical reform along universalist lines, see Ferrera 1993, pp. 233–45.

founded on universalist principles finally came into being, offering protection and services to the whole resident population, regardless of income, gender or occupation. This was the most significant fruit of the 'historic compromise' between Communists and Christian Democrats of those years.[59] Major geographical differences remain in the standards of healthcare between the south and centre-north of the country, but overall the national health service must be judged a considerable success. Indeed, it is the most precious of present-day links between families and the Italian state. This is particularly true in regions like Lombardy, Venetia, Emilia-Romagna and Tuscany, where healthcare structures and medical skills are significantly above the European average. In the last twenty years the devolution of powers and resources away from the central state and towards regional governments has had largely positive results. So, too, has the reform of 1999 which encouraged greater efficiency and control in the spending of healthcare budgets.[60]

However, the welfare system, like other parts of the Italian state, cannot escape the effects of the deformed relationship between state and citizen which I have described above. Indeed, Maurizio Ferrera and others have made a convincing case for regarding Italian welfare as part of a specific southern European model, covering Spain, Portugal, Italy and Greece.[61] Its characteristics are not comforting ones: generous spending on pensions and other benefits for stably employed and trade-unionised workers, but almost no coverage for less-protected elements in the labour market; a model of family life strongly marked by intergenerational solidarities, with families regularly called upon to substitute for the state's deficiencies; and a welfare system marked by 'an elevated level of particularism'. Ferrera notes the low level of 'stateness' in the south European model: 'a state with few recognisably Weberian elements, infiltrated to a considerable degree and easily manipulated by organised interests, especially by political parties'.[62]

The Italian case is also marked by the absence of any clear direction for family policies. There is adequate maternity leave, but poor maternity care; infant schooling for 80 per cent of children between 3 and 5 years old, but crèches for only 5 per cent of the age group up to 3 years; tax deductions for a dependent spouse, but child benefits only for three or more children, and then only for dependent workers. Sometimes it is easy to discern the influence of Catholic ideology. At other times the state's distraction seems to correspond to no particular choice, being rather a series of *ad hoc* and sporadic responses to pressures of different kinds.

[59] For the projects and hopes of those years, see Berlinguer 1979.
[60] Maino 2001; Luzzi 2004. [61] Ferrera 1996; Naldini 2003.
[62] Ferrera 2006, pp. 42–5.

A final word about Italian family law. States, both democratic and not, seek to influence and mould families by means of the law, but rarely do we find an exact correspondence between the family as a social institution and the set of laws affecting it. Mary Ann Glendon has rightly called them 'two moving systems', not necessarily proceeding at the same pace.[63] In the Italian case, we find an extraordinary immobility in the central precepts of family law, lasting more than a century, from 1865 to 1975. The Civil Code (Codice Pisanelli) of 1865 was certainly revolutionary in its unitary intent and in its promulgation of civil marriage, but its version of gender relations, remorselessly patriarchal, enjoyed all too long a life – first in liberal Italy, then under Fascism and finally in the first three decades of the Republic. The code reflected in part the break between church and state at the heart of the Risorgimento, but in its family sections it was cautious indeed, reiterating the indissolubility of marriage and other central elements of canon law.

By the 1960s such a code was no longer sustainable. Italian society and the families that composed it had run far ahead of family law. Breaches were made in the archaic fabric of the code with the Divorce Law of 1970 and the Abortion Law of 1978. On both occasions the Catholic hierarchy and its mass organisations sought to abolish the laws by means of abrogative referenda (1974 and 1981). On divorce they lost clearly, by 40.9 per cent against 59.1 per cent; on abortion overwhelmingly, by 32.5 per cent against 67.5 per cent. Italian families clearly wanted to be free to make their own decisions about family formation and dissolution.

In 1975 came the most important piece of legislation in the Republican period – the reform of family law.[64] The gender codes of the previous century were radically modified. Parity between the two partners in marriage was established, the head of family could be of either sex, all legal discriminations against children born out of wedlock were abolished, and new guidelines were laid down for relations between parents and children. The reform constituted a major public shift towards gender parity and the rights of individuals, both adult and not, within the family. Family law had at last caught up with Italian families.

This legal impetus coincided with the setting up of family advisory clinics in 1975 and was shortly followed, as we have seen, by the creation of the national health service in 1978. Welfare provision and the reform of family law thus went hand-in-hand. However, the impetus was not maintained. In the very different economic and political climate of the 1980s and 1990s, the

[63] Glendon 1989, p. 5.

[64] It is worth noting the extraordinary synchronisation of family law reform in France, West Germany, Sweden and Italy during the course of a very few years, 1973–6; Glendon 1989, pp. 159–88.

Republican state reverted back in many areas to *delegating* to families rather than *providing* for them, thus reinforcing the negative aspects of the southern European welfare model. As Chiara Saraceno has written, here was another type of familism, this time descending from the state towards society, rather than vice versa.[65]

The virtuous circle of the mid-1970s – a new family code, universalist welfare provision and an active civil society – was replaced by one much less conducive to a chain of harmonious connections between families, civil society and the state. Families were thrown back on their own resources, civil society battled unsuccessfully with the *partitocrazia* and citizens expressed high levels of distrust and cynicism towards the state. At the same time, the obsequiousness of all Italian political parties to the Vatican has meant that the sort of progressive family legislation which the Spanish Socialist government undertook from 2004 onwards has been totally lacking in Italy.[66] A dismal overall picture has only in part been mitigated by the high standards of healthcare in many regions of the centre and north of the country.

VI

In this chapter I have concentrated on the nature of the connections between individuals, families, civil society and the democratic state in Italy in the second half of the twentieth century. It seems to me that an analytical framework of this sort constitutes a potentially very rich way to understand the overall trajectory of a country's history. Tracing such lines of connection or disjunction can lead to a broad comparative framework between nations, with each national history displaying differing strengths and weaknesses, and each possessing its own patterns of connectivity.

The Italian case, as I have tried to show, is based upon the following elements: in the first place, cohesive, matrifocal families which reflect the long-standing tradition of strong families in southern Europe and which, in the absence of adequate connections between themselves and civil society, tend to be self-referential; second, a historically weak civil society, especially in the south, and one which was based heavily in the early years of the Republic not on pluralist values but upon the ideological divide between Catholic and Communist sub-cultures; finally, a late-formed, porous and grossly ineffective democratic state, which to a considerable extent reflects the relations between patrons and clients dominant in society as a whole.

[65] Saraceno 1994.
[66] See Mora-Sitja in chapter 9 of this volume.

Like all brief summaries, this one gives rise to distortion. With a few more words at my disposal, I would emphasise two mitigating elements: a modern civil society, made up of active and dissenting citizens, nearly always middle class and often employed by the state; and a national health service which aspires to – but does not always achieve – high-level and egalitarian treatment of all its citizens.

Even with these mitigations, the overall combination of elements outlined above is not a good one, by any standard, and in fact Italian democracy is in very deep trouble. In reflecting on this parlous state of affairs, it is worth underlining a couple of points. The first concerns the state. Without demanding impossible Weberian leaps towards rationality, impartiality, meritocracy and efficiency, there are certain moments in the history of the Italian state when its historians can reasonably express regret, even frustration, that those who held power at the time, offered the clear opportunity of a turning point, were unable or unwilling to make history turn. The first of these is located at the fall of Fascism and the founding of the Republic, between 1943 and 1948. It has intentionally entered little into my story. But there is another which emerges in ever more imperious fashion and demands due consideration, like one of Pirandello's characters angrily in search of his author. In the decade 1968–78, the bases for Republican democracy were made and lost in Italy. Certain aspirations were at least in part fulfilled – the reform of family law, the national health service, the eventual growth of a modern civil society. But others – the dilution of the dependencies inherent in Italian families, the democratic reform of the church, the greater popular participation in both political and economic life, the curbing of Mafia power in many regions of the south – were left unrealised.[67]

Susan Moller Okin, in her *Justice, Gender and the Family*, asked – though she did not answer – one of the key questions underlying the Italian case: 'unless the household is connected by a continuum of just associations to the larger communities within which people are supposed to develop fellow feelings for each other, how will they grow up with the capacity for enlarged sympathies such as are clearly required for the practice of justice?'[68]

Once the so-called 'disturbance' of the years of collective action had disappeared, so too did the possibility of connecting a majority of Italian households to just associations and to the democratic state. Instead, a different model grew up from the 1980s onwards, heavily insistent upon the negative freedom of individual families. From commercial television and other sources came the incessant invitation to families to express themselves primarily in terms of

[67] De Luna 2009. [68] Moller Okin 1989, p. 100.

home-living and consumerism. Silvio Berlusconi presides over this scenario. He is not its inventor – we have to look across the Atlantic for that – but he is its most powerful Italian representative. He is also, to return to my starting point, a Mediterranean patron on a grand scale, offering protection and promotion in return for loyalty and obedience. It will not be easy to dislodge him. The history of the Italian Republic, its deep culture and social structures, are to a great extent on his side.

7 The Netherlands

Anneke van Doorne-Huiskes and Laura den Dulk

I

One of the key features of Dutch society before and for two decades after the Second World War was its division into *zuilen*, religious or ideological groupings or 'pillars', a phenomenon known in Dutch as *verzuiling*, translated variously as 'socio-political compartmentalisation' or, more literally, 'pillarisation'. What did pillarisation actually involve? Dutch society was sharply divided along religious and political lines, splitting the population into four 'pillars': Roman Catholics, Protestants, Socialists and Liberals. Each of these groups lived in a world that was largely separate from the others.[1] What did those worlds consist of?

To begin with, they consisted of religious denominations and political parties. People belonging to the Catholic grouping virtually all voted for the Catholic People's Party. The Protestants voted for Protestant parties. The two non-denominational groups, the Socialists and the Liberals, also had their own political representatives and parties. But the phenomenon of 'pillarisation' went much further than religious or political affiliation. The trade union movement, for example, was also divided into Catholic, Protestant and general (Socialist) unions, and the same applied to organisations of employers and farmers. The press and other media, including radio and later television, were also divided largely along socio-political and religious lines. The education system was – and in a certain sense still is – a textbook example of compartmentalisation. It was not only primary schools that were strictly divided into religious and other ideological categories, but so were secondary schools and even tertiary educational institutions. Although most Dutch universities were non-denominational, three institutions for higher education were founded at the initiative of religious organisations, one Protestant and two Catholic.[2]

Before the Second World War, and for two decades thereafter, many Dutch people lived their whole lives within the context of the 'pillars' and their institutions, which provided them with their main social environment. The elite in

[1] Lijphart 1988. [2] Lijphart 1988.

each grouping, however, were often in close contact with one another. These contacts gradually became institutionalised and served to preserve the unity of the Dutch state and Dutch society, a purpose to which they were well suited.

During this period, these elite classes were entirely male in composition. Women had no access to them. The ban was never expressed in so many words, nor were women explicitly refused entry; it was simply natural for women not to concern themselves with questions of governance, at least not in a public role. It was taken for granted that the elite was an all-male domain, and even Lijphart, in his standard work on 'pillarisation' in the Netherlands,[3] never discusses the role of women or the fact that the elite consisted entirely of men. Nor does he consider the unpaid work of women or their limited place in the world of work.

It should be added, however, that the majority of men in the Netherlands had as little to do with government and public affairs as the female population. It was the elite who governed the country.[4] Although parliamentary democracy functioned effectively, the most prominent members of the elite tended to discuss key social and economic issues in advance. This meant that, despite their religious and political conflicts and major differences of opinion, they were able to cooperate effectively. They were, for example, able to gain majority votes in parliament for such important matters as universal suffrage and state funding for Protestant and Catholic schools. They were able to shape Dutch society in this way because they had loyal and obedient followers, the 'common man' (and woman) within their own groupings. The leading figures in each group were able to persuade their supporters that they were acting for the general good of the country. The tone of communication between the elite and their followers differed significantly from that between the elite classes themselves. The latter was business-like, with mutual relations serving to resolve important issues. Those concerned understood the necessity of compromise and were prepared to negotiate. The tone used with their followers was much more ideological and/or religious in nature. They emphasised such contrasts much more when addressing 'the public at large' than in their contacts with one another, which served to settle vital issues.

The elite also kept a tight grip on the political and social organisations within their groupings. Political parties, trade unions, employers' associations, farmers' cooperatives – all showed signs of oligarchic control. The power exercised by the elite over the main political parties was bolstered by the electoral system introduced by the lower chamber of parliament in 1917. It consisted of proportional representation according to a system of lists, with votes being counted as if the entire country were a single electoral district.[5] The choice of who would stand for parliament was entirely an internal matter for the political parties.

[3] Lijphart 1968. [4] Lijphart 1988, p. 119. [5] Lijphart 1988.

The party leadership – who were also the leaders of the 'pillars' – compiled the lists. Because political parties could bank on a loyal and stable group of followers, the candidates – the vast majority of whom were male in the pre-war years – were elected in the order dictated by the party leadership.

The state operated at a distance in this parliamentary democracy, which was shaped in equal measure by the oligarchic elites. The idea was that the system would protect civil society – or rather, the various civic organisations within the socio-political groupings – from direct state intervention. Subsidiarity, or 'sovereignty within one's own circle', was and still is an important principle in the Netherlands. The principle of subsidiarity implies that government or the state only steps in when individuals and private organisations are unable to solve problems. This principle – Catholic in origin – corresponded to Protestant ideas about the proper social order. The 'circles' in which one moved – the family, schools, trade unions, volunteer organisations – should remain 'sovereign', in other words independent and autonomous. The power of the state should be restricted in these various areas of life.

The organising principles espoused by the denominational (that is, Catholic and Protestant) parties had a major impact on pre-war politics in the Netherlands. Between 1917 and 1940, the denominational parties exerted a major influence on the political complexion of the government, and, until 1939, completely excluded the social democrats. In the years leading up to the Second World War, the Netherlands was a corporatist state *par excellence.*

This patriarchal, corporatist society governed by an elite class made up entirely of men had a major influence on the role played by women in Dutch society. That influence can still be felt to a certain extent, although individualisation and secularisation have radically altered the country since the 1960s. There is still a certain patriarchal, imperious undertone to Dutch society, however, in particular when it comes to male/female relationships. We will return to this subject in the following section.

II

It was in the immediate post-war period that a large number of West European countries laid the basis for the welfare state. William Beveridge's *Social Insurance and Allied Services* (1942) and *Full Employment in a Free Society* (1944) were important starting points for building a welfare state and for overhauling and expanding the social welfare system in the Netherlands no less than in Britain. The purpose of social welfare, in Beveridge's words, was to protect people against the 'Five Great Evils of Want, Disease, Idleness, Ignorance and Squalor'.[6] John Maynard Keynes's *General Theory of*

[6] Hemerijck and Bakker 1994.

Employment, Interest and Money (1937) also emphasised the state's responsibility for full employment – at least for men. Both Keynes and Beveridge based their ideas on the traditional family structure. With men working full time and women staying at home to care for their families, the obligations of the welfare state would in fact be limited. Men's paid employment would also pay for women's unpaid work.[7]

This view of men's and women's roles corresponded entirely with the situation in the Netherlands. Let us take a look at how things stood then. In 1917, Dutch women were enfranchised, at first passively (gaining the right to be elected to office), and then actively (gaining the right to vote in elections). Women voted for the first time in 1922, and from 1919 on they began to trickle into parliament. The first female cabinet minister was not appointed until the 1950s, however, and in 1953 parliament was still discussing whether women should be admitted to the judiciary. They were accepted as judges in the juvenile courts, but were considered 'too emotional' for other positions on the bench.[8] Generally speaking, the rule at the time was that married women belonged at home, taking care of their families, and not in the labour market.

Society in the first half of the twentieth century placed great emphasis on the role of the family and children. The various socio-political groupings, especially the religious ones, had explicit views about the family. Protestant circles, for example, referred to God's intentions for families: 'God wants nothing more and nothing less than love and community based on the intimate bond between man and woman and the ties of blood between parents and children.'[9] Within that divine mission, men and women each had their specific roles. Men had the obligation to provide for their families, and women to care for the home and their loved ones.

The Catholics also had explicit ideas about the family and the roles of men and women. In 1930, Pope Pius XI issued the encyclical *Casti Connubii* banning all forms of contraception. The Dutch Catholic world of the time embraced the encyclical as God's word.[10] Women's purpose was to bear as many children as possible, and there was even a 'Union for Large Families'. Before the war – and even after – it was not unusual for local Catholic priests to call on married couples in their parish and ask them when they were planning to have their next child.

But the idea of the family as the core unit of society reigned not only in Dutch religious circles, but throughout the general pre-war population. The best way to prepare children for their place in society, it was agreed, was to raise them within the family. Although the state was not expected to intervene directly in family life, there were various government policies that affected

[7] Hemerijck and Bakker 1994; see also Thom's discussion in chapter 2, above.
[8] Verwey-Jonker 1985. [9] Van Eupen 1985. [10] Van Eupen 1985.

the family to some extent. For example, government housing policy focused almost entirely on building family dwellings, with scarcely any accommodation available for single persons. A law enacted in 1939 provided for a system of child benefit; this came into force on 1 January 1941.[11] Child benefit provision was fairly sizeable and was explicitly intended to 'promote the natural progression of family life'.[12] In the years leading up to the Second World War, Catholic ministers of social affairs attempted to ban married women from the labour market by law. Although they never succeeded entirely, government organisations and schools were required to dismiss female public servants and teachers on their wedding day. The Dutch welfare state created in the post-war era was based in part on the same ideas about the role of the family and men and women in society. To quote J. Bussemaker and K. van Kersbergen, the 'breadwinner-caretaker' structure continued to underlie much of Dutch social policy.[13] Sainsbury also refers to the Catholic principle of subsidiarity and the Protestant doctrine of 'sovereignty within one's own circle';[14] in both, the family was enshrined in its traditional form. State action was sanctioned in order to protect the family from economic hardship and to help the family's provider – the breadwinner – meet his maintenance obligations.[15] As Sainsbury argues, the principle of maintenance was firmly entrenched in social welfare, and benefits and contributions were designed to take the family as the norm, with a family minimum evolving gradually.

The family was therefore the foundation on which the Dutch welfare state was built in the decades after the Second World War. Men were entitled to social security benefits if, for whatever reason, they were unable to secure an income for their family. Women's social entitlements, on the other hand, were unrelated to their economic performance or their role as wage-earners; on the contrary, their benefits were tied to their marital status, in other words to whether or not they had a husband who was the family breadwinner.[16]

As Bussemaker and Van Kersbergen[17] indicate, it was not considered discriminatory to treat men and women differently with regard to social security benefits; instead, doing so acknowledged the natural differences between men's and women's talents and tasks. Interestingly, this idea has still not disappeared entirely from the Netherlands, even after four decades of individualisation, secularisation and of women being increasingly better educated. The 'ideology of motherhood', which is still very strong in the Netherlands, has its roots in this attitude.

In her analysis of the early Dutch welfare state, Sainsbury too emphasises the family as the unit as regards social security benefits. Married women without

[11] Bosmans 1988. [12] Bosmans 1988. [13] Bussemaker and Van Kersbergen 1994, p. 23.
[14] Sainsbury 1996. [15] Borchorst 1994.
[16] Bussemaker and Van Kersbergen 1994. [17] Bussemaker and Van Kersbergen 1994.

breadwinner status were denied social security benefits, for instance an individual pension or extended unemployment or disability benefit. Legislation prohibited married women from entering the labour market or penalised them when they did, for example by adding up husbands' and wives' income under the family-oriented tax system. In the late 1960s, Sainsbury argues, the Netherlands was a prime candidate for the archetype of the breadwinner model: social entitlements were derived almost entirely from the principle of maintenance and it was the head of the household who was the recipient of the benefits.[18] To avoid any misunderstandings, the man was considered the head of the household.

III

After a long period when a constant share of working women never rose above 30 per cent of the female population aged 15–64, married women began to enter the world of work in greater numbers in the late 1960s, partly owing to a growing shortage of labour in general, and female labour in particular. The traditional dividing lines, though, were still firmly in place: most women worked in lower-level positions in such sectors as education, healthcare and office work.

The 'second wave' of the feminist movement – meaning a more or less organised battle for women's emancipation or, in more radical terms, women's liberation – only hit the Netherlands in 1968. Women were not alone in protesting, however. Questions were being raised about all sorts of social and economic assumptions that had previously been taken for granted. Besides tackling the official, legal obstacles to women's emancipation, the new feminist movement also emphasised cultural, social and psychological barriers. These ideas were fed by new trends and pioneering research in the social sciences. What was also innovative, and somewhat confrontational at the time, was the idea that women were 'imprisoned' in a web of standards, values and expectations as to their role, leading to certain personality traits that developed in early childhood and were nurtured by various socialisation processes. Dependence, a lack of self-confidence and a need for approval were unfavourable traits as regards women's integration into society. The initial aim of the emancipation movement in the late 1960s and early 70s was to get women to recognise these traits by raising their consciousness and to teach them new attitudes and new behaviour.[19]

The sociologist Marjolein Morée wrote an interesting study on working mothers in the period between 1950 and 1990. The title of her thesis says it

[18] Sainsbury 1996; see also Mora-Sitja's discussion in chapter 9, below.
[19] Van Doorne-Huiskes 1979.

all: 'My children didn't notice a thing.'[20] According to Morée, there was virtually complete consensus in the Netherlands of the 1950s that the role of a mother was to care for her children. Children would suffer irreparable damage if their mothers were not constantly there for them. Gradually, a new consensus arose in the 1960s. Mothers of schoolchildren were tolerated in the labour market, partly owing to the labour shortage. There were almost no childcare facilities, however, and working hours were far from flexible. In those days, married women who worked sought to justify their decision to do so. They needed 'justification strategies'.[21] Admitting that they needed a second income to survive would be too threatening to their spouse's status and prestige. If they expressed an intrinsic need for self-fulfilment and opportunities for personal growth, they ran the risk of being labelled 'egotistic'. Calling paid work a 'hobby', however, took the edge off its importance, and was also a useful way of describing the role of paid work in women's lives at that time: it was of secondary importance, something fun to do on the side.

The individual's right to self-development and freedom of choice became more important in the 1960s and 70s. Mothers were no longer considered irreplaceable figures in the child rearing process. Increasingly, women were thought to have the right to pursue gainful employment. That change in attitude was reflected by government, which developed a policy on women's emancipation. In May 1977, the government presented the lower chamber of parliament with its first policy document on women's emancipation. According to that policy, women were free to go to work and earn an income. It should be easier for them to take on paid employment, but they should also have the right to choose otherwise. The document explicitly rejected the idea of an incomes policy that would force both marriage partners to go out to work.[22]

Gradually, in the years thereafter, the government began to emphasise the importance of women's economic independence. That growing emphasis was not accompanied, however, by measures that actually encouraged more women to enter the workforce. For example, childcare facilities were very limited until the early 1990s. In addition, the tax system continued to reward workers (usually men) who had a dependent partner (usually women). Even today, the Dutch tax system has what is sometimes referred to as a 'kitchen sink subsidy', in which breadwinners whose partners do not work or have a very small income are permitted to add that partner's tax-free allowance for income (or notional income) to the tax-free allowance for their own income. Even in the government formed in 2007, the Christian parties were able to pressure their coalition partners into retaining this concession to breadwinners for another fifteen

[20] Morée 1992. [21] Morée 1992, ch. 4, pp. 93–132.
[22] Hooghiemstra and Niphuis-Nell 1993.

years. The discussion concerning such tax facilities illustrates how ambivalent Dutch society feels about dispensing with the old breadwinner model.

During the 1980s, the Dutch employee insurance schemes, which offer sickness, disability and unemployment benefits, gradually became more individualised under the influence of various European Union directives. This meant that working women with husbands or partners were now entitled to individual benefits in the event of sickness, occupational disability and unemployment, even if they were not the breadwinner and regardless of other sources of income in their household. The employee insurance schemes are one of three components that make up the Dutch social security system.

The second component consists of social insurance schemes. The General Old Age Pension Act (Algemene Ouderdomswet, AOW) is one such scheme under which men and women are individually entitled to a benefit from age 65 onward, regardless of their marital status. This piece of legislation guarantees everyone who has lived in the Netherlands for fifty years a basic income, even those who have never paid contributions. The latter is true of quite a number of elderly married women in the Netherlands who have no work history.

The third component of the public social security system consists of social welfare benefits, paid for from taxation. They apply when individuals are in 'reduced circumstances'. The best known among these is the National Assistance Act (Algemene Bijstandswet), which came into effect in 1965; it made it a realistic option, for the first time, for women to end their marriages. Divorcees whose ex-husband failed to pay alimony or who received too little alimony qualified for benefit under this act.

Whether someone is entitled to national assistance and how much benefit they receive depends on their family circumstances. In other words, the income and assets of other family members are considered when determining an individual's eligibility. The Supplementary Benefits Act (Toeslagenwet), introduced in 1987, provides for another social welfare benefit. It gives eligible individuals the right to supplementary benefit if their unemployment, sickness or disability benefit is below the minimum wage. The size of the benefit is once again based on family circumstances. If there are other adequate sources of income in the household, entitlement to the supplementary benefit lapses. In practical terms, this means that fewer women than men actually qualify for benefits under this act,[23] and in a certain sense it also discourages married or cohabiting women from working longer hours.

While individual entitlement to social security benefits was one of the most important emancipation priorities of the 1980s, the key policy issue in the 1990s was how best to combine working and childcare.[24] This growing interest was closely related to new trends in society, for example the increasing

[23] Driessen and Veldman 1997. [24] Sociaal en Cultureel Planbureau 1998.

labour market participation of mothers since 1970, the growing demand for childcare, and the changing workforce, which was no longer dominated by the male breadwinner but increasingly diverse in nature. Government policy at the time focused on enabling working mothers to combine paid work with caring for young children.

The first Incentive Measure on Childcare was introduced in 1990, followed by parental leave in 1991. The Incentive Measure on Childcare was a major policy change designed to encourage childcare facilities for working parents. For the first time in history, the state became actively involved in childcare for children under the age of 4. After years of Incentive Measures, a Childcare Act finally came into force in January 2005. At the same time, the number of statutory leave arrangements increased; ultimately, these were combined into the Work and Care Act (2000) (Wet Arbeid en Zorg). The Work and Care Act gives working parents the right to take sixteen weeks of maternity leave, thirteen weeks of parental leave, ten days of care leave, two days of paternity leave and four weeks of adoption leave.

Despite introducing statutory childcare and leave arrangements, what government emphasised most in its support for working mothers was part-time work. In its view this form of work was a perfect strategy allowing women to combine their working lives with caring for children. Although this was a fairly progressive policy in the early nineties – the aim, after all, was to make it easier for women to enter paid employment – that emphasis smacks, in retrospect, of conservatism. Part-time work gave women the opportunity – albeit a small one – to gain economic independence and enjoy a career. At the same time, however, the emphasis on its part-time character did nothing to change the status quo. Men were still the breadwinners, and women were primarily caregivers and mothers. Women's career opportunities remained limited.

The conservatism of this policy is particularly obvious when we consider the astonishing success of women's part-time work in the Netherlands. In 2008, 75 per cent of all Dutch women in employment worked part time. Compare that to the European average of 31 per cent. Part-time work has even become popular among Dutch men, with 23 per cent working part time, whereas the European average is 7 per cent.[25] The disproportionate popularity of this form of work among women led in 2008 to the establishment of a government task force, the 'Part-time Plus Task Force'. Its job is to propose ways of increasing the number of hours that women work per week. We will return to this matter in the following section.

In the 1990s, government promoted part-time work mainly by protecting the legal status of such workers. Since 1996, employers have been obliged to treat full-time and part-time employees equally with regard to conditions

[25] Statistics Netherlands 2010.

of employment, for example holiday pay and entitlements, overtime pay and training. The Working Hours Amendment Act (Wet Aanpassing Arbeidsduur, WAA) came into force in 2000, giving workers the right to request to work more or fewer hours per week. What is special about this act is that employers are compelled to honour such requests, unless doing so is precluded by conflicting business interests. This implies that every refusal has to be justified by the employer; employees, on the other hand, do not have to justify their request.[26]

This concludes our review of the emancipation of women in the Netherlands. Women are still entering the workforce in growing numbers. In 2008, 71 per cent of Dutch women had a job, compared to a European average of 59 per cent. We have already noted that these jobs represent a relatively small number of working hours, and will look more closely at this phenomenon in the following section. When it comes to education, women in the Netherlands have likewise made very good progress, with a sharp rise in their educational level in recent decades. Indeed, there are currently more female than male students enrolled in higher education programmes. Women are also more likely than men to graduate. For example, of all students graduating with a Master's degree in 2007, 54 per cent were female and 46 per cent male.[27] Women's rising educational level has not yet led to their being well represented in senior management, however; the Netherlands still has a long way to go in that respect.

IV

We have seen that the 'ideology of motherhood' is still deeply rooted in the culture of the Netherlands. This is to some extent due to the country's political and cultural history, as described in the previous sections. In addition, most couples do not feel financial pressure to maintain two full-time or almost full-time jobs. The decision to work part time is based on more than socio-economic circumstances. Working part time can be seen as the cultural expression of the ideology of motherhood and as a compromise between the traditional model – the mother as the ideal care-giver who stays at home to take care of the children – and more modern models of motherhood. What does 'modern' motherhood actually mean? T. Knijn and C. Verheijen distinguish two kinds of mothers: *traditional* mothers and *individualistic* mothers.[28] The latter fits in with the new concept of motherhood, which emphasises such notions as personal development and self-realisation. The two categories are also associated with differences in socio-economic status: the better educated a couple is,

[26] Baaijens, Van Doorne-Huiskes and Schippers 2005.
[27] Statistics Netherlands 2008. [28] Knijn and Verheijen 1991.

and the higher their occupational status, the more likely that the woman is an individualistic mother. When motherhood itself is an expression of personal development, however, it still tends to be expected that women who go out to work should, generally speaking, not place too much emphasis on their jobs. Their work should certainly never be more important or meaningful than having children or being a mother.

As noted above, the pattern of part-time work, a compromise between modern and traditional motherhood, is fairly well entrenched in the Dutch social infrastructure. Part-time employees are well protected in the Netherlands and even high-powered jobs may be part time. In terms of preferences, it seems as if the vast majority of Dutch women work part time by choice. Nearly all working women in part-time jobs prefer to work fewer than the thirty-eight hours regarded as constituting a full-time job in the Netherlands. This is basically because Dutch parents prefer, by and large, to care for and raise their children themselves. If we consider part-time work within the context of the cultural meaning of motherhood, we can also see it as a 'strategy' or – in less deliberate terms – as an opportunity to maintain the traditional model of motherhood, at least in part. The traditional model has never disappeared entirely from Dutch culture; on the contrary, motherhood is still highly valued. Although many women today continue working after having children, in general most women would not dispute that motherhood comes first. Their reasoning is: although I like my job and would miss it enormously, if it proves harmful for my children, I will quit it immediately. And their partners agree with them, even if this means that they have to shoulder the breadwinner burden by themselves. Interestingly enough, economic independence is of secondary importance to Dutch mothers; they are guided by what is best for their children.[29] This is a view held by women and men alike.

Working part time offers many Dutch women the opportunity to enjoy personal development, as befits a modern woman, and to take care of their children themselves, in keeping with tradition. But this compromise comes at a price. Work-centred women, as C. Hakim calls them,[30] who are ambitious and want to have full-time jobs and careers, find it difficult – not just practically but more so in terms of social legitimacy – to combine demanding work and family life. In only 6 per cent of all working couples with children do both partners have full-time jobs. Although work-family leave and childcare facilities are available to a certain extent, it is not easy in the Netherlands to combine motherhood with an interesting career or plans to move into the upper echelons of a professional hierarchy. Work-family facilities are generally used

[29] Portegijs, Hermans and Lalta 2006. [30] Hakim 2001.

to supplement parental – and usually maternal – care. Children whose parents place them in formal childcare usually only spend two to three days a week at a day-care centre. So although work-family policies appear to be embedded in Dutch culture, they do not enable women to have full-time jobs. Work-family facilities are primarily seen as supplementary to the care provided by mothers and fathers themselves.

The positive attitude toward part-time jobs has altered slightly in recent years, at least in government circles. The economic boom and tight labour market have turned part-time work into a public and political issue. For the first time in Dutch history, the argument that women are wasting their talents by continuing to work in little part-time jobs has become more relevant and important. One sign of this change in attitude was the Dutch government's decision to install the Part-time Plus Task Force in 2008. The government wants women to increase their working hours, if not to thirty-eight hours a week – that would be a too big step for Dutch culture – then by an average of four to six extra hours minimum. At least, this is what the government hopes. It has asked the task force to explore the situation of women in part-time jobs and to advise on how to get more women to work longer hours.

To illustrate how the Part-time Plus Task Force works, we present some findings from a pilot study conducted in a number of healthcare organisations.[31] The study focused mainly on hospitals and asked the following key questions. To what extent and for what reasons do women in these organisations work in 'little' – twenty-four hours or less – part-time jobs? Are these women willing to increase the number of hours that they work each week? Under what conditions would they consider an increase in their working hours desirable and feasible? Do managers in these organisations want more women working more hours per week? How likely do they think this is? Have they developed policy measures to get more women working longer hours or even full time?

To answer these questions, the researchers collected qualitative data in interviews with women, supervisors, managers and HR officers. First, we review the part-time situation in the healthcare sector. Many employees in this sector have part-time jobs, especially female employees. In 2007, hospital employees worked an average of 24.6 hours a week; staff in mental healthcare institutions 27 hours a week; employees in disabled care services 23 hours a week; staff in retirement homes 21 hours a week; and home care service workers 17 hours a week. The table below presents the figures on 'little' part-time jobs (24 hours or less a week) and the percentages of such jobs held by women.

[31] Van Doorne-Huiskes, Henderikse and van Beek 2009.

Percentages of 'little' part-time jobs in the healthcare sector, by sex

Subsector	Percentage of little part-time jobs	Percentage occupied by women
Hospitals	34	74
Elderly and disabled care	54	87
Home care	61	92

Source: Keuzenkamp, Hillebrink, Portegijs and Puwels 2009

The most important reason by far for women to work part time in healthcare is the situation at home, their family circumstances. Most nurses, for example, decide to cut down on their working hours after the birth of their first child. Women are explicit about their wish to do so, and it is interesting that women and their husbands/partners agree on the issue of working hours. The general feeling is that it is primarily the woman's responsibility to care for the new-born. Husbands tend to agree and feel responsible for earning an income. Additional arguments are the difficulty that men have working part time ('In his job, part-time work is impossible or only possible at a high price, a loss of career prospects for instance') and the many opportunities to work part time in the healthcare sector.

In line with general findings on women's part-time work in the Netherlands, women working in the healthcare sector prefer to limit their working hours even when their children are older. One key explanation is that they continue to feel responsible for the situation at home. 'My children do not like me to be away from home five days a week' is an oft-heard argument, even when the children concerned are in their teens or even twenties. In the course of time, everyone in the family has got used to the mother's working hours and part-time presence at home, the woman herself being no exception. In the meantime, the gap between her earnings and her partner's has become wider, the couple has become accustomed to the pattern of income and expenses and there is therefore no financial argument to upset their working time routines.

In some areas of the healthcare sector, there are reasons other than women's preference for the prevalence of 'little' jobs. For example, home care or disabled care organisations often make lower-level positions part time. This type of work tends to peak during specific moments of the day and night. Employers argue that it would be too expensive to have full-time employees on the payroll for eight hours when so many of those hours may be unproductive ones. To avoid that situation, the work is divided into smaller blocks of time and offered as little part-time jobs. Quite apart from women's preferences for working fewer hours, this organisational strategy goes a long way to explaining why part-time jobs are so persistent in these areas of the healthcare sector. It is a worrying development in one way, as it is related to the quality of the jobs available to less well-educated women. It is also related to traditional 'frames or definitions' and 'images' of women's jobs in which their work is seen only as a sort of supplement, and not as something that will last throughout their entire life course. Their career prospects are not regarded as very important, nor is the quality of their jobs.

Even in hospitals, where most women generally have qualified jobs, they seem to have little or no ambition to increase their working hours, at least not permanently. They may occasionally work four hours more per week than their official contract indicates, but this only happens when the institution needs them at a specific moment in time. The dominant view is: the number of hours I work fits in with my daily schedule, and I do not want to change that situation. Later perhaps, but not now. Most women agree that they would work longer hours if their income were to fall sharply and they had a pressing need to earn more. They consider this to be an exceptional situation, however, and one that is unlikely to apply to them. None of this means that women do not like their jobs. On the contrary, they are generally very satisfied with their work, love the direct contact with patients and display a caring attitude.

Some women in the survey mentioned the workload as a reason for not working full time. Older women in particular found their jobs fairly demanding and stressful. This is a point that deserves further attention. Is it true that jobs in hospitals and in the healthcare sector are generally too demanding to be full-time appointments? If so, then the push to get women to increase their working hours and participate more fully in the labour market will run into some serious obstacles.

According to our findings, part-time work among female employees has gained wide acceptance among managers in the healthcare sector. There is no formal policy advocating part-time work as such in the sector; the trend seems to have evolved on its own. As a hospital HR officer said: 'We have all sorts of contracts in our hospitals, from just a few hours on a flexible basis to full-time jobs of 36 hours a week, or sometimes more.' Part-time jobs are seen as a fact of life. Not that managers particularly like this situation; they sometimes mention disadvantages, for instance in terms of scheduling, coordination, communication and the transfer of information. Some managers suggest that having several days off a week has a negative effect on the commitment of female employees. This is not supported by what the workers themselves say, however. They all feel very committed to their work, but admit that at times – after a break of for instance four days or more – they are assigned a number of new patients and may miss the patients that they had cared for in previous weeks.

It therefore seems that managers, at least in hospitals, would probably prefer more women to work longer hours. Given the preferences of the nurses and other care personnel, however, they do not see this as a realistic option. As already mentioned, part-time work and all associated complexities are a feature of the sector, which is dominated by female employees. The fact that part-time work is accepted may also explain why managers and employers do not urge women to work longer hours. They may occasionally ask them to work extra hours, for example to fill in for sick colleagues or in an emergency. But generally speaking, managers are glad enough to keep women on board at a time when labour shortages are becoming urgent in the healthcare sector, at least in various specific nursing positions.

This pilot study in the healthcare sector shows how institutionalised part-time work has become in the Netherlands. All the relevant parties – women themselves, their managers and their colleagues – consider it entirely natural that women should work fewer hours after having children. Motherhood explains and justifies their choice. There is, however, another aspect to that justification. Although women voluntarily decide to work fewer hours, Dutch society does pressure them into taking that decision. If they continue to work full time after having a child, they will have more explaining to do to family and friends than if they simply cut back on their working hours. Although women in the Netherlands have an average of only 1.7 children, motherhood has enormous implications for the way they conduct their private lives – an attitude that society until recently sanctioned and condoned as completely legitimate. Halfway through the previous decade, however, the economic boom gave rise to new views on the subject for the first time in the history of the Netherlands. As the government looked to the future and saw the spectre of an ageing population – and labour force – looming in the distance, it began to call on women to make paid employment a bigger part of their lives. Given the country's political and cultural history and its continuing effects, it will take some time for attitudes and behaviour to change. There is also a great deal of ambivalence about this issue. For example, there is still no proper childcare and community school infrastructure in the Netherlands that will truly help mothers combine working with caring for their family.

V

We turn finally to the latest trends in family policies in the Netherlands. Since 2003, when the Christian Democrats returned to office after an absence of eight years, the family has come in for much more attention in social policy-making. As noted above, the coalition of Christian Democrats and Socialists established in 2007 wants to make the Netherlands a more family-friendly country. One question is whether and to what extent their intentions are in fact modern and future-driven, or whether they can – at least in part – be interpreted as the vestiges of an older, historical ideology.

The government now wishes to invest in social cohesion. According to the 2008 Family Policy Document, social cohesion begins at home, the place where care is given and children feel secure. Young people and the family are key themes in the social policies of the Christian Democrat/Socialist coalition government. Since 2007, there has even been a separate minister for youth and families, not an obvious development in a country where, historically speaking, the state has been expected to keep its hands off families, or at least not pursue a social policy focusing specifically on them. We can view this change as a reaction to what is regarded in Christian Democrat circles as 'individualisation taken to the extreme'. By placing too much emphasis on the individual, society has come to put selfish interests first, undermining solidarity and eroding social cohesion. In today's modernising, globalising world with all its uncertainties, the Dutch government's family policy is meant to create the right conditions for giving as many children as possible the best chances in life. The 2008 Family Policy Document emphasises that government can only do so much. The responsibility and authority for organising family life and raising children rests primarily with parents. Government must keep its distance and respect its citizens' private lives. Its role is to facilitate, for example by helping families financially, but also by offering them what the document calls 'parenting support'. But the Family Policy Document also states that government must have the right to challenge parental authority when the child's safety is at risk and the family is unable, temporarily, to care for itself properly. The Dutch government has three main themes in its family policy: more time for families, extra investment in families and better parenting.

One of the key aims of current family policy in the Netherlands is to create more time for families. Interestingly enough, this is not related to any concern about Dutch men and women working too many hours. Indeed, the Netherlands has one of the lowest annual totals of working hours in Europe. The focus on time for family life has historic roots in traditional family values and has recently been heightened by concerns about a potential loss of social cohesion. The 2008 Family Policy Document describes various measures to create more time for family, including the 'modernisation' of existing leave arrangements and encouraging employers to become more family friendly. By 'modernisation', the document means extending parental leave from thirteen to twenty-six weeks per parent, making the take-up of leave arrangements more flexible, and offering parents a small financial compensation while they are on leave.[32] The minister for youth and family would like to introduce a quality certificate for family-friendly employers. The main objective would be to encourage employers to support workers with family responsibilities and to develop best practices.

[32] Moss 2009.

Reflecting on these policy developments, we may well ask whether and to what extent the Netherlands is challenging the traditional breadwinner model or basing its social policy on a modified breadwinner model. There is evidence that the ideology of motherhood still prevails within society. For instance, part-time work remains highly popular and it has proved to be very difficult to encourage women to increase their working hours, as we saw in the case of the healthcare sector. In addition, policy-makers and parents are still very ambivalent on the question of childcare. The dominance of the modified breadwinner model also explains why the debate on work-life issues is still limited primarily to working parents. Consequently, parenthood remains a salient criterion embedded in a normative and cultural context. This has implications for the labour market position and career prospects of working parents. They are, after all, not available to work at all hours. And so motherhood – and perhaps in the future fatherhood too – may well continue to be a career penalty for some time to come.[33]

[33] Correll, Benara and Paik 2007.

8 Scandinavia

Maria Ågren

I

The Nordic countries stand out as a region defined by the common history of its five constituents. While Finland was an integral part of Sweden for several hundred years, Norway and Iceland (together with some other north Atlantic islands) were crucial components of the early modern Danish composite state. The five countries were affected differently by twentieth-century warfare, but there still remains a tangible Nordic culture and Nordic cooperation is facilitated by the linguistic proximity of the three Scandinavian languages, even if English is increasingly used in inter-Nordic exchanges. Other defining characteristics of the Nordic countries are high degrees of secularisation, strong civil societies, gender equality and a political culture of consensus rather than confrontation.[1] Finally, and perhaps most recognised amongst outsiders, the Nordic countries display strong and well-developed welfare states. One of the leading scholars in welfare state research, the Danish sociologist Gøsta Esping-Andersen, has identified the social democratic welfare state found in Scandinavia as one of three ideal type welfare regimes.[2]

At the heart of the welfare state discussion is the relationship between the state and its citizens. What sort of responsibility does the state have for the well-being of its citizens, and when should the state refrain from 'interfering' in the private sphere? Who are the citizens upon whom the state bestows welfare and rights: everybody, or just the grown-ups, or just adult men as heads of families? On all these accounts, the Scandinavian countries position themselves as a special category: they are comparatively 'state friendly', accepting a high degree of state involvement, and they are also (like France) 'universalistic', in

The author extends her thanks to Rolf Torstendahl for his valuable comments on a previous version of this chapter.

[1] Sørensen and Stråth 1997; Christiansen, Petersen, Edling and Haave 2006. While the concept Norden ('The North') includes all five countries, the word Scandinavia denotes Sweden, Denmark and Norway, the three realms that formed the medieval Kalmar Union. On the early modern composite or 'conglomerate' state, see Gustafsson 1998.

[2] Esping-Andersen 1990.

the sense that practically all inhabitants are 'seen' by the state and included in the welfare regime (even those who are wealthy enough not to need it).[3]

The relationship between the family and the state becomes particularly interesting in this context. It is telling that twentieth-century family law varies according to the three main types of welfare regimes – the liberal Anglo-American, the conservative German and the Scandinavian (sometimes described as social democratic).[4] Thus, English family law is characterised by a general antipathy to state intervention in the family sphere, by individualistic property rules and by a high degree of legal flexibility (mitigating some of the harsh effects of a literal application of the code). German family law accepts state intervention in the private sphere but accords different social rights to people within different labour market sectors. It also supports rather than replaces the traditional family model, enforcing the power of husbands over their wives and children. In the Nordic countries, by contrast, state intervention is pronounced. The states seek to establish the same social rights for everyone, often by redistributing resources via the tax system. There has been a clear tendency to construct husband and wife as equal, albeit different, citizens, and to improve the property rights of married women.[5] These patterns strongly suggest that the role assigned to the state in a given country is closely connected to the role allotted to the family in the same country. Families and states are, in a sense, corresponding vessels in welfare regimes.

The more or less systematic differences between various European welfare regimes have caused much scholarly debate, not least about how they can be explained. In this context, it is noteworthy that Esping-Andersen himself conceptualised the rise of welfare states as the response to a historically created problem: the increasingly 'commodified' character of European populations.[6] Bearing in mind, however, that there are several types of welfare states, a better way of phrasing this observation may be to use the plural form and say that welfare regimes constitute varying responses to different, historically created problems. This reformulation prompts us to move further back in time and to look closer at the prehistory of welfare states.

Research into the roots of modern welfare states has, however, tended not to look much further back in time than the late nineteenth century. What came before has been accorded relatively scant interest.[7] The tradition of strong,

[3] See Sarah Howard's contribution to this volume: 'As the Pitt–Jolie affair demonstrates, the French state treats families with munificence and favours a universal approach to many family benefits.'

[4] The importance of social liberalism for the creation of the Swedish and Danish welfare states has been pointed out in Edling 1998, Hedin 2002 and Christiansen, Petersen, Edling and Haave 2006, p. 14.

[5] Bradley 2000; Melby, Pylkkänen, Rosenbeck and Wetterberg 2006.

[6] Esping-Andersen 1990.

[7] See, for instance, Christiansen, Petersen, Edling and Haave 2006, pp. 15ff.

centralised and paternalistic states in early modern Scandinavia has of course been mentioned as an explanation as to why Scandinavians tolerate state interference to a degree that few others do; but, on reflection, it is hard to see how acceptance of high taxes in a situation of war in the seventeenth century can account for acceptance of, for instance, a state prohibition on child flogging 300 years later. What we need are more detailed analyses of early modern family law and its complex connections to early modern and, later, modern state-building. Some such attempts have been made in previous research, but, while yielding important insights, they have nevertheless resulted in misleading descriptions of late nineteenth-century legal reforms as expressions of entirely new ideas about marital relations (the two-breadwinner model) and about the responsibility of states.[8] This is only partly correct and, what is more, such a narrative creates the impression that the modern welfare state is fundamentally different from its early modern and, still more, its medieval precursors, whereas there are significant similarities that may account for long-term patterns. Moreover, a failure to appreciate these similarities will lead to a failure properly to understand the critical importance of the transitional period, around 1800, when the relationship between state and society was put under debate and decisive choices made.

In what follows, I propose to explain the Scandinavian/Nordic model by moving much further back in time than just the late nineteenth century. First, I shall discuss the meaning of central terms such as welfare and social rights. I shall also describe important parts of the early modern institutional setting in Scandinavia in order to show what the relationship between state and families (or citizens/subjects) looked like. I shall then focus upon the historic watershed in Sweden around 1800, when doubts were cast upon the traditional relationship between state and families. Finally, I shall revisit more well-researched developments in the late nineteenth century that bring differences and similarities within the Nordic region to the fore.

II

Inspired by the work of Karl Polanyi, Esping-Andersen defined the objective of modern welfare states as the de-commodification of their population. In this way, Esping-Andersen turned the modern welfare state into the third chapter of the dramatic narrative about how peoples in Europe had first had access to resources with which they could make a decent living, and then been bereaved of these resources and recklessly exposed to the market as the only institution that might (or might not) give them something to live on. The transition from the first to the second chapter represented, in the words of Polanyi, the

[8] Melby, Pylkkänen, Rosenbeck and Wetterberg 2006, pp. 54, 185.

commodification of the labouring population, making men and women into nothing more than things offered for sale in the market place, to be chosen or rejected. However, in the third phase, people were de-commodified as the welfare state introduced social rights: through the support of the state people gained strength and voice so that they could challenge the power of the market.[9]

According to Esping-Andersen, the prime criterion of social rights is the degree to which they 'permit people to make their living standards independent of pure market forces. It is in this sense that social rights diminish citizens' status as "commodities".'[10] In a moment of serendipity, Esping-Andersen summarised his argument by stating that social rights are simply 'freedom, if you like'.[11] When used in this way, freedom does not mean absence of restrictions on one's scope of action. Instead, freedom denotes access to resources that give to the persons concerned some freedom of choice, some leeway that allows them to say no to some of the things that the market has to offer (like prostitution). Freedom is whatever improves a person's fallback position.[12]

Consequently, welfare is wealth but not in the narrow economic sense of the word but, rather, wealth understood as quality of life. Economic assets are necessary to welfare but they are not sufficient; access to education becomes at least as important. Interestingly, with this definition of social rights and welfare, Esping-Andersen comes close to the approach of the Indian economist Amartya Sen, who understands development in the third world as the freedom to develop one's inherent capabilities (rather than GNP growth only).[13]

Understanding welfare and social rights as remedies to the shattering effects of previous commodification (or proletarianisation, as the Marxist tradition would have it) makes good sense precisely because it makes clear that modern states are solutions to historical problems. However, these problems were not exactly the same in all countries. We have to pay attention to the fact that some societies experienced high degrees of commodification early on, while others did not. In some parts of Holland, 60 per cent of the population were wage workers as early as the sixteenth century.[14] In England, at the same time, the range has been estimated at between 25 and 50 per cent, but it has also been pointed out that there was not really a rural proletariat because access to land or use of land remained widely distributed. Around 1700, however, around 60 per cent of the population were wage workers.[15] In the Scandinavian countries,

9 Polanyi 1944. 10 Esping-Andersen 1990, p. 3. 11 Esping-Andersen 1990, p. 221.

12 'Social right' can also be defined more narrowly as the right to benefit from state-organised redistribution of resources. Such a definition is, however, problematic since it makes it dubious whether liberal and conservative welfare regimes do in fact grant any social rights at all. Moreover, such a narrow definition obscures the similarities between modern and earlier welfare regimes that do, after all, exist.

13 Sen 1999. 14 De Moor and van Zanden 2009, pp. 12–13.

15 Humphries 1990, p. 18; Wrightson 2000, p. 36.

by contrast, a significant rise in the number of proletarianised did not occur until after 1750 (Sweden) and 1800 (Norway),[16] and industrialisation proper was a late nineteenth-century phenomenon. As late as 1870, a very significant proportion of the Scandinavian population was employed in agriculture, forestry and fishing.[17]

What was the relationship between societies that experienced the latter alternative – countries with widespread small-scale landholding – and the creation of the modern welfare state? As will be apparent by now, this question is particularly pertinent for the Scandinavian countries. Here, land was relatively easily available, which allowed the working population to retain some leeway and avoid becoming 'properly commodities in the sense that their survival was contingent upon the sale of their labor power'.[18] It was only as and when society was stripped of the 'institutional layers that guaranteed social reproduction outside the labor contract' that commodification occurred, as Esping-Andersen put it.[19] This happened late in Scandinavia.

III

Moving backwards in time, the problem one encounters is that the conceptual tools tailored for modern states (nineteenth and twentieth centuries) are not easily squared with medieval and early modern societies. The notion of 'welfare' would appear not to be directly applicable to such cases, even though some scholars have tried to give it a more trans-historical meaning.[20] Likewise, it is not immediately obvious what a 'social right' would be in a medieval or early modern setting. Often, historians arrive at the conclusion that people in such societies did recognise their responsibility for taking care of the weak and the deserving poor, but historians add that this responsibility was usually not vested in the state (but in the family and/or the local community) and that support was given out of mercy and not as a matter of right. Pre-modern poor relief is frequently contrasted with modern social rights, epitomising the unbridgeable gap between today and yesterday.

This way of conceptualising social rights threatens to lead to a modern-centred, self-congratulatory view of history. The past becomes a foreign country of poverty and social dependence, in stark relief to modern society with its welfare institutions and its insistence on everybody's indisputable right not only to survival but a decent life. By contrast, if social rights are instead

16 Winberg 1977; Sandvik 2005, p. 111. Winberg's results are presented and discussed in Tilly 1984.

17 Christiansen, Petersen, Edling and Haave 2006, p. 356: Iceland 88 per cent, Finland 78 per cent, Sweden 72 per cent, Norway 64 per cent, Denmark 55 per cent.

18 Esping-Andersen 1990, p. 21.

19 Esping-Andersen 1990, p. 21.

20 Green and Owens 2004.

defined as whatever gives to people the freedom to make their living standards independent of pure market forces, it is clear that medieval and early modern societies were replete with such rights. As a matter of fact, it was precisely the eradication of such rights that paved the way for what Polanyi termed the great transformation, and that created the problems which states finally had to solve. The historical narrative on which most welfare state research is predicated presupposes that modern welfare states represent the *reestablishment* of something that was present in early modern societies and subsequently lost.

Various forms of customary rights gave to early modern people the freedom to make their living standard independent of the naked forces of the market. Grazing, gleaning, cutting wood and digging peat and turf are forms of work often connected with rights to commons. In the words of Jane Humphries, 'by providing some members of the laborer's family with alternatives to wage labor, the commons liberated them from the beck and call of the farmers'.[21] Another example to the same effect was the customary notion, still honoured in late eighteenth-century England, that the price of bread should be equitable. The fact that unreasonable prices could be publicly corrected supports the interpretation that this was not just a notion, desperately embraced by the poor, but a more commonly acknowledged right.[22] For customary rights to be comparable to modern social rights it is, of course, imperative that they be fairly strong. It had to be possible, for instance, to enforce them in a court of law. If that was not the case, the borderline between such rights and relief given out of mercy becomes blurred. It did make a difference if a landowner accepted gleaning because he wanted to give a personal favour to someone in the local community, or if gleaning was available to everyone within that local community as a matter of right.

Another type of right that becomes interesting in this context is inheritance rights. To the extent that these are indefeasible, that is to say, if they cannot easily or arbitrarily be annulled, such rights too provide young people with considerable freedom to make their living standard independent of the market. If, for instance, young people stand to inherit a cottage, they will have the freedom not to pick every offer of employment that presents itself in the market. What is more, indefeasible inheritance rights also allow young people to make their living standards independent of parents and kinsmen. If they have a legal right to a stated share in the property of their parents, they will not be susceptible to threats to the effect that the father will 'cut you off with a shilling'. Finally, if inheritance rights are not only strong (because they are enforceable in state courts), but pertain to land and are more or less universally available, they grant a considerable amount of freedom to large sections of the population.

[21] Humphries 1990, p. 41; Wrightson 2000, p. 36. [22] Thompson 1971.

Consequently, such a system of inheritance rights will be not identical to but very much alike a system of universal social rights granted by the state.

As it was set up in the middle ages, and as it continued to work until the late eighteenth century, Swedish-Finnish inheritance law can be said to be an example of this model. Legitimate children's rights to inherit were almost indefeasible, and translated directly to well-defined shares of the estate.[23] Both sons and daughters had inheritance rights to all types of property, even if daughters' shares were only half the size of those of sons. The only grounds on which inheritance rights could be questioned were, as far as we know, if children had failed to pay due respect to their parents, if they refused to support the parents in their old age or if they used violence against them. As a logical consequence of the strong inheritance rights, parents' freedom of testation was limited: only such property as one had not inherited oneself was disposable at will. This is worthy of notice since this was not the case everywhere. Early modern English law gave to fathers a considerable degree of freedom to use their property as they saw fit. Amy L. Erickson has shown that this freedom was often used to give more or less equal shares to all children, sons and daughters alike, but this was a personal choice and nothing a father could be forced to do by law.[24]

The basic rationale of the Swedish-Finnish system was the idea to safeguard land and to make sure that it remained within the lineage from which it had originally come. In contrast to the English system, where land was looked upon as the property of individuals, the Swedish-Finnish system defined inherited land as kin property. Rights of testation did not extend to such land in order to prevent individual members of the lineage from misusing their powers and transferring land to people outside the kin group. Rights of inheritance were strong precisely because it was deemed essential to make sure that land was transferred without interruption between generations. Thus, collective rights and kin interests were at the heart of inheritance law. Paradoxically and perhaps unintentionally, this legal construction meant that the rights of young individuals (to receive an inheritance) were corroborated at the expense of the older generation and of fathers in particular. Fathers could not use 'their' property entirely as they liked.

However, children could not use inherited land entirely as they liked either. There was a strong cultural assumption that children should use the economic resources they had received to support not only the next generation but also the older generation. While parents were more or less obliged to leave their inherited property to their children, children were more or less obliged to take care of their parents in their old age. Thus, the inheritance system was also a form of pension arrangement that balanced the rights of the old against those of the

[23] Admittedly, rights of illegitimate children were weak. [24] Erickson 1993.

young.[25] In this regard, the Norwegian system was very similar to the Swedish-Finnish one. Norwegian law also operated with the notion of lineage property, reducing rights of testation to a minimum and making the system less flexible than, for instance, the English one. Sons inherited twice as much as daughters, but all children had strong rights and could claim their share of the parental property. Landowners transferred their rights to a selected child, against the promise of care and support in their old age, being thus able to retire.[26] Danish inheritance law shows similar traits (for instance, unequal right of inheritance prior to 1857) but this was on the whole less important prior to 1788, since only a small proportion of the population had land of its own.[27]

Medieval and early modern Swedish-Finnish law also protected the land rights of married women.[28] Because of the strong inheritance rights of children, in combination with the low degree of proletarianisation, many girls inherited land from their parents. In order to prevent such land from being usurped or squandered by husbands, who were the ones who effectively managed the entire marital estate including the land of their wives, Swedish-Finnish law defined such land as separate and laid down a number of restrictions on husbands' scope of action. For instance, a husband could not sell his wife's land without first having obtained both her consent and that of her next-of-kin. A sale of land that did not conform to these procedural rules could be vetoed by the wife's kinsmen and subsequently annulled by a court.[29] Norway and Denmark also had laws that prevented a husband from misusing his authority by selling the inherited land of his wife.[30] However, the overall tendency in early modern Norwegian and Danish law seems to have been to define the marital estate (excluding land) as joint property; only to the extent that spouses made an explicit arrangement could property be defined as separate.[31]

Like the rules pertaining to inheritance, the main purpose of the rules governing married women's property rights was to prevent land from leaving the lineage from which it had originally come. Law was oriented towards safeguarding kin interests. At the same time, though, the same rules made the rights of individual women visible and unquestionable, and they also raised awareness about the fact that women's rights might be at peril during marriage. The double-sided nature of these protective structures becomes clear if we look at how seventeenth-century Swedish legal scholars justified them. While someone like Erik Lindschiöld stressed that kinsmen had a legitimate right to control

[25] Ågren 2000, p. 202. [26] Sandvik 2005, pp. 113, 123.

[27] Dübeck 2005, p. 129.

[28] We find examples of this elsewhere in Europe too. For some good examples, see Erickson 1993 (on England), Hardwick 1998 (on Nantes), and Guzzetti 2002 (on Venice).

[29] Ågren 2009. [30] Dübeck 2005, p. 133; Sandvik 2005, p. 114.

[31] Dübeck 2005, pp. 127, 129–30; Sandvik 2005, p. 114.

the fate of land that had devolved upon their kinswomen, Gustaf Cronhielm seems to have been more concerned with the sometimes precarious situation of women and with balancing the unequal power relations between husband and wife. The rules made sense both in the eyes of those who wanted the legal system to sustain traditional rights of kinsmen, and in the eyes of those who were more concerned with the predicament of individual women.[32]

Despite the strong emphasis on land rights vested in kin, neither Sweden-Finland nor Norway were clan societies, inhabited by chieftains who exerted power over their entourage. Since all persons belonged to *two* lineages, the father's and the mother's, and were entitled to inherit from both, no clear-cut clan allegiances or clan-identities ensued. In each situation, the individual could choose whether to adduce his/her affinity with the father's family or with the mother's. Nor were these countries characterised by clan justice, since the state was so closely involved with the judiciary and with upholding family law. Early on, around 1350, the inheritance rules were incorporated in the national legal code pertaining to rural Sweden (where the vast majority of the population lived) and the rules were sustained and enforced by official local courts that were gradually (particularly in the seventeenth century) integrated in the state-supervised system. Thus, society was predicated on a state–family compact which was quite different from what we find in family-oriented societies such as contemporary Spain.[33]

For historical reasons, then, the early modern Swedish-Finnish state (as well as its neighbour Denmark-Norway) had a state-supported system of strong kin rights in land. Somewhat paradoxically, this system both restricted individuals' freedom of choice (testation rights) and strengthened individuals' claims to a share in the family estate. The rights of the old were balanced against those of the young, and the rights of wives were, at least to a certain extent, balanced against those of husbands.[34] This reminds us of some of the most conspicuous characteristics of the modern Nordic welfare state: a state that is not afraid to interfere with what is elsewhere looked upon as private (owners' freedom to do what they like with their property) and a state that not only 'sees' and enforces the rights of fathers but expressly acknowledges the rights of children and wives. The similarities between the old state and the new, particularly in their relationships to families, are too obvious to be ignored. And, contrariwise, the differences between the Nordic states and their British counterpart are also too glaring to be passed over in silence. According to David Bradley, freedom of testation was and remains 'a salient indicator of English individualism' and, still today, there is 'no indefeasible share for children in English law'.[35]

[32] Ågren 2009, p. 80. [33] See Mora-Sitja in chapter 9 of this volume.
[34] Ågren 2009. [35] Bradley 2000, pp. 56–7.

IV

We are entitled to look upon early modern Nordic societies as welfare regimes of sorts. They used family law, upheld by state courts, to create rights that gave to many people some modicum of freedom from market dependence: the young could count on an inheritance, the old could count on care and support from the young, and women could count on protection of their property rights during marriage. One could argue (and I shall pursue this line later in the present chapter) that freedom from market dependence was bought at the cost of close dependence on one's relatives.

But while it is indisputable that Nordic societies represented a sort of welfare regime, it is also indisputable that these regimes were far from static. In the case of Sweden, for instance, the welfare regime declined significantly in the course of the eighteenth and the early part of the nineteenth centuries, as increasing numbers of rural youngsters were unable to keep 'a foot on the land'.[36] The same thing happened in Norway, leading first to proletarianisation and then to mass emigration.[37] These developments were the result of economic and demographic factors interacting with parts of the legal system that had, until this time, caused little concern. Now, they turned into major problems, problems that eventually forced themselves on the political sphere and the legislature. I shall next pursue this theme in the case of Sweden.

At the beginning of the eighteenth century, there were still relatively few persons in Sweden who were *obesuttna*,[38] that is to say, who had very little or no land with which to support themselves and who, for that reason, had to rely on waged work.[39] The overwhelming majority of the population consisted of peasant families, one third of whom owned the land they tilled. Around 1700, the remaining two-thirds were tenants of the crown or nobility, but their numbers declined as the opportunity to purchase state land was made available.[40] From the middle of the century, however, population growth set in and more peasant children survived. Because of the strong rights of inheritance, still in force, everybody had a claim to a part of the parental property. Statutory law made it illegal, however, to subdivide farms below a certain limit since this was believed to jeopardise the tax incomes of the state.[41] Therefore, families were

[36] For this expression, see Wrightson 2000, p. 36. [37] Sandvik 2005, p. 111.

[38] This Swedish concept denotes those who had too little land to be taxed for it. Thus, it is a fiscal concept, but it is frequently used as a social term, to designate those of small or no means.

[39] Gadd 2000, p. 23.

[40] In Norway, the proportions were 30 per cent owned by the occupiers, 50 per cent owned by the crown and 20 per cent owned by the nobility (in 1660). In Denmark at the same time, a much smaller share was owned by occupiers and a much larger share by the nobility. Sandvik 2005, p. 114.

[41] Similar laws applied in Norway. Sandvik 2005, p. 113.

exhorted to let one or possibly two children take over the farm, and to pay off the other children for their shares. At the same time, land prices started rising as the combined effect of more lenient taxation and better prospects for profit in agriculture. Land turned into an object of investment, which was good for some people in society, but to the child who was chosen successor this entailed difficulties to pay the siblings what was due to them.

The effects of these developments were complex and are still not fully understood. We do know, however, that they tended to create or exacerbate socio-economic differences within the rural population. While this has long been recognised in research, less attention has been devoted to the crucial role played by shortcomings in family law. Indeed, the socio-economic developments of the eighteenth and early nineteenth centuries made very clear what the weak points of 'the old welfare regime' were.

First, while it was true that everybody had strong rights of inheritance, these rights only applied to such land as the father or mother had inherited. By contrast, a child could claim nothing in land that the parent had purchased in the market. Parents could choose to let such land too devolve upon the child but, legally, there was nothing to prevent them from transferring it by will to someone else, leaving the child with next to nothing. In a society with a relatively static land market, this rule was probably of little importance but as the land market grew more volatile – as it did in the eighteenth century – the risk of such a scenario loomed larger.

Secondly, while it was true that all children (of the same sex) had equal rights of inheritance, it proved increasingly complicated to let that principle translate into equally valuable pieces of property. With rising land values, it was easier said than done to pay a market price for the siblings' shares. The parental generation would often support the successor in his (seldom her) efforts to keep the price at a low level. The reason for this was simple: the old couple was going to stay on at the farm until the time of death, being supported by the successor and his family. Consequently, it was not in their interest to have the farm encumbered by debts. Instead, they would be more inclined to endorse arrangements that improved the economic position of the new farmer.

Thirdly, while it was true that the judiciary provided protection for married women's property rights, this only applied to a woman's inherited lands and not to money or chattels she had brought into the marital estate. No such thing as the trust (developed in English law) was available to safeguard women's rights to property other than land (money, chattels), which meant that her husband was at complete liberty to use such property as he liked. This legal lacuna was not new, but it attained a special significance in the eighteenth century when some children had to agree to have their inheritance in the form of property other than land – and daughters were more likely to fall into this category. Furthermore, the legal protection of married women's inherited lands was undermined as the legislature abolished the requirement for relatives' consent to the husband's sale of such lands. Consequently, while the protection of married women's inherited lands was weakened, the protection of their money and chattels had always been non-existent, making, on balance, the legal and economic situation of many women precarious. In a situation where many men (farmers, officers, etc.) were pressed for money, the temptation to use the wife's property must have increased.[42] Similar trends have been charted for Norway.[43]

Although revised on many points in the first half of the eighteenth century, the Swedish legal code still shared fundamental assumptions with its medieval precursor. It continued to take for granted that the society for which it was written consisted of landowners only – men and women – and paid very scant attention to the interests of those who had no such material resources. A closer observance of these interests would have prompted other types of legal rules, better suited to create social rights for the broad majority of people. Such rules could have included, for instance, a right for married women to a share in their husband's property – an invaluable right to a woman who had no property of her own at all. Such rules could also have included the trust – for women with property that did not take the form of land – or a larger share in the common spousal property (in the eighteenth century, the wife's share was still only half the size of the husband's). Finally, such rules could have dealt with the awkward discrepancy between children's strong claims to a share in inherited land and their non-existent rights to purchased land. None of this was available, and around 1800 it was up to legislators to choose which way to go: to keep the narrow focus or to broaden the vision to include everyone in society.

V

In the last year of the eighteenth century, a relatively obscure Swedish judge wrote a book on Swedish jurisprudence. He remarked that the Swedes (among whom he probably included the Finns) held their legal code in very high esteem. In the law, they saw the best defence against all forms of oppression and arbitrary rule. As a consequence, the Swedes were most keen to have the legal code continuously amended and updated so that all parts of life were regulated in it, and all rules that applied were included in it. Somewhat surprisingly, perhaps, the judge did not concur with this view himself. He saw it as misguided and even as an expression of prejudice. It is wrong to believe, he stated, that human beings can only act in an acceptable way if guided by a code of laws. When enlightened by common sense and conscience, human

[42] Ågren 2009, ch. 4. [43] Sandvik 2005, pp. 114–17.

beings can organise large parts of their life in free agreement with each other and without the interference of state law. Thus, the fact that the code of 1734 left out important parts of life and was therefore deemed insufficient by many observers did not impress Judge Lind. Such parts could be dealt with in other ways than through legislation, he maintained.[44]

What Lind must have had in mind were various sorts of informal deals and contractual arrangements. If the law is not comprehensive and updated in every detail, that need not be a problem because, according to his argument, people will appreciate the need for arrangements that safeguard their rights and those of their family members. Indeed, it is clear from eighteenth-century legal practice that various forms of agreements and arrangements were developed and deployed to protect widows' rights and the rights of orphaned children. Young people intent upon marrying were also said (in the 1840s) to set up pre-nuptial agreements to make their respective rights and duties clear and undisputable. Such practices made sense in a situation of increasing socio-economic differentiation and a growing commercial sector. It was to families who did not have all their property in the form of inherited land that the legal code provided insufficient protection. Thus, the socio-economic landscape had changed, and so had the strategies people developed. It was in this context that the role of binding state law appeared on the agenda.[45]

Judge Lind's opinions are interesting, not only for the lucidity with which they were formulated but also because he was not the only one to hold these views in the first half of the nineteenth century. There were others who also disliked the idea of regulating everything in detail through the legal system and who opted for free agreements between citizens. For instance, when a proposal for a new bill of testation was put before parliament (around 1850), suggesting that children needed to be protected from their callous parents (who were prepared to will away their purchased property to the detriment of their children), several parliamentarians argued for the freedom of owners to do what they liked with what was theirs. One parliamentarian commented that 'the more we legislate with the objective of restricting the natural right of ownership, the worse the outcome will be'. Another argued that 'as for the property that I have acquired through my own labour, I want to be allowed to use it as I like', while a third added that the unrestricted right of parents to give purchased property to whomever they liked served as an incentive for children to treat their parents well. Freedom and natural rights figured prominently on the agenda of these men, who also explicitly advocated the liberal English concept of ownership as a model to follow.[46] They lived at a time when many believed that it was appropriate for the state to recede from society and when, as a consequence,

[44] Lind 1799, ch. 1. [45] Ågren 2009, ch. 4. [46] Ågren 2009, pp. 191–2.

voluntary associations mushroomed, taking over some of the responsibilities previously vested in the central state and its legal system.[47]

But their voices were not the only ones to be heard in these nineteenth-century debates. While the freedom of disposition was a crucial part of ownership, others conceded, it was also necessary to modify that same freedom to make it conducive to the general objectives of civil society. In this particular case, the problem was that 'he who does not have any inherited property, can deprive his children of all his [non-inherited] property, while he who has nothing but inherited property, does not have any freedom of disposition at all, but must accept leaving the property to a distant, anonymous relative [if he does not have children]'. This situation was not conducive to the general objectives of civil society, the legal committee of parliament argued in 1858, and it was *not* enough to leave everything to the 'free agreement' of citizens. Instead, it was incumbent on somebody to take action and 'modify freedom'.[48]

In this case, somebody was the law. The parliamentarian Cederström argued that it was better for the law to prescribe how property be divided between children than for fathers to make painful decisions. Since the law speaks on behalf of society as a whole, individuals become more willing to accept its orders than those of fathers. Consequently, it was legitimate for the law to ordain that a certain share of the parents' property must be left to the children (regardless of whether the property was inherited or purchased). In a similar vein, the lawyer Staaf argued for legal regulation rather than individual agreement with respect to spouses' property rights. The law must decide exactly what the rights of wives are and not leave this to the parties or their parents to decide. When people are in love, they cannot conceive of anything they would not be prepared to give to their beloved, and they seldom take necessary precautions. Therefore, Staaf said, it is vital that the wise legislator take precautions on their behalf.[49]

These speakers clearly articulated an issue that often remains under debate in contemporary societies. To what extent should the state, through the legal system (family law, taxation law, social security law, etc.), take a more overarching responsibility for the lives of its citizens, and to what extent should the state refrain from assuming this sort of responsibility? Is it perhaps better to let citizens organise their lives as they prefer, and give to them as much freedom as possible? With the latter view, it is not a great problem if the law does not provide an exhaustive description of every problem that may occur in social life. Flexible judges can accommodate such laws with contracts and agreements that are adapted to specific situations and needs. With the former view, by contrast, it is logical to want the code to be more or less all-encompassing,

[47] Jansson 1985. [48] Ågren 2009, p. 192. [49] Ågren 2009, p. 194.

to expect from it that it should express values embraced by the majority of the population, and to demand of judges that they follow the law to the letter. Law should be the mouthpiece of society, as Cederström phrased it, and can, at times, be conceived of as a guardian for those who do not know their own good, as Staaf suggested.

According to Lind's grumblings, many ordinary Swedes preferred the law to be as exhaustive and all-encompassing as possible and they did this because they abhorred arbitrary rule. If his observation was correct, there was strong support not only for the rule of law in a general sense but for binding state regulation in the field of family law. Many of the legal reforms that were carried through in the first half of the nineteenth century can indeed be seen as expressions of the more interventionist ideal espoused by legislators such as Cederström and Staaf. Testamentary law was changed to the effect that no more than 50 per cent of all property was available for testamentary dispositions (even if all property had been purchased), and marital property law was changed to the effect that wives now acquired a right to 50 per cent of the common marital estate (as compared to one third previously). These outcomes have to be understood against the backdrop of socio-economic developments in the previous century, which had made 'the old welfare regime' less universalistic and, in consequence, created problems of poverty.

Even if these reforms did not provide final solutions to the entire, complicated issue known at the time as pauperism and later as the social question,[50] it is clear that they were intended as partial remedies. They were seen as ways of helping those who had little or no property and who, therefore, were exposed to the vagaries of the market. Among these, children who did not receive an inheritance – because their parents had no property at all or because their parents' property was not inherited – figured prominently in the debate. So did married and widowed women. Widows, particularly those of soldiers, were overrepresented among the poor at the time.[51] Married women, whose bankrupt husbands had alienated their property, were also depicted as being in special need of the concerns of an enlightened legislator. When the image of such a legislator was invoked rather than that of citizens making free agreements with each other (for the benefit of their wives and children), it was an implicit way of defining the entire field of family law as the responsibility of the state. It was *once again* defined as being within the remit of the state – medieval law having already expressed a concern with the situation of married women and their property rights, and constructed robust inheritance rights for all children of legitimate birth.

[50] Larsson Kraus 2009 shows that, already in the 1840s, there was a clear awareness in Sweden of the social problems later described as 'the social question'. See also Hedin 2002 for later developments.

[51] Skoglund 1992.

In these early nineteenth-century debates, the value of women's work in society was mentioned as an argument for why inheritance law and marital property law must be reformed. This was perceived to be an issue of equity: men and women make different kinds of contributions to society, debaters claimed, but they all contribute. Therefore, it would be unjust not to reward them on an equal basis. It was also argued that women's situation in society needed to be improved to make them loyal to the country. If we continue to treat half of the population with unfairness, Swedish parliamentarians argued, we cannot take their continued commitment and contributions for granted.[52] In their efforts to improve women's rights, some Norwegian debaters stressed rural women's hard work and sound sense for economics in a way strikingly similar to what we find in Sweden.[53] These arguments show that a concern with women's economic situation in society was at the heart of the matter, and this is hardly surprising – as we have already seen, women were consistently worse off than men in a situation where not everybody could receive an inheritance in the form of land and where property other than land was less well protected by the law. The arguments also make clear how investment of labour was seen as inherently valuable. Very likely, this high appraisal of work should be attributed to the Lutheran heritage and its understanding of daily work as the fulfilment of a vocation given by God.[54]

It is clear that Sweden was at a crossroads during these years, in the sense that people held widely different views on what needed to be done. While one side argued that the problems in society should be left to the discernment of individuals equipped with conscience and common sense, the other side maintained that family law should be reformed and *a new general welfare regime* created. While the first opinion is strikingly similar to the ideological positions behind the Anglo-American welfare regime of the twentieth century, the second one resembles those of the modern Scandinavian welfare state.

VI

From the middle of the nineteenth century until 1929, marital law was again the object of reform in Scandinavia. This time, it was deemed important to create some degree of legal uniformity within the Nordic countries, partly because of inter-Nordic migration. Therefore, Nordic legislators not only surveyed existing law in the countries concerned, but were also at great pains to harmonise old legal traditions to formulate new coherent laws. In this process, civil society organisations (like the women's movement) were allowed to have a say, but so were lawyers, politicians, clergymen and physicians. Their common

52 Ågren 2009, p. 185. 53 Sandvik 2005, pp. 116, 122.
54 Christiansen, Petersen, Edling and Haave 2006, p. 10; Ågren 2009, pp. 198–9.

exertions resulted in what has been called the Nordic model of marriage. The model's defining characteristics were, on the one hand, strong emphasis on equality between the sexes and on the rights of the individual family member and, on the other hand, insistence on the crucial roles played by the nuclear family and by the housewife.[55]

As has been convincingly shown, Nordic legislators did not take the male breadwinner model as a point of departure in their work. Instead, it is clear that they conceived of both husband and wife as performers of valuable work and as contributors of economic assets to the marital estate. The fact that husbands tended to be the ones who earned a living through waged or salaried work did not alter this view of the couple. Women's unpaid work in the household was expressly defined as valuable, on a par with the work of their husbands, and married women's rights to gainful employment and independence were stressed in the new legislation. By contrast with Germany, where there was a marriage bar for women, Nordic women were encouraged to work, and what they did, whether at home or in the market, was described as valuable contributions to society. The reason for this difference seems to have been that Nordic legislators and politicians eagerly sought to make the family more attractive in the eyes of women. It was humiliating for a woman to be legally and economically subordinated to her husband, legislators argued, especially since increasing numbers of women did work and could be expected to understand economic matters. Unless something was done about their position, women would surely refrain from getting married, with adverse effects on population growth, legislators feared.[56] This concern with demographic decline was fuelled by mass emigration around 1900, but it continued to be a decisive factor in twentieth-century social democratic politics, for instance in the writings of Gunnar and Alva Myrdal. In their preoccupation with biopolitics, Sweden and France displayed many similarities.[57]

Despite the existence of a common model of marriage, there were some differences between the Nordic countries that surfaced during the process of legal integration. For instance, while Swedish and Finnish law and politics focused more on improving the rights of working women, Norwegian mothers were not encouraged to be active in the labour market to the same extent.[58] While the state, along with the church and medical science, was more involved with regulating marriage and the marital economy in Sweden and Finland, Norway was less enthusiastic about all forms of interference in private life

[55] Melby, Pylkkänen, Rosenbeck and Wetterberg 2006, p. 14.

[56] Melby, Pylkkänen, Rosenbeck and Wetterberg 2006, pp. 22, 176–8, 289, 307.

[57] See Sarah Howard's chapter in this volume. Cf. also Elgán 1994 for a systematic comparison of Swedish and French abortion and contraception politics in the first half of the twentieth century.

[58] Haavet 2006, p. 189; Melby, Pylkkänen, Rosenbeck and Wetterberg 2006, pp. 11, 23.

and more concerned with upholding individual freedom.[59] While alimony was never granted after divorce, because women were expected to be able to support themselves, that expectation does seem to have been more pronounced in Sweden and Finland than in Denmark and Norway. On the other hand, divorce rules were more liberal in the latter two countries.[60] Thus, the west/east divide within Scandinavia proved important in the early 1900s, and remains a reality today. After a short period of popularity, the housewife ideal has dwindled in Sweden since the 1960s,[61] and the Christian Democrats' recent offer to 'parents' (by which mothers are meant) – that they can stay at home with their small children against a small monthly allowance – has been received with lukewarm enthusiasm. Norwegian spouses, by contrast, often adopt a more traditional division of labour.

But even more interesting, perhaps, is the strong continuity between the early twentieth-century legal reforms and those that were initiated around 1800. When Nordic legislators argued for a two-breadwinner model in the early twentieth century, they were *not* proposing an entirely new model. As has been shown already, the argument that women perform valuable work in society and must be duly remunerated was put forward in the early nineteenth century too. On both occasions, the argument was used to improve women's economic and legal rights, and the ultimate objective was to make women loyal to their families and to the society of which they too were members. A new contract was set up between families and state around 1900, but this relied heavily on the one struck 100 years earlier (which, in its turn, relied on the medieval/early modern contract). In both cases, confidence in the state and in state law was conspicuous, and so were ideas about men's and women's productive roles in society.

VII

As Esping-Andersen has argued, the Nordic countries do constitute a special type of welfare state regime, characterised by comprehensive and universally available social rights provided by the state. Admittedly, there are important differences within the region, for instance with respect to gender issues. To a large extent, however, these differences follow a west/east divide, created historically through the two early modern composite states of Denmark-Norway and Sweden-Finland. This fact suggests in itself that an investigation into the origins of the Nordic model of welfare must go much further back in time

[59] Melby, Pylkkänen, Rosenbeck and Wetterberg 2006, pp. 132–5, 152. See also Hedin 2002 for an analysis of how Swedish liberals gradually adopted a more positive view of state intervention (around 1900).

[60] Melby, Pylkkänen, Rosenbeck and Wetterberg 2006, p. 175. [61] Åmark 2002.

than is usually attempted. Such an investigation cannot only be preoccupied with political alliances struck in the twentieth century, nor with disparities in economic wealth between different countries around 1900.[62] It must also focus upon the long-term relationship between families and states, in order to disentangle new traits from very old ones. This is what I have endeavoured to do in the present chapter. Let me summarise and elaborate three of my more important arguments.

My first point concerns time and timing. It is obvious that the length of the period of commodification (to use Polanyi's word) is crucial to the welfare state as it was created in the late nineteenth and early twentieth centuries. Countries like Holland and England had already experienced two or three hundred years of a large commodified population, that is to say, with a population that had to rely on the labour market for its survival. The Nordic experience was very different, with late proletarianisation and a tradition of multitask occupations, all of which made for a less complete process of commodification. Even if the labour market did expand in the eighteenth and nineteenth centuries, it was never as dominant for such a long time as it was in Holland and England. Very likely, this made commercial solutions and 'the free agreement between citizens' less palatable to many Scandinavians who were used, in a sense, to regarding access to land as a given. This is not to deny the existence of poverty, economic hardship and an embryonic working class in early modern society. But the latter did not become numerous until the last decades of the nineteenth century, which was very close to the creation of the modern welfare state. The short time-span between proletarianisation and the welfare state lends credibility to the argument that medieval and early modern views on the correlated responsibilities of families and state did have an impact on what welfare models were chosen after 1900. The short time-span also suggests that the alleged heavy workload of women, mainly in the agrarian sector, did have an impact on how women's roles and contributions were conceptualised around 1900. Women were not depicted as indolent no-goods or as domestic angels, and it is likely that this affected how their rights were construed in modern society.

The distinction between pre-modern and modern is hard to sustain when confronted with historical realities. Rather than sharp breaking points and distinct watersheds, we see gradual shifts from one form of welfare regime to another, each of which had much in common with its predecessor. The Swedish early modern welfare regime had its roots in medieval times. This system was undermined by socio-economic developments in the eighteenth century but was then consciously recreated in the early nineteenth century, to be re-enforced once again around 1900. It is clear that there was a long tradition of investing the state, as it was embodied in the legislature and the

[62] Esping-Andersen 1990; Sommestad 1998.

judiciary, with social responsibilities, and of giving to the state and the law the job of protecting individuals and monitoring family relations.

My second point concerns the relationship between social and property rights. These are often conceived of as oppositional in the scholarly literature. Social rights are what people with little or no property need to lead decent lives; by contrast, people with property do not need and do not want social rights, since they confer a stigma upon the person receiving them. Social rights are also oppositional to property rights in the sense that states often need to levy taxes to create social rights, and such taxes will invariably have a negative effect upon those with (much) property. It should come as no surprise that one of the driving forces behind the modern Swedish welfare state, the social democratic minister of finance Ernst Wigforss, tried to reform inheritance law and to increase taxation on inherited assets precisely in order to accomplish socio-economic equality.[63]

But if social rights are understood as everything that 'permits people to make their living standards independent of pure market forces', it is clear that this is precisely what property rights do, and what various customary rights can also do. Therefore, the opposition between social rights and property rights is not logically necessary. In societies where some people have property and others do not the opposition can materialise, but in less-differentiated societies it becomes hard to make the distinction at all. More to the point, if property rights are circumscribed in a way that restricts owners' freedom to do what they like with what is theirs and if, by extension, others than owners can lay a claim to certain aspects of private property, the distinction between holders of property rights and holders of social rights becomes blurred. This was what happened in early modern Sweden-Finland, where owners were barred by kinsmen and children from using their inherited land as they preferred. This was also the situation in England as long as customary rights to commons were strong.

The difference between the modern welfare regime and its medieval and early modern predecessors has misleadingly been exaggerated because modern social rights (often associated with social democratic government in Scandinavia) have erroneously been compared with old and denigrating poor relief systems. This comparison suggests that the notion of a *right* to a decent living was absent in the past – when people did care for those in need it was only out of mercy. In the Nordic countries, however, the notion of a right to a decent living was a cornerstone of inheritance law, and inheritance of land was (with the possible exception of Denmark) widely available. Inheritance law was not esoteric doctrine but practised by families on an everyday basis and upheld by state courts. This was the state–family compact particular to

[63] Wigforss 1951 (1980), pp. 154, 272–80.

early modern society, and with this before our eyes it becomes easy to see how closely social rights and property rights were intertwined.

My third point concerns the differences between the modern Scandinavian welfare state and its precursor that do, after all, exist. While it is true that both systems give to the state the responsibility for safeguarding people's ability to make a living independent of pure market forces, they do not do this in exactly the same way. First, it is clear that the modern state has the ambition to reach out to everybody, that citizens expect the state to achieve its objectives in this respect and that media monitor these matters closely. Even though the medieval state may once have had the same ambition – to safeguard everybody's right to a living by constructing very strong kin rights to land – the system was not all-encompassing in the seventeenth century and it was not possible to hold any state official publicly responsible for this. The system worked well for those who belonged to a landholding family, but much less so for those who had other forms of property or no property at all. Even though the landless (*obesuttna*) were still quite few in 1700, they did exist.

Secondly, while the medieval and early modern Scandinavian system presupposed close ties and dependences within families, households and kin groups, the modern system is more geared towards individuals and their independence and rights. The modern welfare state empowers individuals in a way that mitigates their dependence on and responsibility for the kin group. Some observers will even say that the state completely eradicates that dependence, making, for instance, the weak and the old the responsibility of 'society' rather than of family and relatives. Other observers will counter by saying that this is exactly why the modern welfare state has been able to liberate women, who used to be the ones expected to take care of relatives. The individual has been liberated not only from dependence upon pure market forces but also from other forms of dependence and duties.

Since the medieval and early-modern welfare regimes were predicated on the strong interdependence of members belonging to the same kin group, the lack of such interdependence in modern Scandinavian society is arguably the most conspicuous long-term change that has taken place in the state–family relationship. It is also something that makes Scandinavian society different from countries such as Italy and Spain, where the family is a source of support but also dependence.[64] When asked what they think about their new country, immigrants from more family-oriented countries sometimes comment, with a tinge of regret, on what they see as an absence of strong and warm family ties in the Nordic countries. Maybe a time-traveller from pre-modern Scandinavia would make the same, not entirely approving comment.

[64] See Ginsborg in chapter 6 and Mora-Sitja in chapter 9 of this volume.

9 Spain

Natalia Mora-Sitja

I

The family is one of the social structures more resistant to abrupt changes, but in the second half of the twentieth century the European family underwent many important transformations. It is not difficult to identify common trends across many countries in relation to family changes: an increase in the divorce rate, an increase in the number of unipersonal households, the decreasing weight of the polynuclear family and the appearance of new forms of cohabitation. Spain is not alien to these shifts, but the metamorphosis of the Spanish family happened, in comparison to other European countries, very late and very quickly, in parallel with a delayed but accelerated period of industrialisation and economic growth.

The centrality of the family in Spanish life has shown tremendous resilience. The definition of what constitutes a family has evolved, and in the last decade we have witnessed the emergence of two conflicting family models. One, ideologically emanating from the Catholic church or even the standard definitions provided by the United Nations, would consider the family as a unit structured around a married heterosexual couple. The other model, a more liberal approach, departs from an egalitarian view of relationships in the private sphere, and accepts same-sex relationships and less conventional household structures. There is still, in spite of these different approaches, a common view of what essentially constitutes a family: a study of different family associations, of both traditional and liberal views, has identified a common definition of a family as a unit that shares a life project, involves relationships of reciprocity and mutual help and is oriented towards happiness.[1]

Looking at the historical evolution of family policies should be a fruitful process. Political changes usually bring with them changes in family legislation, since these can have an immediate impact on society, and even sideline political or economic structures that are more difficult to transform.[2] In Spain, this can clearly be applied to the Second Republic and to the new regime built

[1] Ayuso Sánchez 2009. [2] Iglesias de Ussel 1990, p. 235.

by Franco at the end of the Civil War: the emphasis of national-Catholicism on the family could well be regarded as a way to establish a very clear break with the recent past of the Second Republic and to exert a direct influence on society. However, the other major political shift in Spain, the transition to democracy, was not accompanied by a substantial redefinition of family politics. Indeed, for the first two decades of democracy after Franco's death, family was never at the centre of any party's political programme. This is what has led Julio Iglesias de Ussel to state that the family in Spain is 'lacking any political reflection'.[3]

In this chapter, I shall analyse family politics and family policies since the end of the Civil War in 1939 until the present day. This will involve describing the legal and socio-economic factors influencing family structures in three distinctive historical periods: early Francoism – from 1939 to 1959; the decades of reform and transition to democracy – 1959 to 1977; and democratic Spain. A common theme will be the exploration of the alignment of family policies and legislation with social realities, and the two-way relationship between state institutions and society.

II

It has often been argued that during the Second Republic (1931–9) the institutional framework was too progressive and modern for a backward society, and that this created the many cleavages that led to the Civil War. The treatment of the family during those years was certainly quite revolutionary and ahead of its time. The Second Republic, through a very strong separation of church and state and important changes in civil law, redefined family institutions and in doing so tried to promote social change. The state gave women the right to vote, abolished religious marriage, legalised divorce, banned prostitution, promoted gender equality, equalised the rights of legitimate and illegitimate children, decriminalised adultery, regulated abortion and created birth control and family planning centres.[4] It is not an overstatement to say that many of these reforms were revolutionary in the 1930s, since several of the policies mentioned above would only be approved by Western European democracies decades later.

Against the backdrop of the progressive spirit of the Second Republic, Francoist family policies represented an abrupt reactionary backlash. Family policy under Franco's regime had two clear objectives: population growth and social control. Demographic growth was perceived to be central to economic development, and a very important target to make up for the losses of

[3] Iglesias de Ussel 1990, p. 236. [4] Flaquer and Iglesias de Ussel 1993, p. 60.

the Spanish Civil War (1936–9). War casualties (and executions outside combat during and after the war) had decimated the young adult male population; and emigration, in the form of exile, further contributed to this, while seriously eroding human capital in Spain. Franco needed prosperity to support his regime, and in this sense a population boost could not only trigger economic growth in the post-war years, but could also be seen as a sign itself of prosperity. Franco often referred in his speeches to a future Spain inhabited by 40 million people, a target that would not be reached in Franco's lifetime, not even in the twentieth century, and one that certainly seemed very far from the 26 million that Spain had in 1940. The church became the main transmitter of the demands for procreation, and reminded women – at mass or during confession – of their conjugal duty and of the need to have as many children as God wanted. But religion or morality were not the only reasons provided to encourage procreation: the use of any illicit method to limit the number of children was considered a social crime and a sign of 'lack of patriotism'.[5] Interestingly enough, Franco himself would only have one child, a daughter, and his two brothers also had one child each, so that the Francos' demographic contribution to Spain could be considered deficient. Their sister Pilar, however, made up for it by having ten children.[6]

The legal framework and social policies also worked towards this pro-natalist goal: the regime illegalised abortion in 1941, and the Penal Code of 1944 forbade the production, sale and consumption of any contraceptive method. On top of these laws sat a series of measures to help economically families with many children.[7] As early as 1938, the Nationalist government set up a programme of family subsidies that established payments for each child, the payment per child being highest the higher the number of children. These subsidies were not means tested in any way. In addition, since 1945 workers could receive a wage complement (*plus de cargas familiares*) from their employers depending on the number of children they had and on whether they had to maintain their wives or not. These payments were unified in 1954 under the so-called *ayuda familiar*, a monetary payment per number of children and dependent wife. And in all cases, these payments would be paid to the head of the household; only in very exceptional circumstances would the mother – even if she was a paid worker – be entitled to receive them. After 1941, married couples could also access loans on very good conditions, with repayments decreasing with each new child born, and the potential loan amount would be higher should the working woman commit to stop working after getting married. These loans were replaced in 1948 by a monetary payment upon marriage.

[5] Manrique Arribas 2007, p. 10. [6] Payne 1992, p. 11.
[7] What follows is extracted from Valiente Fernández 1996.

The most visible pro-natalist policies in official rhetoric were those that rewarded large families, defined in 1943 as one that had to maintain at least four children. These families received, in addition to the family transfers, preferential treatment in taxes, public transport, loans, access to public housing or land and stays at leisure centres managed by the state. There were several national and provincial prizes for the Spanish families with most children, and it was common to publicise the picture of the winning family with all their children, in order to give a graphic representation of the successful strategy to increase population. The first prize, in 1954, was won by a couple that had nineteen children. However, Franco's pro-natalist policies clashed with the reality of a very dire economic situation. Thus, while in the 1940s nuptiality increased – and the age at marriage decreased – birth rates did not increase, which speaks for itself of the economic problems that acted as a constraint on Spanish families.[8]

Social control, the second objective of Francoist family policies, refers to the embracing of the family as an organic part of the new order that could be manipulated and subordinated to the state's interests. The new regime emphasised the centrality of the family to its institutional framework in many different ways. The *Fuero del Trabajo*, which was one of the Fundamental Laws of the Francoist regime – approved as early as 1938, before the end of the Civil War – recognised in its article XII.3 'the family as a natural primary cell and foundation of society, and at the same time as a moral institution endowed with an inalienable right and superior to any positive law'.[9] This was reiterated in the *Fuero de los Españoles* of 1945, another Fundamental Law, followed by 'marriage will be one and indissoluble. The State will give special protection to large families.'[10] The family was also assigned a political role: the three institutions through which 'Spanish people could participate in legislative initiatives' were 'the family, the municipality, and the syndicate'.[11] Franco often referred to the family in his speeches to the nation: in his new year's eve speech of 1953, he said that the family was the cornerstone of the nation, and added that 'at our homes' threshold we leave the world's hypocrisies, in order to enter the temple of truth and sincerity … Our Nation has been, more than the sum of individuals, a sum of households, of families with a common surname, with their generations and their natural and sacred hierarchies.'[12]

As this shows, Francoism defined the nation (and hence the state) as the sum of family homes, and in this sense we can think politically about the family

[8] Reher 1997b, pp. 154, 175, 185. [9] *Fuero del Trabajo* 1938, my translation.
[10] *Fuero de los Españoles* 1945, chapter II, article 22, my translation.
[11] *Ley de Principios del Movimiento Nacional*, 17 May 1958, my translation.
[12] *New Year's Eve Speech*, 31 December 1953, my translation.

during Francoism within an Aristotelian framework, to use the terminology proposed by Paul Ginsborg.[13] The importance of kinship, the role of the family as a constitutive cell of the state and the clear separation of the private and public spheres are all elements in Aristotle's view of the relationship between the family and the state. The deep connections and organic relationship between the family and society were also highlighted in the National Congress of the Spanish Family in 1959, where society was described as a living organism: 'Most of the ills that beset modern society are basically due to the weakening of the familial bond. When the familial institution loses strength, society suffers, and when it gets close to disintegration, society becomes anarchic.'[14] This organic link between the family and the state seems to have been a common theme in other European dictatorships.[15]

Relationships within the family were highly hierarchical, and on top of the hierarchy rested the father. According to a secondary education textbook of the time, the 'authority of the father does not come from his physical strength, or from his social or economic superiority. It comes directly from God. Of this authority, we can say it is of Divine institution. Thus, the father is, within the family, a representative of God's paternal authority. And the mother's authority is through participating in that of her husband.'[16] Inequality within the household was not only reflected in the official rhetoric, but also in the law. The abolition of all the Republican legislation meant a return to the Civil Code of 1889, which prevented women from taking any decisions within the family, and established the obligation for them to obey their husbands, and to follow them if they wanted to change place of residence.[17] The power invested on the father during Francoism somehow mirrored that invested on Franco – *Caudillo por la Gracia de Dios*, or Leader by the Grace of God – who would act as *pater familias* of Spanish society.

The roles of men and women were clearly delineated: the promotion of the male breadwinner model relegated women to their role as housewives, and emphasised maternity as their function within society. The public sphere was, as in the Aristotelian model, for adult males, and the private sphere for women and children.[18] Women were to play a very important role in the indoctrination of their children. The perfect mother was not only to bring up her children 'under the best health and hygienic conditions, but also to provide them with an excellent education and the right moral guidelines'.[19] While women were to be the cornerstone of family life, and within the walls of their households they

[13] Ginsborg 1995.
[14] *I Congreso Nacional de la Familia Española*, Madrid, 18 February 1959.
[15] Ginsborg 2000, p. 420. [16] Quoted in Manrique Arribas 2007, p. 18, my translation.
[17] Sarasúa and Molinero 2008, p. 5. [18] Ginsborg 1995, p. 257.
[19] Quoted in Manrique Arribas 2007, p. 12, my translation.

were to exercise leadership and ideological influence, they were not expected to enter political life, or indeed to provide any space for political discussion within the family. Their role was to offer a stable and, more importantly, a depoliticised private sphere. Mothers were, according to an official publication of 1951 entitled *The Ideal Mother*, 'the best forgers of fatherlands and empires. The best way a woman has to serve her fatherland is to provide her with children and convert them into heroes and patriots ready to give their lives if needed. This is the great and magnificent mission of the Spanish mother, her great task, her best service.'[20] The *Sección Femenina* (Women's Section) of the Falange (the Spanish Fascist Party) is generally perceived as crucial in preserving and exacerbating this traditionalist view of the Spanish woman, although some studies suggest instead that the Sección Femenina offered women a unique political alternative and encouraged them to be independent and to enter higher education.[21]

The family was thus to be the reproducer of social values, and as such it had to contribute to the stability of the regime and to the political apathy so promoted by the Francoist regime. The family was put at the service of the new state, and the individual was put at the service of the family.[22] The only set of ideas allowed to enter family life were those of Catholicism, which constantly permeated society both as a justification to the pro-natalist policies and as an objective in themselves, being a set of values that was not perceived to challenge the regime, or that indeed underpinned it. Civil society, meanwhile, was barely given any room to breathe in the early years of Francoism. The Francoist state, while having abandoned pretensions to becoming a totalitarian state, was defined in opposition to the liberal state, and as such dominated most spheres of civil society.

III

Both family and civil society would experience important transformations in the late 1950s and particularly in the 1960s. At the risk of being somewhat reductionist, I shall argue that the crucial trigger was the socio-economic change brought about by the regime's new economic policy, exemplified by the Stabilisation Plan of 1959. The Plan consisted of a set of liberalising economic measures, and it unleashed all the growth potential that Spain had accumulated in the first two decades of Francoism, decades lost in terms of economic growth. During the 1960s, Spain would be the second fastest growing economy in the world – after Japan – even though that was at a period of exceptional

[20] Quoted in Manrique Arribas 2007, p. 9, my translation.
[21] Enders 1998; Ofer 2005. [22] Flaquer and Iglesias de Ussel 1993, p. 61.

growth rates across Europe. Several important developments accompanied growth: emigration – both abroad and from the Spanish countryside to the cities – the influx of tourism, foreign investment and the rise of a consumer society. The family was not left untouched by such changes: due to the very favourable economic conditions, average age at marriage decreased considerably until the late 1970s, and at the same time the marriage rate reached a historical maximum. Increases in nuptiality led to modest increases in the birth rate, but since the mid-1960s marital fertility started to stabilise and later decrease.[23] The evolution of the birth rate in Spain since the 1960s – in parallel with similar trends across Europe – reveals that Spanish women were increasingly using more effective contraception methods, despite the still prevailing pro-natalist ideology and the legal measures against birth control, with abortion banned and contraception illegal.[24] Declining fertility and the increase in mobility of the Spanish population also led to a reduction of family size and an increase in the proportion of nuclear households compared with the more traditional extended family forms, although Spain's family size remained comparatively high (4.4 in 1966) and the transition to a nuclear family model was slow relative to the speed of economic change.[25] Overall, however, the Spanish family became nuclear, with fewer children, and urban, in opposition to the 'archetypical extended, prolific, and rural' family approved by Franco's regime.[26]

Urbanisation, economic development and openness also led to changes in civil society. Victor Pérez-Díaz has argued that economic growth, coupled with increasing international ties through trade and tourism, helped to shape a new civic culture and a new civil society that, in spite of being initially sponsored by the regime, eventually came to undermine it. In this sense, Pérez-Díaz is saying that the transition to democracy began in the early 1960s with the emergence of liberal democratic traditions in society. The development of a civil society is, in this account, the mechanism that relates socio-economic development and democratic transitions, hence its importance to understanding the political change in Spain upon Franco's death.[27] Pérez-Díaz's story of the transition to democracy is one that emphasises 'pressure from below', as opposed to the 'reform from above' prioritised by other accounts that define democracy as a settlement between political elites and focus on the role of key political actors. Pérez-Díaz does not dismiss the importance of political changes at the top level, but according to him the function of civil society is to guarantee that these changes will find popular support and that the new democratic system will stabilise.

[23] Reher 1997b, p. 186. [24] Iglesias de Ussel 1990, p. 275.
[25] De Miguel 1996, p. 60. [26] Ginsborg 2000, p. 422. [27] Pérez-Díaz 1993.

IV

The relevant question for this chapter is whether there is a connection between the family, civil society and the state during Spain's transition to democracy. If we start with an analysis 'from above', the institution we cannot ignore is the church, whose support for Franco's regime weakened in parallel with the dwindling influence the church had on daily life and family matters. The changing attitude and role of the church stemmed from different factors, amongst which the Second Vatican Council and the secularisation of Spanish society are probably the most important. Iglesias de Ussel has also argued that the socio-economic changes of the 1960s, and the changes in attitudes towards the family during the 1960s, undermined the church's privileged position and eventually forced the church to abandon its prerogatives on family legislation. He refers in particular to the jurisdiction the church had over nullity and separation cases, and how in the context of increasing numbers of such cases brought before ecclesiastical courts, it became clear that the procedure was expensive, probably corrupt and clearly obsolete.[28] But beyond moral and behavioural changes, whether approved from above or instigated from below, what was the relationship between family and political change in Spain? And what was the link between families and the civil society that has been described above as setting the base for a democratic transition?

I shall argue that families directly influenced political change and the direction it would take. Several studies have emphasised, for example, the persistence across successive generations in membership of and support for political parties.[29] In Francoist Spain, with a negligible political culture, there were not many spaces to discuss politics or express political preferences. Even amongst supporters of the regime, and with the exception only of the Falangists, who were quite active politically, the degree of political involvement of parents appears to have been minimal.[30] It has been suggested that, since politics were expelled from public debate, it is plausible that any discussions on political issues were moved to private *loci*, such as the family, which censorship could not reach. There are many different types of evidence that seem to indicate that this was the case. The electoral map of the first democratic elections, for example, was quite similar to that of the last democratic elections during the Second Republic fifty years earlier, pointing at a potential transmission of political ideals across generations.[31]

[28] Iglesias de Ussel 1991, p. 287.

[29] Lane 1959. See Caspistegui Gorasurreta and Periola Narvarte 1999 for an analysis of the transmission of traditionalist values amongst Basque Carlist families, and Pérez-Díaz 1999, p. 118, for a study on normative consensus between generations in Spain in the 1990s.

[30] Maravall 1978, p. 128. [31] Jaime Castillo 2000, p. 77.

In his book on political dissent, José Maravall offers an insight into the influence of parents on their offspring's political involvement, and his study shows that student radicalism was associated with ideologically deviant families. While not wanting to reduce this connection to a simple intergenerational continuity or ideological reproduction, Maravall acknowledges that conversations on politics, and the transmission of paternal perceptions of the post-war period, mattered for the ideological shaping of their children, who nonetheless tended to hold political orientations much to the left of their parents.[32] The expansion of higher education after 1965, however, seems to have changed the sources of students' political ideas: young activists started to find their ideological roots outside the family, and usually within the student movement.[33]

Perhaps more than the transmission of political ideas alongside a left–right spectrum, it was the transmission of the memory of the Civil War from one generation to another which mattered, and that was often done within the family. Families acted as transmitters of a historical memory of the Civil War and its traumas, and of a 'fear of the past'. As Paloma Aguilar's excellent study on *Memory and Amnesia: The Role of the Civil War* has demonstrated, historical memory was very important in the 1970s, since the generation that came to power and led political changes were the sons (and to a less extent the daughters) of those who had fought the Civil War. They did not have direct memories of the Civil War, but they had perceptions of the past, transmitted by their elders, and they consciously drew lessons from them, mostly converging in the idea that a war had to be avoided at all costs.[34]

If we look at family associations, families might appear to have had an additional – and more tangible – role in civil society and in the creation of a democratic culture in the 1960s and 1970s. Family associations started to mushroom in the 1960s, particularly after the Associations Law of 1964 and the legal recognition accorded in 1958 to the idea that the regime's 'organic democracy' was organised around the family, the municipality and the syndicate. The legal recognition of family associations as a legitimate interest group was somehow endorsing their right to representation. But where these innocuous associations became important to the transition to democracy was in their role within the 'citizenship movement' of the mid-1970s, and particularly within the Head of Households' Associations, which were of a local nature and as such functioned as a school of democratic values. They would eventually merge into Neighbours' Associations, which would play an important role during the transition.[35]

We have seen the different forms – ideological and associative – in which families may have provided an input to the shape of the democratic transition

[32] Maravall 1978, p. 123. [33] Maravall 1978, pp. 137–8.
[34] Aguilar 2002, pp. 31–4. [35] Ayuso Sánchez 2009.

in Spain. Given the scale of the political reforms after Franco's death in 1975, it seems pertinent to ask what was, conversely, the effect that institutional change had on families.

One view, put forward by Iglesias de Ussel, would be that the political transition was accompanied by revolutionary changes in family law.[36] The family model of the past, and the system of values it entailed, was slowly but firmly dismantled after Franco's death. In the first few years most legal measures were on sexual matters: the new legislation allowed the distribution of contraceptives (1978), decriminalised adultery – which had mostly punished female marital infidelity – and abolished the requirements of maidenhood and known decency before a woman could be acknowledged as the victim of a rape. Further changes were approved in the early 1980s regarding marriage and the rights of children, of which the most controversial was the legalisation of divorce in 1981. Other measures included the equalisation of the rights of children born within and outside marriage (1981), and the concession of equal rights and standing to husbands and wives, thereby eliminating the former subordination of the wife to the husband (1981).

These were reforms that basically did away with the family model and values of Franco's regime. Iglesias de Ussel nicely delineates the reasons why they did not generate significant political controversy.[37] He refers to both the actions and strategies of the political parties and the church, who managed to reach consensus on family matters, and to the fact that social changes had already begun to take place during late Francoism. The lack of a strong Christian Democrat Party has also been put forward as a reason why the political leaders of the emerging democracy were able to keep on good terms with the church, since they did not see religious matters as a political ideology in competition with their own programmes.[38]

Amongst the steps taken deliberately by the political class, I would emphasise the careful writing of the Constitution to avoid creating any cleavages. This was a great lesson from the past, and an attempt to avoid the negative impact that had resulted from the anti-religious nature of the Second Republic's Constitution. The Spanish Constitution of 1978 does not define family in any way, and refers to family legislation only tangentially. The Constitution has an article (art. 39) guaranteeing the 'Protection of family and childhood', but the emphasis here is on the rights of children, born in or out of wedlock. The explicit idea of 'family' in the Constitution is just that of a unit with parents and children. Marriage is referred to in a different article (art. 32), where it just says that 'men and women will have the right to get married with full legal equality' (32.1) and that 'the law will regulate marriage, the rights and duties

[36] What follows is from Iglesias de Ussel 1991.
[37] Iglesias de Ussel 1990, p. 275.
[38] Pérez-Díaz 1993, p. 170.

of the spouses, and the causes of separation'.[39] This last point left it open for the Congress to legislate divorce in 1981, and the first point (by referring only to equality within marriage, but by not defining marriage explicitly as a union between a man and a woman) has more recently (2005) allowed the legalisation of same-sex marriage – although it is unlikely that this was an intended or even a predicted consequence by the Constitutional fathers. In essence, the fact that the Constitution was not addressing controversial policies was used politically, and Adolfo Suárez, head of the government between 1976 and 1981, asked for an endorsement of the Constitution by saying: 'It is not true that the Constitution allows abortion, proclaims divorce, does away with the family, no longer guarantees freedom of education or undermines the unity of Spain.'[40] Yet it was this lack of definition that facilitated radical changes in family legislation in subsequent years.

Another potential explanation of why changes in family legislation did not generate more controversy is that they were just a way of catching up with social reality. The socio-economic changes witnessed by Spain since the 1960s, and the accompanying evolving attitudes, had in a way brought society ahead of the legislative framework. Henceforth, when laws changed, they excited little reaction. As Felipe González, head of the government from 1982 to 1996, said in 1986 reflecting on the transition to democracy: 'If society demonstrated anything, it is that, well before the death of Franco, it had taken up attitudes that no longer corresponded to the super-structural crust represented by the Franco order. If this had not been the case, democratic change would not have been possible.'[41]

V

Yet, in spite of the post-1975 changes in family law, and the new understanding of the family they carried with them, Spain was for many years after Franco's death characterised by a lack of family politics, and this gives us the second lens through which to analyse the post-transition period.[42] Valiente analysed political programmes and political initiatives between 1975 and 1996, and observed that none of the main political parties, whatever their colour, paid attention to family issues. This was particularly surprising of the Unión de Centro Democrático (UCD, the centre-right party that politically led the democratic transition until 1982). Similar conservative parties in Europe at the time showed a strong interest in family issues, and yet UCD's electoral programmes only contained a couple of statements on the family as a basic social institution

[39] *Constitución Española* 1978. [40] Quoted in Iglesias de Ussel 1991, p. 292.
[41] Quoted in Iglesias de Ussel 1991, p. 286.
[42] See Valiente Fernández 1996 for the views that follow.

and a 'centre for education, solidarity, and cohabitation', but did not go beyond that and did not promote any public policies affecting the family.[43] For the Partido Socialista Obrero Español (PSOE, the Socialist Party, governing from 1982 to 1996), Valiente found almost no references to the family in any of its seven electoral programmes until 1996.

In practice, this lack of interest in the family meant that in many ways the traditional family view prevailed. The fiscal treatment of families until the late 1980s is a good example of a policy that had an implicit model of household in mind. Until 1989, married couples were obliged to present joint tax returns. Given the progressive nature of income tax in Spain, having to declare a 'family income' fiscally penalised the lower income earner within the couple, who was usually the wife, since this second earner's salary would bring the household earnings to a higher income bracket for tax purposes. On the one hand, one could argue that this policy disincentivised marriage. On the other, given how deeply rooted marriage was in Spanish society, its most important effect was probably to discourage women from entering the labour market, particularly in low-paid or part-time jobs. Although litigation is rare in Spain, the law was challenged in the Constitutional Court – the highest court – by a married couple, and compulsory joint tax declarations were declared unconstitutional in February 1989, since when it has been an option for married couples to opt for a joint or individual tax return.

Valiente argues that the lack of family politics between 1975 and 1996 can be explained as a reaction in opposition to the strong family orientation during Franco's dictatorship, and as a rejection of something closely associated with the authoritarian period and with an essential component of the Francoist official discourse. She even extends her analysis to the Popular Party (PP), the main opposition party until 1996: the PP's political programmes contain many more references to the family than the PSOE's, but the parliamentary activity of the party's representatives shows little interest or concern with family issues, with very few proposals or parliamentary questions on family policies. In order to understand why the PP has acted so differently regarding the family to its European counterparts we need to look again at the heritage of Francoism: the PP has had to work hard to present an image of a genuinely democratic party, as opposed to being seen as an heir to Francoism with an opportunistic support for democracy; and this has not been an easy task given the presence in the party of some who were prominent political figures during Francoism, most notably its founder Fraga Iribarne, who had been one of Franco's ministers. Anything that could be related to that authoritarian past, such as the family, was carefully avoided by the PP.

[43] Valiente Fernández 1996, p. 157.

One could argue that, since Valiente's article in 1996, the two main Spanish political parties have been more proactive regarding family policies, and different opinions within society over family issues have surfaced and become much more visible.[44] The shift towards setting a national framework of support for the families occurred during the two legislatures of the PP (1996–2000 and 2000–4), with the passing of several measures – unanimously supported by all political parties – regarding conciliation of work and family life, accompanied by fiscal policies in support of families with children, and childcare services.[45] The PSOE's government – in power since 2004 – continued with similar measures, but additionally promoted reforms in family law that triggered quite a lot of controversy and debate, and brought the family back to the public domain. By 2005 the Congress had approved a new law to fast-track divorce (commonly known as the 'express divorce law'); had elaborated a plan and legal framework to crack down on gender-based – or domestic – violence; and had modified the Civil Code to allow same-sex marriage, including the adoption of children by same-sex couples. In little over a year, the Socialist government had shaken the foundations of the Spanish family, by redefining both marriage and the procedure for its dissolution, and by recognising domestic violence – kept until then under the umbrella of the private sphere – as a public problem. The Catholic church, and the sectors of civil society most closely associated with it, reacted quickly, and in June 2005, the streets of several Spanish cities witnessed massive demonstrations against 'the erosion of marriage and family values', headed by a banner that read 'family matters'.[46] The protest was organised by the Foro Español de la Familia (Spanish Family Forum), a self-declared non-confessional organisation comprising many Spanish family associations, and the march was headed by its representatives, several bishops and several very prominent PP politicians, although not its president Mariano Rajoy. Since then, there have been many similar demonstrations – although less numerous – and the defence of the traditional family has been the excuse for the church to become again involved in politics, something it had not done for many years since Franco's death. In the run-up to the 2008 elections, the church bitterly criticised the PSOE and openly asked for electoral support to the 'lesser evil', assumed to be the PP, adding that 'without morality, there is no democracy'.[47]

The PP, meanwhile, has challenged the same-sex marriage law in the Constitutional Court, but has not done much else politically to back its usual rhetorical claims against the family models promoted by the PSOE. The 2008 Electoral Programme of the PP, for example, contained no mention whatsoever of any intention to modify the legal framework surrounding marriage, abortion

[44] Valiente Fernández 1996. [45] Salido and Moreno 2007.
[46] *El Mundo*, 20 June 2005. [47] *El País*, 31 January 2008.

or 'express divorce'.[48] In an electoral campaign interview, Mariano Rajoy, the PP's candidate for the presidency, only mentioned that, should he win, he might abolish the right of adoption for same-sex couples, but would not abolish the same-sex marriage law, since, he added, his electoral programme was not 'dictated by the bishops'.[49] It might be the case that the PP is still careful not to be associated with too conservative or right wing postures, for fear of being considered a reactionary party.

VI

The socio-economic and political changes I have been describing, combined with other shared developments with the rest of Europe, have reshaped family structures, family relationships and the role of the family in the economy. So where does the Spanish family, compared with the average European family, stand now? Spain has been defined as a country of very strong family ties, while demographic and household formation patterns place it in the so-called Mediterranean model of family structures, of which Italy is the other most prominent exponent.[50] The particularities of this model include a high degree of cross-generational cohabitation, strong kinship links – translated into a high frequency of social contacts and help to relatives – and widespread family and child-oriented attitudes.[51] The family is, in Spain, at the core of social life, and it has persistently come out as the most valued institution in various national surveys. But the strength of the family, while clearly perceived and valued by most Spaniards, might be masking the weaknesses of public services towards the family and of the presence of the family in the public sphere. An anecdote can illustrate this point. When Anthony Giddens visited Spain in 1998 to disseminate his work on *The Third Way*,[52] a book that dealt directly with family politics, a Spanish journalist told him, during the course of a public debate, that his views on the family and society could not be applied to Spain, and that 'here [in Spain] we do not have the problems that for example the United Kingdom has'. To which Giddens's reply was as straightforward as it could be: 'Are you saying the Spanish family has no problems? I can't believe it. What was then the demonstration I saw on Wednesday [against domestic violence] about? Why does Spain have the lowest birth rate in the world? And why are there no women sitting here among us?'[53]

The last two questions formulated by Giddens highlight the other two salient indicators of the Spanish family model: despite increasing female participation rates in the last three decades, Spain still presents one of the lowest female

[48] *Programa Electoral del Partido Popular* 2008. [49] *El País*, 9 February 2008.
[50] Naldini 2003. [51] Jurado Guerrero and Naldini 1996. [52] Giddens 1998.
[53] *El Mundo*, 29 November 1998, my translation.

employment rates in Europe, combined with one of the lowest fertility rates. Furthermore, in Spain the difference between the number of children desired and the number attained, or the discrepancy between desired and achieved fertility, is bigger than in any other European country.[54] Cross-generational cohabitation, interpreted by some as a sign of harmony between parents and children, very often reveals the economic obstacles that young people face in being able to afford abandoning the parental household. The age at leaving home in Spain is one of the highest in Europe, and it usually coincides with marriage.[55] This makes variables such as marriage, work, independent housing and age at leaving home much more correlated in Spain than in northern European societies.[56]

The conciliation of family life and work appear as the Achilles' heel of the 'strong' family model. This weakness stems partly from the politics on gender inequality put forward by different governments, which have been directed at guaranteeing equal employment opportunities and equal work conditions for men and women, but have at the same time sidelined family policies and equality within the household. As a result, and despite a considerable increase in part-time employment opportunities in the last two decades, the proportion of Spanish women working part time is very low by European standards. Given that part-time work is very often a strategy to combine a career and motherhood, it is not surprising that Spain also emerges as one of the countries with the lowest staying-on rate in the labour market after child bearing.[57] When Spanish women have children, they have to choose between carrying on working full time or leaving the job market. It has been suggested elsewhere that very low fertility might be associated with a rapid shift towards high levels of gender equality in individual institutions – such as the labour market – in combination with persistent low levels of gender equality within the family and in family-oriented institutions.[58] This might indeed be applicable to Spain, where again governments appear reluctant to regulate directly the domain of the family, even when their policies are targeting family outcomes.

The consequence of leaving the family 'untouched' is that provisions for the family are very low, precisely where the family is more important. And this brings us to the relationship between the family and the welfare state: most sociological studies of the family in Spain would highlight that the family has become the main provider of welfare, care and even insurance, since the growth of the welfare state has not been accompanied by a proportional expansion of family provisions. This is a trend that started in the 1960s: although half of the social expenditures in early Francoism were

[54] Van Peer 2002. [55] Holdsworth 2000.
[56] Reher 1997a, p. 114, and Holdsworth and Irazoqui Solda 2002.
[57] Gutiérrez-Domènech 2005. [58] McDonald 2000.

directed towards the family, the nominal values of these measures were not changed after the early 1960s. Thus, although the policies were the same, due to inflation their impact became smaller and smaller, and the real value of the family programmes began to decrease just before the transition to democracy. In 1965, family transfers were 2.6 per cent of GDP; ten years later they were only 1 per cent, and they still stand now amongst the lowest in Europe.[59] The family in Spain has also received comparatively little attention as a percentage of total social expenditure: in 1991 it stood at 0.6 per cent of all social transfers, the lowest figure in the European Union; almost negligible compared to the 10.3 per cent spent in Denmark, and still very low when confronted with the 3.6 per cent spent in Italy.[60]

Thus the family emerges, in Spain, as the true pillar of the welfare system.[61] This is seen very clearly for example in the care of the elderly. In 1991, around 44 per cent of people over 60 in Spain cohabited with one of their children, whereas in northern countries or in the United States the figure is around 10 per cent.[62] The Spanish model, therefore, is one where parents take care of their children for a longer period of time, and in exchange they receive care from their children when they are old.

Strong family ties have also shaped the Spanish labour market. Spain presents one of the lowest internal migration rates in Europe: in 2001, only around 10 per cent of the Spanish respondents to the Eurobarometer Survey declared that they had moved to another region in the previous ten years, and a similar number declared the intention of doing so in the next five years.[63] Given that the decade covered in the survey included a period of high unemployment rates – of above 20 per cent in 1994 – and given that regional disparities in employment opportunities differ considerably in Spain,[64] this low regional labour mobility is hard to explain in terms of economic opportunities and push and pull factors. Unless one resorts to the role that family networks provide, particularly in three key stages of a professional career. First, the family is very often – in above 60 per cent of cases – the source of information for employment opportunities.[65] Second, the proximity of the family is crucial for women who want to work and have children: 77 per cent of working mothers have a close relative living in the same locality, who in most cases helps them with childcare.[66] Finally, although one could argue that the dependence on the family is constraining career opportunities and hence increasing the probability of

[59] Iglesias de Ussel and Meil Landwelin 2001, p. 61.
[60] Valiente Fernández 1996, p. 159. [61] Pérez-Díaz 1999, pp. 48–9.
[62] Reher 1997a, p. 119.
[63] Paci, Tiongson, Walewski, Liwi'nski and Stoilkova 2007, p. xviii.
[64] Paci, Tiongson, Walewski, Liwi'nski and Stoilkova 2007, p. 11.
[65] Paci, Tiongson, Walewski, Liwi'nski and Stoilkova 2007, p. 53.
[66] Tobío Soler 2002, p. 160.

unemployment, the family also emerges as the most important institution to mitigate the negative consequences of joblessness. The 1980s provide a very interesting example. In that decade, unemployment rates in Spain averaged 20 per cent, and reached 24 per cent in the early 1990s. These figures hide people who were working in the black economy and others who were essentially moving from one precarious job to another, but in essence they describe a flow of generally young people who were in search of job stability and could not find it. Despite such disruptive unemployment rates, the decade advanced without any major social upheavals, the only exception being a general strike in 1988 that nonetheless did not prevent the Socialist Party from renewing its absolute majority in 1989. The main reason behind this 'social calm', it has been argued, was that there was an institution in charge of reducing the costs of this system. The family provided food, living space and if possible job opportunities, and at the same time allowed people's self-esteem to remain intact by giving them a sense of belonging to a group.[67] Moreover, unemployment disproportionately affected 'secondary workers' – women, older workers and those who were not heads of household – for whom the family was a form of unemployment insurance.[68] The family, its traditions and its structures have therefore had an impact on the economy. Spain, like Italy, has shown much more persistence of political-economic power bases linked to the family firm, partly explained by differences in legislation but also because the weakness of the central state has given strength to strong regionally focused families.[69] In the light of the importance of the family to professional and family life even after leaving the parental home, it is not surprising to see figures of over 60 per cent of the population in 2001 declaring that they have lived in their local community since birth, a percentage unmatched by any other European country.[70]

The links between family and civil society are much more difficult to pinpoint than those between the family and the state or the family and the economy. All studies converge in defining Spanish civil society as weak. For example, if we consider involvement in different types of voluntary associations, ranging from sports clubs to trade unions or even political parties, Spain ranks amongst the lowest in Europe, just above Hungary, Portugal, Poland and Greece, and slightly below Italy.[71] This has led some to say that 'civic anaemia is endemic in Spain'.[72] Many different explanations claim to account for this civic apathy: anthropological approaches focusing on the individualism of Spanish people, socio-economic reports emphasising the high rates of unemployment and late entry of females into the workforce, or analyses that

[67] Pérez-Díaz 1999, pp. 120–1. [68] Alba-Ramírez and Freeman 1990.
[69] Colli, Fernández Pérez and Rose 2003.
[70] Paci, Tiongson, Walewski, Liwi'nski and Stoilkova 2007, p. 48.
[71] Wallace and Pichler 2008, p. 268. [72] McDonough, Barnes and López Pina 1998, p. 1.

describe historical institutional constraints on the formation of interest groups, reaching as far back as the beginnings of liberalism in the nineteenth century but obviously stressing as well the legacy of the Francoist authoritarian period.[73] There are, on top of these theories, explanations that have focused on the family to justify the deficiencies of Spanish civil society. David Reher, for example, argues that societies with weak family ties tend to have a strong civil society, and those with strong family ties a weak civil society.[74] The causal link seems to be the prevalence of loneliness, which only associationism can combat in those places where the family does not prevent it.

A specific study of family associations in Spain delivers very similar conclusions to those of Reher: a classification of different European countries according to the degree of development and participation in public life of family associations ranks Spain – alongside Greece – amongst those where family associationism is rare and has a weak impact on civic life. The paradox in Spain is that the family is very highly valued and there is a strong 'familial culture', but unlike many other countries, there is no public space in Spain to discuss family matters: the Spanish National Associations Register, for example, includes 'family associations' in the same category as consumers' associations and groups for the elderly. Ayuso Sánchez suggests that maybe the cause of the weakness of family associations in Spain is to be found precisely in the cultural strength of the family, and in the fact that the family itself already promotes a sort of private associationism that renders the extra-familial 'family' organisations unnecessary.[75]

The picture that emerges from these last reflections, within the tripartite framework of the role of the civil society, the family and the state, is one where, to start with, and despite all its recent transformations, the family remains a very powerful institution. The Spanish family is likely to move in the same direction as the families of other European countries, but it will also probably remain stronger than the European average. As Reher has shown, historical developments and path dependence are very strong forces in shaping family structures, and it is likely that differences amongst European families will prevail.[76] Civil society, conversely, is weak, and does not therefore serve the function of establishing a link between individuals, families and the state. The state, meanwhile, remains hesitant – although less so than a couple of decades ago – to enter the realm of the family and to engage in family politics. The dramatic fall in fertility rates and the consequent ageing of the population might serve as a stimulus for the state to revisit its position. But exclusively pro-natalist

[73] See Encarnación 2001, pp. 69–73, for an expanded explanation of each of these.

[74] Reher 1997a, p. 126. [75] Ayuso Sánchez 2009, p. 115.

[76] Reher 1997a. Jurado Guerrero and Naldini 1996 also show that there is no convergence between southern and central/northern European families.

solutions – such as the payment of 2,500 euros for every child born (approved in 2007 and abolished in 2011) – will not change the way the family shapes the labour market and women's professional careers, or indeed the way family and society interact. The recent developments indicate that the PSOE, which in the last ten years has been more hesitant than the PP to promote family-related initiatives, might be trying to redefine the family in a more modern way in order to promote family policies without being accused of conservatism. Once a different family emerges, one that fully embraces a same-sex couple and their children, we may witness a return to family politics.

References

Agamben, Giorgio (1998). *Homo Sacer: Sovereign Power and Bare Life*, Stanford.

Ågren, Maria (2000). 'Contracts for the old or gifts for the young? On the use of wills in early modern Sweden', *Scandinavian Journal of History* 25:3, pp. 197–218.

(2009). *Domestic Secrets. Women and Property in Sweden 1600–1857*, Chapel Hill.

Ågren, Maria and Erickson, Amy L. (eds.) (2005). *The Marital Economy in Scandinavia and Britain 1400–1900*, Aldershot.

Aguilar, Paloma (2002). *Memory and Amnesia: The Role of the Spanish Civil War in the Transition to Democracy*, New York.

Alba-Ramírez, Alfonso and Freeman, Richard B. (1990). 'Jobfinding and wages when long run unemployment is really long: the case of Spain', *NBER Working Paper*, 3409.

Alberti, Leon Battista (1969). *The Family in Renaissance Florence*, ed. R. Neu Watkins, New York.

Amar, Cécile (2009). *Fadela Amara: le destin d'une femme*, Paris.

Amara, Fadela and Zappi, Sylvia (2003). *Ni putes ni soumises*, Paris.

Åmark, Klas (2002). 'Familj, försörjning och livslopp under 1900-talet', in Helena Bergman and Peter Johansson (eds.), *Familjeangelägenheter: modern historisk forskning om välfärdsstat, genus och politik*, Eslöv, pp. 236–78.

Ancellin, Jacqueline (1997). *L'action sociale familiale et les caisses d'allocations familiales. Un siècle d'histoire*, Paris.

Arendt, Hannah (1958). *The Human Condition*, Chicago.

Arlacchi, Pino (1992). *Gli uomini del disonore*, Milan.

Attias-Donfut, Claudine (ed.) (1995). *Les solidarités entre générations. Vieillesse, famille, état*, Paris.

Authors Collective (ed.) (1970). *Storefront Day Care Centers. The Radical Berlin Experiment*, Boston, Mass., available at www.bpb.de/publikationen/98DK3M.html.

Ayuso Sánchez, Luís (2009). 'Emergencia y configuración del asociacionismo familiar en España', *Revista Internacional de Sociología* 67:1, pp. 107–33.

Baaijens, C., van Doorne-Huiskes, A. and Schippers, J. (2005). 'Do Dutch employees want to work more or fewer hours than. they actually do?', in B. Peper, A. van Doorne-Huiskes and L. den Dulk (eds.), *Flexible Working and Organisational Change. The Integration of Work and Personal Life*, Cheltenham, pp. 201–21.

Bagnasco, Arnaldo (2006). 'Ritorno a Montegrano', in Edward C. Banfield, *Le basi morali di una società arretrata*, Bologna, pp. 7–34.

Bairner, A. (ed.) (2005). *Sport and the Irish. Histories, Identities, Issues*, Dublin.

Banfield, Edward (1958). *The Moral Basis of a Backward Society*, Glencoe, Ill.

Barbagli, Marzio and Saraceno, Chiara (eds.) (1997). *Lo stato delle famiglie in Italia*, Bologna.

Barca, Federico et al. (1994). *Assetti proprietari e mercato delle imprese*, 2 vols., Bologna.

Beck, Ulrich and Beck-Gernsheim, Elisabeth (1995). *The Normal Chaos of Love*, Cambridge.

Bergman, Barbara (1996). *Saving our Children from Poverty: What the United States Can Learn from France*, New York.

Berlinguer, Giovanni (1979). *Una riforma per la salute*, Bari.

Berlusconi, Silvio (2000). *L'Italia che ho in mente*, Milan.

Bernhard, Ernst (1969). 'Il complesso della Grande Madre', in E. Bernhard, *Mitobiografia*, Milan, pp. 168–79.

Bernstein, Basil (1971). *Class, Codes and Control*, London.

Béroud, Sophie and Mouriaux, René (1997). *Le souffle de décembre. Le mouvement social de 1995: continuités, singularités, portée*, Paris.

Berthoud, R. and Gershuny, J. (eds.) (2000). *Seven Years in the Lives of British Families: Evidence from the British Household Panel Survey*, Abingdon.

Beveridge, William (1942). *Social Insurance and Allied Services*, London.

(1944). *Full Employment in a Free Society*, London.

BFI (1940). *Housewives' Choice. British Women on the 'Home' Front* (1926–55), British Film Institute, London.

Biraben, J. N. and Dupâquier, J. (1981). *Les berceaux vides de Marianne: l'avenir de la population française*, Paris.

Birg, Herwig (2001). *Die demographische Zeitenwende*, Munich.

Blanden, Jo and Gregg, Paul (2004). *Family Income and Educational Attainment: A Review of Approaches and Evidence for Britain*, Discussion Paper No. 41, Centre for the Economics of Education, London.

Bobbio, Norberto (1987). *The Future of Democracy*, Cambridge.

(1990). 'La fine della prima Repubblica', *Europeo* 46, 28 December, p. 107.

Bobbitt, Philip (2002). *The Shield of Achilles: War, Peace and the Course of History*, London.

Boeckenfoerde, Ernst-Wolfgang (1976). *Staat, Gesellschaft, Freiheit*, Frankfurt.

Bonini, C. and Del Porto, D. (2008). 'Per una poltrona negata a un fedelissimo Mastella disse: ti faccio il mazzo quadrato', *La Repubblica*, 17 January.

Bonnet, C. and Chambaz, C. (2000). 'Les avantages familiaux dans le calcul des retraites', *Solidarité et santé* 3, pp. 47–63.

Borchorst, A. (1994). 'Welfare state regimes, women's interests and the EC', in D. Sainsbury (ed.), *Gendering Welfare States*, London, pp. 26–44.

Bosmans, J. (1988). 'Het maatschappelijk-politieke leven in Nederland 1918–1940', in Th. van Tijn, P. de Rooy and D. Damsma (eds.), *Geschiedenis van het moderne Nederland*, De Haan, pp. 398–443.

Bourdieu, Pierre (1998). *Acts of Resistance: Against the New Myths of Our Time*, Cambridge.

Boverat, Fernand (1924). *Une politique gouvernementale de natalité. Étude présentée sur sa demande à M. le président du conseil des ministres par l'alliance nationale pour l'accroissement de la population française*, Paris.

Bowlby, John (1951). *Child Care and the Growth of Love*, Harmondsworth.

Bradley, David (2000). 'Family laws and welfare states', in Kari Melby, Anu Pylkkänen, Bente Rosenbeck and Christina Carlsson Wetterberg (eds.), *The Nordic Model of Marriage and the Welfare State*, Copenhagen.

Brisson, Dominique (2004). *Guide de la famille et de la vie quotidienne*, Paris.
Bull, Malcolm (2007). 'Vectors of the Biopolitica', *New Left Review* 45, pp. 7–25.
Bussemaker, J. and Kersbergen, K. van (1994). 'Welfare states: some theoretical reflections', in D. Sainsbury (ed.), *Gendering Welfare States*, London, pp. 8–25.
Caritas/Migrantes (2009). *Dossier statistico 2009. XIX° Rapporto sull'immigrazione*, Rome.
Carter, Erica (1997). *How German is She? Postwar West German Reconstruction and the Consuming Woman*, Ann Arbor.
Caspistegui Gorasurreta, Francisco Javier and Pierola Narvarte, Gemma (1999). 'Entre la ideología y lo cotidiano: la familia en el carlismo y el tradicionalismo (1940–1975)', *Vasconia* 28, pp. 45–56.
Cassese, Sabino and Franchini, Claudio (eds.) (1994). *L'amministrazione pubblica italiana*, Bologna.
Cavalli, Alessandro and De Lillo, Antonio (1993). *Giovani anni '90*, Bologna.
Centraal Bureau voor de Statistiek (2008). *Statline 2008*, Den Haag/Heerlen.
(2010). *Nederland langs de Europese meetlat*, Den Haag/Heerlen.
Cesareo, Vincenzo et al. (1995). *La religiosità in Italia*, Milan.
Chaumier, Serge (1999). *La Déliaison amoureuse. De la future romantique au désir d'indépendance*, Paris.
Chauvel, Louis (2000). 'Comment se manifeste la solidarité intergénérationnelle?', in François Charpentier (ed.), *Encyclopédie protection sociale. Quelle refondation?*, Paris, pp. 138–59.
Chauvière, Michel and Sassier, Monique (eds.) (2000). *Les implicites de la politique familiale*, Paris.
Christiansen, Niels Finn, Petersen, Klaus, Edling, Nils and Haave, Peter (eds.) (2006). *The Nordic Model of Welfare: A Historical Reappraisal*, Copenhagen.
CNAF (2004a). 'Rétrospectif de la branche famille', *Horizon 2015* 2, p. 5.
(2004b). 'Évolution des prestations sociales et familiales sous conditions de ressources, *Horizon 2015* 2, p. 2.
Cobb, Richard (1998). 'The experiences of an Anglo-French historian', in Richard Cobb, *Paris and Elsewhere*, London.
Colli, Andrea, Fernández Pérez, Paloma and Rose, Mary B. (2003). 'National determinants of family firm development? Family firms in Britain, Spain, and Italy in the nineteenth and twentieth centuries', *Enterprise and Society* 4, pp. 28–64.
Comand, Maria Pia and Santucci, Maddalena (1995). 'Il consume addomesticato', in Francesco Casetti (ed.), *L'ospite fisso*, Milan, pp. 155–82.
Commaille, Jacques (1998). *Les enjeux politiques de la famille*, Paris.
Commaille, Jacques, Strobel, Pierre and Villac, Michel (2002). *La politique de la famille*, Paris.
Connolly, Linda (2002). *The Irish Women's Movement: From Revolution to Devolution*, Basingstoke.
Cook, Hera (2004). *The Long Sexual Revolution: English Women, Sex and Contraception in England 1800–1975*, Oxford.
Coote, Anna and Campbell, Beatrix (1982). *Sweet Freedom*, Oxford.
Corcoran, Mary, Gray, Jane and Peillon, Michel (2008). 'Ties that bind? The social fabric of daily life in new suburbs', in T. Fahey, H. Russell and C. T. Whelan (eds.), *Quality of Life in Ireland: The Social Effects of Economic Boom*, Dordrecht, pp. 175–98.

Correll, S. J., Benard, S. and Paik, In (2007). 'Getting a job: is there a motherhood penalty?', *American Journal of Sociology* 112:5 (March), pp. 1297–338.

CSO (2007). *Census 2006. Vol. 11: Disability, Carers and Voluntary Activity*, Cork: Central Statistics Office, available at www.cso.ie/census/census2006results/volume_11/Volume11_2006.pdf.

d'Iribarne, Philippe (2006). *L'étrangeté française*, Paris.

Dalla Zuanna, Gianpiero and Micheli, Giuseppe A. (eds.) (2004). *Strong Family and Low Fertility: A Paradox?*, Dordrecht.

Damon, Julien (2008). *Les politiques familiales*, Paris.

Darby, P. (2005). 'Gaelic games and the Irish immigrant experience in Boston', in A. Bairner (ed.), *Sport and the Irish. Histories, Identities, Issues*, Dublin, pp. 85–101.

Daunton, Martin (2002). *Just Taxes*, Cambridge.

De Búrca, M. (1999). *The GAA: A History*, 2nd edn, Dublin.

De Luna, Giovanni (2009). *Le ragioni di un decennio*, Milan.

De Miguel, Jesús M. (1996). 'Desarrollo o desigualdad? Análisis de una polémica sociológica de medio siglo en España', *Reis* 75, pp. 55–108.

de Moor, Tine and van Zanden, Jan Luiten (2009). 'Girl power: the European marriage pattern and labour markets in the North Sea region in the late medieval and early modern period', *Economic History Review* 63:1, webpublication 2009, final February 2010, pp. 1–33.

De Rita, Giuseppe (1988). 'L'impresa famiglia', in Paolo Melograni and Lucetta Scaraffia (eds.), *La famiglia italiana dall'Ottocento ad oggi*, Rome and Bari, pp. 383–416.

de Singly, Françoise (1993). *Sociologie de la famille contemporaine*, Paris.

Delaney, Liam and Fahey, Tony (2005). *The Social and Economic Value of Sport in Ireland*, Economic and Social Research Institute, Dublin, available at: www.esri.ie/publications/search_for_a_publication.

Deniaux, E. (1993). *Clientèles et pouvoir à l'époque de Cicéron*, Rome.

Dente, Bruno (1989). 'La cultura amministrativa italiana negli ultimi 40 anni', in B. Dente (ed.), *Politiche pubbliche e pubblica amministrazione*, Rimini, pp. 139–72.

Diamanti, Ilvo (2009). 'Italia 2009: un paese che riscopre la protesta', *Il Venerdì di Repubblica*, 11 December, pp. 18–25.

Dibos-Lacroux, Sylvie (2007). *Pacs. Le guide pratique*, Paris.

Diena, L. (1960). *Gli uomini e le masse*, Turin.

Dolan, F. M. (2005). 'The paradoxical liberty of bio-power: Hannah Arendt and Michel Foucault on modern politics', *Philosophy and Social Criticism* 31, pp. 369–80.

Donzelot, Jacques (1979). *The Policing of Families*, trans. Robert Hurley, New York.

Doorne-Huiskes, J. van (1979). *Vrouwen en beroepsparticipatie. Een onderzoek onder gehuwde vrouwelijke academici*, Utrecht.

Doorne-Huiskes, J. van, Henderikse, W. and van Beek, A. (2009). *From Small to Larger Part-Time Jobs: Views from Employers and Employees*, Paper presented at the Conference 24orMore, Amsterdam, 5–6 Nov. 2009.

Dortier, Michel (2002). *Familles: permanences et métamorphoses*, Paris.

Douglas, J. W. B. (1972). *The Home and the School*, London.

Driessen, M. and Veldman, A. (1997). 'Inkomenszekerheid', in R. Holtmaat and T. Loenen (eds.), *Vrouw en Recht*, Nijmegen, pp. 127–39.

Dübeck, Inger (2005). 'Property and authority in Danish marital law', in Maria Ågren and Amy L. Erickson (eds.), *The Marital Economy in Scandinavia and Britain 1400–1900*, Aldershot, pp. 127–40.
Duchen, Claire (1994). *Women's Rights and Women's Lives in France, 1944–1968*, London.
Dumond, G. F. (1991). *Le festin de Kronos*, Paris.
Durham, Martin (1991). *Sex and Politics. The Family and Morality in the Thatcher Years*, Basingstoke.
Edling, Nils (1998). 'När folkhemmet var liberalt', *Tvärsnitt* 4, pp. 28–37.
Eisenstadt, S. N. and Roniger, L. (1984). *Patrons, Clients and Friends*, Cambridge.
Elgán, Elisabeth (1994). *Genus och politik. En jämförelse mellan svensk och fransk abort- och preventivmedelspolitik från sekelskiftet till andra världskriget*, Uppsala.
Encarnación, Omar G. (2001). 'Civil society and the consolidation of democracy in Spain', *Political Science Quarterly* 116:1, pp. 53–79.
Enciclopedia Cattolica (1952). Volume V, Rome, Vatican City.
Enders, Victoria Lorée (1998). 'Problematic portraits. The ambiguous historical role of the SF of the Falange', in Victoria Lorée Enders and Pamela Radcliff (eds.), *Constructing Spanish Womanhood: Female Identity in Modern Spain*, New York, pp. 375–97.
Erickson, Amy Louise (1993). *Women and Property in Early Modern England*, London.
Esping-Andersen, Gøsta (1990). *The Three Worlds of Welfare Capitalism*, Cambridge.
(1999). *Social Foundations of Postindustrial Economies*, Oxford.
Eupen, Th. A. G. van (1985). 'Kerk en gezin in Nederland', in G. A. Kooy (ed.), *Gezinsgeschiedenis: Vier eeuwen gezin in Nederland*, Assen.
Fahey, Tony (1999). 'Religion and sexual culture in Ireland', in F. X. Eder, L. Hall and G. Hekma (eds.), *Sexual Cultures in Europe: National Histories*, Manchester, pp. 53–70.
Fahey, Tony, Hayes, Bernadette C. and Sinnott, Richard (2006). *Conflict and Consensus: A Study of Values and Attitudes in the Republic of Ireland and Northern Ireland*, Leiden and Boston.
Fahey, Tony and Layte, Richard (2008). 'Family and sexuality', in T. Fahey, H. Russell and C. T. Whelan (eds.) *Quality of Life in Ireland. The Social Impact of Economic Boom*, Dordrecht.
Fahey, Tony, Delaney, Liam and Gannon, Brenda (2005). *School Children and Sport in Ireland*, Dublin.
Fenouillet, Dominique (2008). *Droit de la famille*, Paris.
Fernandez-Cordon, Juan Antonio (1997). 'Youth residential independence and autonomy: a comparative study', *Journal of Family Issues* 6, pp. 567–607.
Ferrarella, L. (2003). 'Previti condannato, ma non per la Sme', *Corriere della Sera*, 23 November.
Ferrera, Maurizio (1993). *Modelli di solidarietà. Politica e riforme sociali nelle democrazie*, Bologna.
(1996). 'The "southern model" of welfare in social Europe', *Journal of European Social Policy* 1, pp. 17–37.
(2006). *Le politiche sociali. L'Italia in prospettiva*, Bologna.
Ferriter, Diarmaid (2009). *Occasions of Sin. Sex and Society in Modern Ireland*, London.
Figgis, J. N. (1913). *Churches in the Modern State*, London.

Finch, Janet (1989a). *Family Obligations and Social Change*, Oxford.
(1989b). 'Kinship and friendship', in R. Jowell et al. (eds.), *British Social Attitudes. Special International Report*, Aldershot, pp. 87–104.
Fine, Agnès and Sangoï, Jean-Claude (1991). *La population française au XIXe siècle*, Paris.
Finn Heinrich, V. (ed.) (2007). *CIVICUS Global Survey of the State of Civil Society*, vol. I, Bloomfield.
Finn Heinrich, V. and Fioramonti, L. (eds.) (2008). *CIVICUS Global Survey of the State of Civil Society*, vol. II, Bloomfield.
Fisher, Kate (2000). '"She was quite satisfied with the arrangements I made": gender and birth control in Britain 1920–1950', *Past and Present* 169, pp. 161–93.
Flaquer, Lluís and Iglesias de Ussel, Julio (1993). 'Familia y análisis sociológico: el caso de España', *Reis* 61, pp. 57–75.
Flockton, C., Kolinsky, E. and Pritchard, R. (eds.) (2000). *The New Germany in the East*, London.
Foucault, Michel (2004). *La naissance de la biopolitique. Cours au Collège de France (1978–1979)*, Paris.
(2008). *The Birth of Biopolitics. Lectures at the Collège de France, 1978–1979*, London.
Fraser, Nancy (1990). 'Rethinking the public sphere: a contribution to the critique of actually existing democracy', *Social Text*, No. 25/6, Durham, N.C.
GAA (1971). *Report of the Commission of the GAA*, Dublin.
(2002). *Strategic Review. Enhancing Community Identity*, Dublin.
(2004). *Annual Report, 2004*, Dublin (available from www.gaa.ie/about-the-gaa/publications-and-resources/).
(2005). *Annual Report, 2005*, Dublin (available from www.gaa.ie/about-the-gaa/publications-and-resources/).
(2007). *Annual Report, 2007*, Dublin (available from www.gaa.ie/about-the-gaa/publications-and-resources/).
(2008). *Annual Report, 2008*, Dublin (available from www.gaa.ie/about-the-gaa/publications-and-resources/).
(2009). *Inclusion and Integration Strategy, 2009–2015*, Dublin (available from www.gaa.ie/about-the-gaa/publications-and-resources/).
Gadd, Carl-Johan (2000). *Det svenska jordbrukets historia, vol. III: Den agrara revolutionen 1700–1870*, Stockholm.
Gégot, Jean-Claude (1989). *La population française aux XIXe et XXe siècles*, Paris.
Gerlach, Irene (1996). *Familie und staatliches Handeln*, Opladen.
(2000a). 'Generationsgerechtigkeit im politischen Prozess', in I. Gerlach and P. Nitschke (eds.), *Metamorphosen des Leviathan? Staatsaufgaben im Umbruch*, Opladen.
(2000b). 'Politikgestaltung durch das Bundesverfassungsgericht am Beispiel der Familienpolitik', in *Politik und Zeitgeschichte* (B 3–4/2000), available at www1.bpb.de/publikationen/5VS1I2,3,0,Politikgestaltung_durch_das_Bundesverfassungsgericht_am_Beispiel_der_Familienpolitik.html#art3.
(2004). 'Die Familienpolitik der Rot-Gruenen Koalition', *WSI: Gewerkschaftliche Monatshefte* 55, pp. 411–18.
Gershuny, Jonathan and Berthoud, Richard (eds.) (2004). *Seven Years in the Lives of British Families: Evidence on the Dynamics of Social Change from the British Household Panel Survey*, Bristol.

Gershuny, Jonathan and Sullivan, Oriel (2003). 'Time use, gender, and public policy regimes', *Social Politics* 10:2, pp. 205–28.
Giddens, Anthony (1992). *The Transformation of Intimacy: Sexuality, Love and Eroticism in Modern Societies*, Cambridge.
(1998). *The Third Way*, Cambridge.
Gillis, John R. (1999). ' "A triumph of hope over experience": chance and choice in the history of marriage', *International Review of Social History* 44, pp. 47–54.
Ginsborg, Paul (1990). *A History of Contemporary Italy: Society and Politics, 1943–1988*, Harmondsworth.
(1995). 'Family, civil society and the state in contemporary European history: some methodological considerations', *Contemporary European History* 4, pp. 249–73.
(2000). 'The politics of the family in twentieth-century Europe', *Contemporary European History* 9:3, pp. 411–44.
(2001). *Italy and its Discontents. Family, Civil Society, State, 1980–2001*, London.
(2005). *Silvio Berlusconi. Television, Power and Patrimony*, London.
(2006). 'I due bienni rossi: 1919–1920 e 1968–1969. Comparazione storica e significato politico', in Associazione Biondi-Bartolini and Fondazione Giuseppe di Vittorio (eds.), *I due bienni rossi del Novecento: 1919–1920 e 1968–1969*, Rome, pp. 13–36.
Glendon, Mary Ann (1989). *The Transformation of Family Law*, Chicago.
Godet, Michel and Sullerot, Évelyne (2009). *La famille: une affaire publique*, Paris.
Goffi, Tullo (1962). *Morale familiare*, Brescia.
Gordon, Peter and Doughan, David (2001). *Dictionary of British Women's Organisations, 1825–1960*, London.
Goudsblom, J. (1967). *Dutch Society*, New York.
Green, David R. and Alasdair Owens (eds.) (2004). *Family Welfare. Gender, Property, and Inheritance since the Seventeenth Century*, Westport.
Greenhalgh, S. (2003). 'Science, modernity and the making of China's one-child policy', *Population and Development Review* 29, pp. 163–96.
Guazzini, G. (1987). 'Dimensione ideale della famiglia e calendario ideale delle nascite', in Rosella Palomba (ed.), *Vita di coppia e figli*, Florence, pp. 39–51.
Gustafsson, Harald (1998). 'The conglomerate state: a perspective on state formation in early modern Europe', *Scandinavian Journal of History* 23, pp. 189–213.
Gutiérrez-Domènech, Maria (2005). 'Employment after motherhood: a European comparison', *Labour Economics* 12:1, pp. 99–123.
Guzzetti, Linda (2002). 'Dowries in fourteenth-century Venice', *Renaissance Studies* 16:4, pp. 430–73.
Haavet, Inger Elisabeth (2006). 'Milk, mothers and marriage: family policy formation in Norway and its neighbouring countries in the twentieth century', in Niels Finn Christiansen, Klaus Petersen, Nils Edling and Peter Haave (eds.), *The Nordic Model of Welfare: A Historical Reappraisal*, Copenhagen, pp. 189–214.
Habermas, Jürgen (1989) [1962]. *The Structural Transformation of the Public Sphere: An Inquiry into a Category of Bourgeois Society*, Cambridge.
Hajnal, John (1965). 'European marriage patterns in perspective', in D. V. Glass and D. E. C. Eversley (eds.), *Population in History*, London, pp. 101–43.
Hakim, C. (2001). *Work-Lifestyle Choices in the 21st Century. Preference Theory*, Oxford.
Halsey, A. H., Heath, A. F. and Ridge, J. M. (1980). *Origins and Destinations: Family Class and Education in Modern Britain*, London.

Hank, K., Tillmann, K. and Wagner, G. G. (2001). 'Ausserhaeussliche Kinderbetreeuung in Ostdeutschland', MPIDR Working Paper WP 2001–003, Rostock.
Hardwick, Julie (1998). *The Practice of Patriarchy. Gender and the Politics of Household Authority in Early Modern France*, Philadelphia.
Harris, José (2003). 'From Richard Hooker to Harold Laski: changing perceptions of civil society in British political thought, late sixteenth to early twentieth centuries', in J. Harris (ed.), *Civil Society in British History. Ideas, Identities, Institutions*, Oxford, pp. 13–37.
Hassan, D. (2005). 'Sport, identity and Irish nationalism in Northern Ireland', in A. Bairner (ed.), *Sport and the Irish. Histories, Identities, Issues*, Dublin, pp. 123–39.
Hassenteufel, Patrick and Martin, Claude (1997). 'La représentation des intérêts familiaux en Europe: Allemagne, Belgique, Grande-Bretagne, France, Portugal', Rapport de recherche pour la Commission Européenne (DG 5), Brussels.
Hedin, Marika (2002). *Ett liberalt dilemma. Ernst Beckman, Emilia Broomé, G H von Koch och den sociala frågan 1880–1930*, Stockholm.
Hegel, G. W. F. (1991) [1820]. *Elements of the Philosophy of Right*, ed. A. W. Wood, Cambridge.
Hemerijck, A. C. and Bakker, W. E. (1994). 'De pendule van perspectief. Convergentie en divergentie in het denken over de verzorgingsstaat', in G. Engbersen, A. C. Hemerijck and W. E. Bakker (eds.), *Zorgen in het Europese huis. De grenzen van nationale verzorgingsstaten*, Amsterdam.
Hendrick, Harry (1997). *Children, Childhood and English Society, 1880–1990* (New Studies in Economic and Social History), London.
Hennessy, Peter (2000). *The Prime Minister: The Job and its Holder since 1945*, London.
Hessische Staatskanzlei (2003). *Die Familienpolitik muss neue Wegen gehen!*, Wiesbaden.
Hilliard, Betty (2003). 'The Catholic church and married women's sexuality: habitus change in late 20th century Ireland', *Irish Journal of Sociology* 12:2, pp. 28–49.
Hirigoyen, Marie-France (2006). *Femmes sous emprise: les ressorts de la violence dans le couple*, Paris.
HMSO (1948). *Making Citizens*, London.
Hobbes, Thomas (1996) [1651]. *Leviathan*, ed. Richard Tuck, Cambridge.
Hochard, Jacques (1961). *Aspects économiques des prestations familiales*, Paris.
Holdsworth, Clare (2000). 'Leaving home in Britain and Spain', *European Sociological Review* 16, pp. 201–22.
Holdsworth, Clare and Irazoqui Solda, Mariana (2002). 'First housing moves in Spain: an analysis of leaving home and first housing acquisition', *European Journal of Population* 18, pp. 1–19.
Hooghiemstra, B. T. J. and Niphuis-Nell, M. (1993). *Sociale Atlas van de vrouw. Deel 2*, Sociaal en Cultureel Planbureau, Rijswijk.
Houseaux, F. (2003). 'La famille, pilier d'identités', *INSEE première* 937, Paris, pp. 1–27.
Howard, Sarah (2006). *Les images de l'alcool en France, 1915–1942*, Paris.
Hug, Chrystel (1999). *The Politics of Sexual Morality in Ireland*, Basingstoke.
Humphries, Jane (1990). 'Enclosures, common rights, and women: the proletarianization of families in the late eighteenth and early nineteenth centuries', *Journal of Economic History* 50:1, pp. 17–42.
Huteau, Serge (2006). *Le contrôle des associations subventionnées,* Voiron.

Iannelli, Cristina and Paterson, Lindsay (2006). 'Social mobility in Scotland since the middle of the twentieth century', *Sociological Review* 54:3, pp. 520–45.

Iglesias de Ussel, Julio (1990). 'La familia y el cambio politico en España', *Revista de Estudios Políticos* 67, pp. 235–59.

(1991). 'Family ideology and political transition in Spain', *International Journal of Law and the Family* 5, pp. 277–95.

Iglesias de Ussel, Julio and Meil Landwerlin, Gerardo (2001). *La política familiar en España*, Barcelona.

Inglis, Tom (1998). *Lessons in Irish Sexuality*, Dublin.

Insegnamenti pontifici (1964). Vol. I, *Il matrimonio*, Rome.

Ipsen, Carl (1996). *Dictating Demography. The Problem of Population in Fascist Italy*, Cambridge.

Isnenghi, Mario (1994). *L'Italia in piazza: i luoghi della vita pubblica dal 1848 ai nostri giorni*, Milan.

ISTAT (1995). *Statistiche giudiziarie penali 1994, Annuario no. 3*, Rome.

(2007). *Italy in Figures*, Rome.

Jackson, Julian (2003). *France: The Dark Years, 1940–44*, Oxford.

Jaime Castillo, Antonio M. (2000). 'Familia y socialización política. La transmisión de orientaciones ideológicas en el seno de la familia española', *Reis* 92, pp. 71–92.

Jansen, M. (2002). 'Kein feministisches Projekt', *WSI: Gewerkschaftliche Monatshefte* 53, pp. 589–96.

Jansson, Torkel (1985). *Adertonhundratalets associationer. Forskning och problem kring ett sprängfyllt tomrum eller sammanslutningsprinciper och föreningsformer mellan två samhällsformationer, ca 1800–1870*, Uppsala.

Journal official (1998). Compte-rendu intégrale des séances de vendredi 9 octobre 1998, Paris.

Julliard, Jacques (2005). *Le malheur français*, Paris.

Jurado Guerrero, Teresa and Naldini, Manuela (1996). 'Is the south so different? Italian and Spanish families in comparative perspective', *South European Society and Politics* 1:3, pp. 42–66.

Kamerman, S. B. et al. (2003). *Social Policies, Family Types and Child Outcomes in Selected OECD Countries*, OECD working paper, Paris.

Kedward, Rod (2005). *La vie en bleu. France and the French since 1900*, London.

Keuzenkamp, S., Hillebrink, C., Portegijs, W. and Puwels, B. (2009). *Deeltijd (g)een probleem: Mogelijkheden om de arbeidsduur van vrouwen met een kleine deeltijdbaan te vergroten*, Sociaal en Cultureel Planbureau, The Hague.

Keynes, J. M. (1937). *The General Theory of Employment, Interest and Money*, London.

Kirchhof, P. (2005). 'Wollen wir eine im Erwerbsleben sterbende oder im Kind vitale Gesellschaft sein?', Diözesankomitee der Katholiken im Bistum Münster Neujahrsempfang, Münster.

(2006). *Das Gesetz der Hydra*, Munich.

Kirchhof, P. and Schmidt, Renate (2004). *Familienpolitik fuer eine lebendige Gesellschaft*, Berlin.

Knight, Barry (2008). 'Civil society in western and southern Europe', in V. Finn Heinrich and L. Fioramonti (eds.), *CIVICUS Global Survey of the State of Civil Society*, vol. II, Bloomfield, pp. 163–80.

Knijn, T. and Verheijen, C. (1991). *Kiezen of delen. Veranderingen in de beleving van het moederschap*, Amsterdam.
Kocka, Jürgen (2004). 'Civil society from a historical perspective', *European Review* 12, pp. 65–79.
Kolinsky, E. and Nickel, H. M. (eds.) (2003). *Reinventing Gender. Women in East Germany since Unification*, London.
Krasensky, Patrick and Zimmer, Patrick (2005). *Surtout ne changez rien*, Paris.
Kreyenfeld, M. (2002). 'Crisis or adaptation reconsidered: a comparison of East and West German fertility patterns in the first six years after the "Wende"', MPIDR Working Paper WP 2002–032, Rostock.
(2004). 'Sozialstruktur und Kinderbetreuung', MPIDR Working Paper WP 2004–009, Rostock.
Kuller, C. (2004). *Familienpolitik im foederativen Sozialstaat. Die Formierung eines Politikfeldes in der Bundesrepublik 1949–1975*, Oldenbourg.
Kynaston, David (2009). *Family Britain, 1951–1957 (Tales of a New Jerusalem)*, London.
Lane, R. E. (1959). 'Fathers and sons. The foundations of political beliefs', *American Sociological Review* 24, pp. 502–11.
Larkin, Maurice (1974). *Church and State after the Dreyfus Affair: The Separation Issue in France*, London.
Larsson Kraus, Jonas (2009). *Att odla ett samhälle. Råby räddningsinstitut och 1840-talets sociala ingenjörskonst*, Uppsala.
Le Bras, Hervé and Todd, Emmanuel (1981). *L'invention de la France: atlas anthropologique et politique*, Paris.
Lees, Sue (1997). *Ruling Passions: Sexual Violence, Reputation and the Law*, Buckingham.
Lefebvre, Alain and Méda, Dominique (2006). *Faut-il brûler le modèle social français?*, Paris.
Lijphart, A. (1968). *The Politics of Accommodation: Pluralism and Democracy in the Netherlands*, Berkeley.
(1988). *Verzuiling, pacificatie en kentering in de Nederlandse politiek*, Haarlem.
Lind, Lars Fr. (1799). *Domarens pröfning efter Sweriges lag, eller Sättet, at utröna lagens rätta förstånd, mening och grund*, Stockholm.
Lovenduski, Joni (2005). *Feminising Politics*, Cambridge.
Lunn, Pete (2007). *Fair Play? Sport and Social Disadvantage in Ireland,* Economic and Social Research Institute, Dublin, available at www.esri.ie/publications/search_for_a_publication/.
Lunn, Pete and Layte, Richard (2007). *Sporting Lives. An Analysis of a Lifetime of Irish Sport*, Economic and Social Research Institute, Dublin, available at www.esri.ie/publications/search_for_a_publication/.
(2008). *Irish Sports Monitor. Second Annual Report*, Economic and Social Research Institute, Dublin.
Luzzi, S. (2004). *Salute e sanità nell'Italia repubblicana*, Rome.
McDonald, Peter (2000). 'Gender equity in theories of fertility transition', *Population and Development Review* 26:3, pp. 427–39.
McDonough, Peter, Barnes, Samuel and López Pina, Antonio (1998). *The Cultural Dynamics of Democratization in Spain*, Ithaca, NY.
Mackintosh, Mary and Barrett, Michele (1982). *The Anti-Social Family*, London.

Macnicol, John (1986). 'The effect of the evacuation of schoolchildren on official attitudes to state intervention', in Harold Smith (ed.), *War and Social Change*, Manchester, pp. 3–31.

Maier, F. (2005). 'Reconciliation of work and private life in German', EGGSIE – EC's Expert Group on Gender, Social Inclusion and Employment, EWERC Univ. of Manchester, Manchester.

Maino, Franca (2001). *La politica sanitaria*, Bologna.

Mair, Peter (1997). *Party System Change. Approaches and Interpretations*, Oxford.

Malena, Carmen (2008). 'Does civil society exist?', in V. Finn Heinrich and Lorenzo Fioramonti (eds.), *The CIVICUS Global Survey of the State of Civil Society, vol. II: Comparative Perspectives*, Bloomfield, pp. 183–200.

Malerba, Giuseppina (1993). 'La donna nella famiglia e nel lavoro: i risultati di una analisi cross-country', in G. Rossi and G. Malerba (eds.), *La donna nella famiglia e nel lavoro*, Milan, pp. 49–90.

Manrique Arribas, Juan Carlos (2007). 'La familia como medio de inclusión de la mujer en la sociedad franquista', *Hispania Nova. Revista de Historia Contemporánea* 7, pp. 1–30.

Maravall, José (1978). *Dictatorship and Political Dissent. Workers and Students in Franco's Spain*, London.

Math, Antoine (2004). 'Doit-on aider les familles? Les familles nombreuses?', *Informations sociales* 108, pp. 3–20.

Maugeri, Mariano (2009). *Tutti gli uomini del viceré*, Milan.

Maurin, Louis (2006). 'Le boom du PACS', *Alternatives économiques* 253, pp. 1–55.

(2009). *Déchiffrer la société française*, Paris.

Mayer, Karl Ulrich and Schulze, Eva (2009). *Die Wendegeneration. Lebensverlaeufe des Jahrgangs 1971*, Frankfurt.

Melby, Kari, Pylkkänen, Anu, Rosenbeck, Bente and Wetterberg, Christina Carlsson (eds.) (2006). *Inte ett ord om kärlek. Äktenskap och politik i Norden ca 1850–1930*, Göteborg.

Melis, Guido (1996). *Storia dell'amministrazione italiana, 1861–1993*, Bologna.

Merlin, Pierre (1989). *Les banlieues des villes françaises*, Paris.

Mermet, Gérard (2009). *Francoscopie*, Paris.

Messu, Michel (1992). *Les politiques familiales. Du natalisme à la solidarité*, Paris.

Mill, John Stuart (1991). *The Subjection of Women* [1869], in Mill, *On Liberty and Other Essays*, Oxford.

Millet, Emmanuelle (2005). *Pour en finir avec les violences conjugales*, Paris.

Minonzio, Jérôme (2006). 'L'Union nationale des associations familiales (UNAF) et les politiques familiales. Crises et transformations de la représentation des intérêts familiaux en France', *Revue française de science politique* 56:2, pp. 205–26.

Minonzio, Jérôme and Pagis, Julie (2009). *Entreaide familiale et solidarités entre générations*, Paris.

Mitchell, Allan (1979). *The German Influence in France after 1870: The Formation of the French Republic*, Chapel Hill.

Mitterrand, François (1988). *Lettre à tous les Français*, Paris.

Moeller, R. G. (1993). *Protecting Motherhood. Women and the Family in the Politics of Postwar West Germany*, Berkeley.

Morée, M. (1992). *Mijn kinderen hebben er niets van gemerkt. Buitenshuis werende moeders tussen 1950 en nu*, Utrecht.

Moss, P. (ed.) (2009). *International Review of Leave Policies and Related Research 2009*, Employment Relation Research Series no. 102, Department for Business Innovation and Skills, London.

Mushaben, Joyce Marie (2004). 'Girl power: women, politics and leadership in the Berlin Republic', in J. Sperling (ed.), *Germany at Fifty-Five*, Manchester, pp. 183–205.

Naldini, Manuela (2003). *The Family in the Mediterranean Welfare States*, London.

Nees, Albin (2005). *Das Bundesverfassungsgericht und die Familienpolitik in Deutschland*, available at www.deutscher-Familienverband.de.

NESF (2003). *The Policy Implications of Social Capital*, Forum Report no. 28, National Economic and Social Forum, Dublin.

Newson, John and Newson, Elizabeth (1965). *Patterns of Infant Care in an Urban Community*, Harmondsworth.

(1968). *Four Years Old in an Urban Community*, London.

Nic Ghiolla Phádraig, M. (1976). *Survey of Religious Beliefs and Practices in Ireland, vol. III: Moral Attitudes*, Dublin.

Nicholas, Tom (1999). 'The myth of meritocracy: an inquiry into the social origins of Britain's business leaders since 1850', Working Paper No. 53/99, Department of Economic History, London School of Economics, London.

Nichols, Peter (1973). *Italia, Italia*, London.

Niephaus, Y. (2003). *Der Geburteneinbruch in Ostdeutschland nach 1990*, Opladen.

Nota Gezinsbeleid 2008 (2008). *De kracht van het gezin*, Jeugd en Gezin, Programmaministerie, Den Haag.

Nussbaum, Martha (1992). 'Nature, function and capability: Artistotle on political distribution', in G. E. Mccarthy (ed.), *Marx and Aristotle*, Maryland, pp. 175–212.

Ofer, Inbal (2005). 'Historical models – contemporary identities: the secci6n femenina of the Spanish Falange and its redefinition of the term "femininity"', *Journal of Contemporary History* 40:4, pp. 663–74.

Ogden, Phillip E. and Huss, Marie-Monique (1982). 'Demography and pronatalism in France in the nineteenth and twentieth centuries', *Journal of Historic Geography* 8:3, pp. 283–98.

Okin, Susan Moller (1989). *Justice, Gender and the Family*, New York.

Opielka, Michael (2002). 'Familie und Beruf eine deutsche Geschichte', *Aus Politik und Zeitgeschichte*, 22–3.

Orfei, Ruggero (1976). *L'occupazione del potere*, Milan.

Paci, Pierella, Tiongson, Erwin R., Walewski, Mateusz, Liwi'nski, Jacek and Stoilkova, Maria M. (2007). 'Internal labor mobility in central Europe and the Baltic region', *World Bank Working Paper*, 105.

Papkostas, Apostolis (2001). 'Why is there no clientelism in Scandinavia? A comparison of the Swedish and Greek sequences of development', in Simonetta Piattoni (ed.), *Clientelism, Interests and Democratic Representation*, Cambridge, pp. 31–53.

Parquet, Muriel (2009). *Droit de la famille*, Paris.

Payne, Stanley (1992). *Franco. El perfil de la historia*, Madrid.

Pedersen, Susan (1993). *Family, Dependence and the Origins of the Welfare State*, Cambridge.

Penn, Mark J. (2007). *Microtrends: The Small Forces Behind Today's Big Changes*, London.

Pérez-Díaz, Víctor (1993). *The Return of Civil Society. The Emergence of Democratic Spain*, Cambridge, Mass.

(1999). *Spain at the Crossroads. Civil Society, Politics, and the Rule of Law*, Cambridge, Mass.

Piattoni, Simonetta (ed.) (2001). *Clientelism, Interests and Democratic Representation*, Cambridge.

Pick, Daniel (1989). *Faces of Degeneration. A European Disorder c. 1848 – c. 1918*, Cambridge.

Pietropolli Charmet, Gustavo (1995). *Un nuovo padre*, Milan.

Pillebout, Jean-François (2007). *Le Pacs*, Paris.

Pinl, C. (2001). 'Wieviele Ernaehrer braucht das Land?', *Blaetter for deutsche und international Politik* 46, pp. 1123–30.

Pitkin, Howard (1985). *The House that Giacomo Built*, Cambridge.

Polanyi, Karl (1944). *The Great Transformation. The Political and Economic Origins of our Time* [1944; Swedish transl. 1989], Lund.

Pollard, Miranda (2000). 'Vichy, abortion: policing the body and the new moral order in everyday life', in Sarah Fishman and Laura Lee Downs et al. (eds.), *France at War. Vichy and the Historians*, Oxford, pp. 191–205.

Portegijs, W., Hermans, B. and Lalta, V. (2006). *Emancipatiemonitor 2006*, Sociaal en Cultureel Planbureau, Den Haag.

Pritchard, R. (2000). 'Pre-school education and childcare in East Germany', in C. Flockton (ed.), *The New Germany in the East: Policy Agendas and Social Developments Since Unification*, London, pp. 123–47.

Putnam, R. D. (2000). *Bowling Alone: The Collapse and Revival of American Community*, New York.

Ramaux, Christophe et al. (2006). *Emploi éloge de la stabilité*, Paris.

Reher, David (2004). 'Family ties in Western Europe: persistent contrasts', in Gianpiero Dalla Zuanna and Giuseppe Micheli (eds.), *Strong Family and Low Fertility: A Paradox?*, Dordrecht, pp. 45–76.

Reher, David S. (1997a). 'Familia y sociedad en el mundo occidental desarrollado: una lección de contrastes', *Revista de Occidente* 199, pp. 112–32.

(1997b). *Perspectives on the Family in Spain, Past and Present*, Oxford.

Report of the Committee of Inquiry into the Care of Children (Curtis committee) (1946). Cmnd 6922, HMSO, London.

Report of the Committee on One-Parent Families (Finer committee) (1974). Cmnd 5629, HMSO, London.

Report of the Royal Commission on Population (1949). Cmnd 7695, HMSO, London.

Reyer, J. and Kleine, H. (1997). *Die Kinderkrippe in Deutschland. Sozialgeschichte einer umstrittenen Einrichtung*, Freiburg.

Riley, Denise (1983a). '"The serious burdens of love?" Some questions on child-care, feminism and socialism', in Lynne Segal (ed.), *What Is to Be Done about the Family*, Harmondsworth.

(1983b). *War in the Nursery: Theories of the Child and Mother*, London.

Ristau, M. (2005). 'Der oekonomische Charme der Familie', *Politik und Zeitgeschichte* 23/4, Bundeszentrale fuer Politische Bildung, available at www.bpb.de/publikationen/7IWEQ7.html.

Rosci, Elena (1994). 'Le lunghe adolescenze dell'Italia di oggi', in Paul Ginsborg (ed.), *Stato d'Italia*, Milan, pp. 301–3.

Rosental, Pierre-André (2003). *L'intelligence démographique: sciences et politiques des populations en France (1930–1960)*, Paris.
Rowbotham, Sheila (1973a). *Woman's Consciousness, Man's World*, Harmondsworth.
(1973b). *Hidden from History: 300 years of Women's Oppression and the Fight against it*, London.
Ruddle, Helen and Mulvihill, Ray (1999). *Reaching Out. Charitable Giving and Volunteering in the Republic of Ireland*, Dublin.
Rugh, A. B. (1984). *Family in Contemporary Egypt*, Syracuse, NY.
Runciman, David (2006). *The Politics of Good Intentions. History, Fear and Hypocrisy in the New World Order*, Princeton.
Sainsbury, D. (1996). *Gender, Equality and Welfare States*, Cambridge.
Salido, Olga and Moreno, Luís (2007). 'Bienestar y políticas familiares en España', *Poíitica y Sociedad* 44:2, pp. 101–14.
Sandvik, Hilde (2005). 'Decision-making on marital property in Norway', in Maria Ågren and Amy L. Erickson (eds.), *The Marital Economy in Scandinavia and Britain 1400–1900*, Aldershot, pp. 111–26.
Sans, R. (2004). 'Das Bundesverfassungsgericht als familienpolitischer Ausfallbürge', available at www.familienhandbuch.de/cmain/f_Programme/a_Familienpolitik/s_519.html.
Saraceno, Chiara (1994). 'The ambivalent familism of the Italian welfare state', *Social Politics* 1, pp. 60–82.
Sarasúa, Carmen and Molinero, Carme (2008). 'Trabajo y niveles de vida en el franquismo. Un estado de la cuestión desde una perspectiva de género', in Cristina Borderías (ed.), *La historia de las mujeres: perspectivas actuales*, Barcelona, pp. 309–55.
Sardon, Jean-Paul (2005). 'L'évolution du divorce en France', in J. P. Sardon et al. *La population de la France*. Bordeaux, pp. 717–50.
Sarkozy, Nicolas (2004). *La République, les religions, l'espérance,* Paris.
Sauvy, A. (1980). *Vues et illusions sur la France de demain*, Paris.
Saviano, Roberto (2006). *Gomorra*, Milan.
Schizzerotto, Antonio (2007). 'La casa: ultimo lembo dell'impero maschile italiano?', in Elena dell'Agnese and Elisabetta Ruspini (eds.), *Mascolinità all'italiana*, Turin, pp. 143–66.
Schlegel, Uta (2000/4). 'Politische Einstellungen Ostdeutscher Frauen', Berlin, available at www.rosaluxemburgstiftung.de/fileadmin/rls_uploads/pdfs/manuskripte1.pdf.
Sciolla, Loredana (1997). *Italiani. Stereotipi di casa nostra*, Bologna.
Scoppola, Pietro (1989). *La Repubblica dei partiti*, Bologna.
Sen, Amartya (1999). *Development as Freedom*, Oxford.
Signorelli, Amalia (1986). 'Patroni e clienti', in C. Pasquinelli (ed.), *Potere senza stato*, Rome, pp. 151–62.
(2000). 'Componenti e percorsi dell'emancipazione femminile nell'Italia meridionale', in Anna Oppo et al. (eds.), *Maternità, identità, scelte. Percorsi dell'emancipazione femminile nel Mezzogiorno*, Naples, pp. 1–12.
Skoglund, Anna Maria (1992). *Fattigvården på den svenska landsbygden år 1829*, Stockholm.
Smith, Timothy (2004). *France in Crisis. Welfare, Inequality and Globalization since 1980*, Cambridge.

Sociaal en Cultureel Planbureau (1998). *Sociaal en Cultureel Rapport 1998; 25 jaar sociale verandering*, Sociaal en Cultureel Planbureau, Den Haag.

Sommestad, Lena (1998). 'Human reproduction and the rise of the welfare states: an economic-demographic approach to welfare state formation in the United States and Sweden', *Scandinavian Economic History Review* 46:2, pp. 97–116.

Sørensen, Øystein and Stråth, Bo (eds.) (1997). *The Cultural Construction of Norden*, Oslo.

Souffron, Kathy (2007). *Les violences conjugales*, Paris.

Souty, G. and Dupont, P. (1999). *Destin de mères, destins d'enfants*, Paris.

Spencer, Stephanie (2005). *Gender, Work and Education in Britain in the 1950s*, Basingstoke.

Spengler, J. J. (1979). *France faces Depopulation: Postlude Edition 1936–1976*, Durham, NC.

Statistics Netherlands (2008). *Statline 2008*, The Hague and Heerlen.

(2010). *Nederland langs de Europese meetlat*, The Hague and Heerlen.

Summerfield, Penny (1998). *Reconstructing Women's Wartime Lives: Discourse and Subjectivity in Oral Histories of the Second World War*, Manchester.

Szreter, Simon and Fisher, Kate (2003). '"They prefer withdrawal": the choice of birth control in Britain, 1918–1950', *Journal of Interdisciplinary History* 34:2, pp. 263–91.

(2010). *Sex before the Sexual Revolution: Intimate Life in England 1918–1963*, Cambridge.

Terrier, Jean and Wagner, Peter (2006). 'Civil society and the problématique of political modernity', in Peter Wagner (ed.), *The Languages of Civil Society*, New York, pp. 9–27.

Thatcher, Margaret (2010). Online archive of the Margaret Thatcher Foundation, www.margaretthatcher.org/speeches, London.

Thélot, C. and Villac, M. (1998). *Politique familiale: bilan et perspectives. Rapport à Mme. la ministre de l'emploi et de la solidarité et au ministre de l'économie, des finances et de l'industrie*, Paris.

Therborn, Gøran (2004). *Between Sex and Power. Family in the World, 1900–2000*, London.

Thom, Deborah (2009), '"Beating people is wrong": domestic life, psychological thinking and the permissive turn', in Lucy Delap, Ben Griffin and Abigail Willis (eds.), *The Politics of Domestic Authority since 1800*, Basingstoke.

Thomas, James (2002). *Diana's Mourning: A People's History*, Cardiff.

Thompson, E. P. (1971). 'The moral economy of the English crowd in the eighteenth century', *Past and Present* 50, pp. 76–136.

Tilly, Charles (1984). 'Demographic origins of the European proletariat', in David Levine (ed.), *Proletarianization and Family History*, Orlando.

Tobío Soler, Constanza (2002). 'Conciliación o contradicción: cómo hacen las madres trabajadoras', *Reis* 97, pp. 155–86.

Tocqueville, Alexis de (2000) [1835/40]. *Democracy in America*, ed. Harvey Mansfield and Delba Winthrop, Chicago.

Touraine, Alain et al. (1996). *Le grand refus. Réflexions sur la grève de décembre*, Paris.

Trägårdh, Lars (ed.) (2007). *State and Civil Society in Northern Europe. The Swedish Model Reconsidered*, New York.

Trappe, H. (1995). *Emazipation oder Zwang? Frauen in der DDR zwischen Beruf, Familie und Sozialpolitik*, Berlin.
Trigilia, Carlo (ed.) (1995). *Cultura e sviluppo*, Rome.
UNICEF (2008). *Global Child Care Transition*, UNICEF Innocenti Research Centre, Florence.
Valiente Fernández, Celia (1996). 'Olvidando el pasado: la política familiar en España (1975–1996)', *GAPP* 5–6, pp. 151–62.
Van Parijs, Philippe (1998). 'The disfranchisement of the elderly, and other attempts to secure intergenerational justice', *Philosophy and Public Affairs* 27, pp. 292–333.
Van Peer, Christine (2002). 'Desired and achieved fertility', in M. Macura and G. Beets (eds.), *Dynamics of Fertility and Partnership in Europe. Insights and Lessons from Comparative Research*, vol. II, New York, pp. 117–44.
Verwey-Jonker, H. (1985). 'De man/vrouw relatie: een machtsbalans', in G. A. Kooy (ed.), *Gezinsgeschiedenis. Vier eeuwen gezin in Nederland*, Assen and Maastricht, pp. 138–66.
Wallace, Claire and Pichler, Florian (2008). 'More participation, happier society? A comparative study of civil society and the quality of life', *Social Indicators Research* 93:2, pp. 255–74.
Wellings, Kaye et al. (1994). *Sexual Behaviour in Britain, The National Survey of Sexual Attitudes and Lifestyles*, London.
Wigforss, Ernst (1951). *Skrifter i urval 8. Minnen 1914–1932* (published in 1980), Stockholm.
Williams, Fiona (2004). *Rethinking Families*, Calouste Gulbenkian Foundation, London.
Willmott, Peter and Young, Michael (1957). *Family and Kinship in East London*, London.
Winberg, Christer (1977). *Folkökning och proletarisering. Kring den sociala strukturomvandlingen på Sveriges landsbygd under den agrara revolutionen*, Lund.
Winter, J. M. (1980). 'The fear of population decline in Western Europe 1870–1940', in R. W. Hiorns (ed.), *Demographic Patterns in Developed Societies*, London, pp. 171–98.
Wrightson, Keith (2000). *Earthly Necessities. Economic Lives in Early Modern Britain*, New Haven.
Wrigley, E. A. (1985). 'The fall of marital fidelity in nineteenth-century France: exemplar or exception?', *European Journal of Population* 1, pp. 31–60, 131–9.

Index

For EU product safety concerns, contact us at Calle de José Abascal, 56–1°,
28003 Madrid, Spain or eugpsr@cambridge.org.

www.ingramcontent.com/pod-product-compliance
Ingram Content Group UK Ltd.
Pitfield, Milton Keynes, MK11 3LW, UK
UKHW020327140625
459647UK00018B/2049
9780521128018